Marxism and Literary History

Marxism and Literary History

JOHN FROW

BASIL BLACKWELL

First published in the United Kingdom in 1986

Basil Blackwell Ltd
108 Cowley Road, Oxford OX4 1JF, UK

British Library Cataloguing in Publication Data

Frow, John
    Marxism and literary history.
    1. Communism and literature
    2. Literature—History and criticism—Theory, etc.
    I. Title
    801   PN51

    ISBN 0-631-14863-9

Typeset by N.K. Graphics
Printed in the United States of America

For Toby and Eleanor

Preface

IN THIS BOOK I try to theorize the concepts of system and history for a Marxist theory of literary discourse. This theorization is conceived as part of a semiotically oriented intervention in cultural politics. I am not interested in producing a general Marxist theory of literature or·in contributing to an aesthetics; and I do not attempt a philosophical purification of these categories. They are difficult categories and I seek to make them more so; but the point is to make them fit tools for critical and political uses.

I use the concept of system in the sense of a nontotalized formation which sets epistemological and practical limits to discourse, and which is thereby productive of discourse; it does not have here its speculative or its systems-theoretical sense of a closed and self-regulating totality. In addition, I seek consistently to deploy the concept in counterpoint to its ongoing deconstruction.

In the same way, the concept of history does not carry the sense of an enfolding narrative continuum or of the given ground of human action. It is used to theorize the discontinuous, nonteleological dynamic of the literary system and the multiple temporalities of texts within complex sets of intertextual relations.

The theoretical framework and intent of the book is a nondogmatic and nonorthodox Marxism which I hope will require no apology. I work within an antihumanist, antihistoricist, and anti-Hegelian tradition, but am also intellectually close to the post-structuralism of Foucault and Derrida. The interplay and sometimes the strain between these traditions will be evident (I hope fruitfully) throughout the book.

My argument is Marxist above all in its commitment to the concept of class and class struggle and to considering the intrication of power in symbolic systems. Chapter 1 seeks to situate this commitment politically and intellectually. I then borrow from Hegelian Marxism the device of prefacing a construction of theoretical categories with a reflection upon the prehistory of those categories. In the rest of Chapter 1 and in Chapter 2 I develop a selective genealogy by constructing what I take to be the problematics of historicist, structuralist, and post-structuralist Marxist literary theory. In particular, I elaborate a cumulative critique of the categories of representation and ideology, the epistemological categories which have been used diversely to explore the workings of literary discourse. In Chapter 3 I then propose an alternative model of discourse. The concept of ideology is thought, in nonrepresentational terms, as a *state* of discourse; and discourse itself is thought not through the Saussurean opposition of the systemic to the nonsystemic but as a structured regulation of practices. I draw here in particular upon the work of Bakhtin, Halliday, Pêcheux, and Foucault.

This reworking of the category of discourse affects the way in which literary discourse can be thought. In Chapter 4 I construct a second genealogical line, that of Russian Formalism, in order to lay the foundations for a workable concept of the literary system. What I have tried to redeem from Formalist theory is a category of system which is in principle capable of accounting both for the structuring role of discursive authority and for the constitutive function of change and discontinuity. Chapter 5 further explores the modes of temporality and the institutional status of the literary system. It constructs a model of the negative intertextual dynamic of the system, but seeks also to qualify the historical generality of the model.

Chapter 6 develops the concept of intertextuality, which is central to thinking relations of discursive authority and discursive transformation. Through a series of analyses I pose the question of how the interaction between code and message, system and text, which constitutes the abstract dynamic of literary change, works as a principle of textual construction and can be identified in a reading. In Chapter 7 the categories of text and reading are then moved from the level of specific entities and processes to the level of systemic categories. The text is defined as a relational structure which is variably constituted through its integration in particular historical systems; and reading is defined in terms of institutional organizations of interpretive interest.

Clearly one of the dangers this approach runs is that of objectifying the category of system. In the last chapter, Chapter 8, I take the system to be itself the product of particular processes of construction. Through readings of an exchange between Derrida and Foucault and of Derrida's essay on the *parergon,* I raise the question of the possibility of setting limits to interpretation, of the real effectivity of limits, and of the function of limits and frames in the constitution of the literary as a historically specific discursive domain. These are, more generally, questions about the politics of reading.

I HAVE WORKED for the past ten years in the Comparative Literature program at Murdoch University. The structure of the program and the university's commitment to interdisciplinary work have made teaching there a consistently rewarding experience. Most of what I know I have learned from my colleagues and my students; Horst Ruthrof in particular has been constantly supportive.

A number of people have read and commented on all or part of the manuscript in its various stages. I owe particular thanks to Mayerlene Frow and Wolfgang Holdheim for their contribution to an earlier version of the text, and more recently to Anne Freadman, Wlad Godzich, Bill Green, Ian Hunter, Noel King, Meaghan Morris, Ian Reid, and Lesley Stern. Didier Coste and the Asociación Noesis generously provided me with shelter in which to complete the manuscript, and Cynthia Baker worked with great dedication to produce it in a final form.

Christine Alavi made the writing of the book possible.

I am grateful to the following journals for permission to reprint material they have previously published: *Clio; Comparative Literature; Comparative Criticism* 5 (published by Cambridge University Press); *Economy and Society; Journal of Aesthetic Education; Journal of Literary Semantics; Literature and History; New Literature Review; Oxford Literary Review; Raritan; Southern Review* (Australia).

Contents

A NOTE ON TRANSLATIONS

Wherever possible I have used a readily available English translation, modifying it where necessary; these modifications are indicated in the notes. All translations from French, German, and Spanish have been checked against the original texts. In cases where verbal detail is of particular importance, I have given the original text together with a translation. Where no translation is specified, the translation is my own.

1

Introduction

Any beginning is determined by the exclusions it operates and the conclusions it repeats. A beginning is not an origin; there can be no founding or finding of first principles which would be prior to the working out of those principles in the course of an argument. The primitive categories of this book could be established only in an infinite regression, because they both constitute and are constituted in ramified processes of conceptual and political exchange. To begin is to interrupt these exchanges, to take a point in a series and disregard what precedes it. A beginning is always a coming between—an intervention, or a mediation.

This means on the one hand that a beginning is the more or less differential repetition of a series of other texts, that it is structured by its inscription within limits and within textual chains. But it is also, in Edward Said's sense, a point of departure, a determinate production of difference.[1] This is one of the theses about literary history that this book will attempt to argue: that textual events are not arbitrary in relation to the system which structures their occurrence. It is true that they are not contained by this system (they cannot be reduced to its terms since they may exceed them), but what makes them possible is *this* system, not any other. When texts are displaced into other literary systems, they are reconstituted in a more complex articulation which establishes a more complex limit on interpretation. Limits are not necessarily to be respected, of course. The patron god of hermeneutics, the bearer of messages from the greater gods, was also the god both of boundaries and of the crossing of boundaries, and the patron of a special mercantile class of what Homer called "professional boundary-crossers."[2] The kind of theory I want to develop will take note both of the determinacy of boundaries and of the need to transgress them, to be disrespectful of the limits of proper authority.

The question of beginning, says Said, conceals four different questions: those of *training* (the institutional context of writing); of the *material* which is worked; of the intertextual *point of departure;* and of the *disciplinary specificity* of textual production.[3] These are, again, essentially questions about limits—that is, about how discursive limits are imposed and particular objects of discourse delimited. But they are also about how beginning-interventions can interrupt these limits and transform discursive objects. I will pose them as the question of three distinct contexts and three distinct crises in which this book seeks to intervene.

The first concerns the context of literary criticism as an institution and as a set of institutionally regulated practices. To see the activity of literary criticism in this way is to reverse the traditional patterns of methodological reflection, which have been concerned with the epistemological protocols governing reading, and to tie the practice of reading instead to the procedures of an apparatus of disciplinary training. In recent years such a reversal has increasingly led to a recognition of the ways in which the constitution of Literature, as an apparently self-contained order of canonic texts, has been a function of the workings of this apparatus. The shift in attention involved here has been manifested unevenly across different national cultures. In France and Germany in the late 1960s and early 1970s, it took the form of proposals for reform of the university and of local pedagogic structures (for example, the two volumes of *Ansichten* and *Neue Ansichten einer künftigen Germanistik*) as well as of a critique of the role of the educational apparatus in the reproduction of class relations (such as the work of Pierre Bourdieu and of Renée Balibar). In the United Kingdom it has taken the form both of a prolonged battle against an entrenched and reactionary Leavisite orthodoxy and of analyses, following on the work of Raymond Williams, of the historical and institutional conditions of demarcation and maintenance of the Literary. In the United States the rapid installation of deconstruction as a new and depressingly depoliticized orthodoxy has been accompanied on the one hand by a pervasive sense of the "loss of the social value and vision of the humanities"[4] and on the other by a sharpened awareness of the disciplinary status of the practices of literary study.

I use the word *discipline* in Foucault's sense of an organization of relations, techniques, and rules which is to be thought not as a repressive apparatus but as a machine for the production of specific behaviors and discourses. Stanley Fish has tried to theorize the concept of the profession in a similar way, arguing that there can be no transcendence of any particular professional system since even alternative or oppositional practices are internal to the system.[5] The argument is, I think, compelling; what is less attractive is the tendency to which it gives rise to conflate an argument for the givenness of the professional system with an argument for acceptance of the actual state of this system. The discussion of professionalism has been much more useful when it has opened the concept out to a comparative study of the historical constitution of professionalism. Samuel Weber, for example, following Bledstein, has outlined the ideology by which from the late nineteenth century onward the "professional" defined the services he rendered as incommensurable with and irreducible to commodity relationships. In order to sustain this ideology, that is "in order for the authority of the professional to be recognized as autonomous, the 'field' of his 'competence' had to be defined as essentially self-contained, in accordance with the 'natural' self-identity of its 'objects.' "[6] Fields are constructed by an initial attention to the borders which demarcate them; but the visibility of limits then tends to be replaced by the detail of rules derived from the founding principles.[7] Said similarly argues that the professional elaboration of the interior of a field tends to block off critical methodological considerations: "A principle of silent exclusion operates within and at the boundaries of discourse; this has become so internalized that fields, disciplines, and their discourses have taken on the status of immutable durability."[8] In particular, the formation and monumentalization of a canon acts as "a blocking device for methodological and disciplinary self-questioning."[9] This process has very direct political consequences, which Said spells out elsewhere: literary critics' "passive devotion to masterpieces, culture, texts, and structures posited simply in their own 'texts' as functioning yet finished enterprises, poses no threat to authority or to values kept in circulation and managed by the technocratic managers."[10]

A Marxist intervention in the discipline of literary studies cannot hope to escape the disciplinary constraints which enable the production of theory, but it can claim to be able to turn back upon these constraints, to indicate the political consequences of boundaries, and to formulate strategies for change. To reflect upon the institutional conditions of constitution of theoretical categories is at once to perform a critique of and to be complicit with the functions of a discipline. These functions can be schematically summarized as the organization and closure of a body of knowledge; the establishment of a canon and a set of methodological paradigms; the administration of forms of accreditation and exclusion; the controlled transmission of knowledge to "disciples"; the establishment of hierarchies of authority; and the definition of appropriate positions of utterance. Building the disciplinary position of enunciation into the theory—without which the effects of this position remain an uncontrolled and uncontrollable secret[11]—is therefore a methodological and tactical necessity; but it is also a way of qualifying any claim of Marxist theory to critical exteriority.

The second context in which this book is situated is directly political. A first version of the book was written in the United States at the end of the Vietnam war. It is rewritten today in a world in which the extermination of the human race is a present possibility. The time between these two writings has witnessed a global crisis of capitalism which has produced massive unemployment and shifted the balance of financial power even further against the Third World; the installation of reactionary regimes in most major Western nations; the extension of the power of U.S. imperialism, both through the increasing control exercised by transnational corporations, the international monetary organizations, and the state-sponsored trade in arms, and through direct military intervention, concentrated most recently in Central America and the Caribbean; the increasingly specular identification of the Soviet Union and the United States; the invasion of Afghanistan and the suppression of the Solidarity movement in Poland; the moral failure of the Cultural Revolution in China and the political failures of Eurocommunism; the political demoralization of large sections of the Western intelligentsia; and, overshadowing everything else, the building up of the arsenal of nuclear weapons to an apparently uncontrollable extent, together with the strengthening of the state and its powers of repression and surveillance to which this gives rise. None of these processes is my immediate concern, but they are my *ultimate* concern. While I insist throughout this book that the study of literary discourse must be nonreductive and must attend to the specificity of literary structures and systems, I also insist that the study of literary texts cannot and should not be separated from ordinary political struggle. Certainly, as Bernard Sharratt writes, "it is too easy to argue for a chain of connections linking one's academic or cultural 'interventions' in England to some putative global strategy of liberation, an alliance at a distance or a sectoral solidarity,"[12] just as it is equally facile to be dismissive of academic theorization. Connections between practices are never given but have to be constructed, with great difficulty and great possibilities of waste. But what is always given is that the practices of literary study are political through and through.

The third relevant context in which this book intervenes is that of Marxist theory and the so-called crisis of Marxism. The crisis is in the first place political and has to do with the possibility of Marxist intellectual work in the absence of a credible mass movement informed by Marxist principles; with the transformation of Marxism in the Soviet Union into an ideology providing legitimation for new forms of class domination;[13] and with challenges mounted, above all by the women's movement, against the monolithic and authoritarian tendencies in Marxism. But this political crisis shades off into a theoretical crisis, caused above all by the inability of the Althusserian paradigm to sustain its momentum or rework itself in the face of criticisms from both its opponents and its adherents. For all its failings, this paradigm was the one current in contemporary Marxist thought with the potential for drastically rethinking the aporias of classical Marxism. The various humanist or culturalist or dogmatic Marxisms which survive it—and this includes most of the Hegelian Marxisms prevalent in the United States—are intellectually moribund and politically sterile.

The political and theoretical radicalism of Marxism can no longer be taken for granted. Nor can it be assumed to be a united whole with its core categories surviving intact (but this means as well that it is not the imaginary monolith constructed by its enemies). Anyone now working with and committed to Marxist theory will have to use concepts which are insecure, tentative, exploratory; will have to recognize the need to draw upon bodies of thought elaborated outside Marxism, and often this will demand an arduous process of reworking alien categories; will have to be deeply suspicious of some of the central categories of Marxism itself. This book is nevertheless an essay *in* Marxist literary theory. I mean by this to claim a position in relation both to a theoretical tradition and to socialist practice. *Marxist* designates not a belief system but a tool which should be discarded when it no longer works adequately. My present judgment is that it can be made to work and that, together with feminism (a problematic "together"), it is the only body of thought capable of giving theoretical guidance to socialist practice (and this includes guidance in the struggle against the repressive regimes of state capitalism and authoritarian party structures). In particular, it is a compelling alternative to the various forms of liberal humanism which in their indefinite deferral of political positioning have been able to offer no serious resistance to the depredations of a power which is neither liberal nor humane.

THE POSSIBILITY of a Marxist literary theory is given in the promise and the ambiguity of the central Marxist metaphors relating the symbolic order to the total social process. The promise is that questions of signification and epistemology can be shifted to a different plane, where they would be reconstrued as questions about the relations between levels or moments of social structure and within a hierarchy of social practices. The ambiguity lies in the initial distinction between levels of the real and between the real and the symbolic. This distinction can either be abolished in a dialectical reintegration of the symbolic order in the real, and the recognition that the real is itself constantly produced and reproduced, or it can be perpetuated as a more powerful unilinear model of causality which relegates the symbolic order to the status of a determinate effect.

Classical Marxist literary theory (from Plekhanov and Mehring, through such disparate writers as Caudwell, Lukács, Fischer, and Sanchez Vasquez, to the official proponents of the doctrine of realism—Weimann, Träger— or heterodox aestheticians like Morawski) has shown a surprising unity in its conception of literary signification; and this unity is provided by its acceptance of the metaphor of the determination of the superstructure by the economic base as an ontological model. The mode of this determination has been thought in radically different ways (as reflection, correspondence, interaction, homology, analogy, affinity, expression, testimony, modeling), but the structure of the terms involved is relatively constant. In its simplest and most mechanical acceptance, the metaphor implies a division of reality into two parts, one of which is more real than the other; the literary text belongs to the superstructure and so has a purely epiphenomenal status with respect to the socioeconomic base. This is, however, no more than a starting point for classical Marxist theory. The originality of the tradition lies in its grafting of this division onto the structure of literary discourse, so that rather than the text's being a purely determinate and secondary phenomenon, it internalizes the division between base and superstructure and superimposes it on the traditional dichotomy of form and content.

Let me illustrate this with a passage from Henri Arvon's exposition of the matter:

> Marxist aesthetics . . . is forced to admit the priority of content, which then creates the need for an appropriate form . . . The relations between content and form correspond to the more general relations between the economic base and the ideological superstructure; content is the governing factor and though form in the final analysis is always necessarily subservient to it, it is not thereby shorn of all autonomy whatsoever.[14]

Content is "prior" because it is, or is the representative of, reality *within* the work. But this leads to a profoundly ambivalent ontology of the text. Insofar as content is more real than form, it is both a literary fact and a nonliterary fact (it is reality itself); it is both inside and outside the text, and so the text straddles two realms, two distinct orders of being—reality and fiction. The signified of the text lies outside the sign; or more precisely, the literary sign incorporates the referent into itself, since the content is grasped as both signified and referent.

Content is thus the presence of an absence, signifying the absent presence of reality, and the text is torn between the phenomenality of the signifier and the quasisubstantiality of the signified. Substance enters the text through the presence of content, but it is absent insofar as content is also an absence (that is, insofar as it also belongs to the order of literary discourse). This implies, further, that it is only this ambivalently external/internal factor which is fully historical. Historicity is denied to the *structure* of the text (the "form" which is "subservient" to content) and is displaced onto that absence which manifests itself as a ghostly concreteness. Hence the inevitable disjuncture between a formal analysis of the text, which can apprehend only the inessential, and an analysis of content, which can come to terms with the essential historicity of the text only by basing itself on that which is not the text (the writer's grasp of reality). The categories of traditional bourgeois aesthetics—the opposition of inside/outside, the text as a stasis outside of time—are thus covertly reintroduced. Since content, which is prior and determinant, is never really contaminated by its immanence within the formal organization of the text (the shell which encloses it without touching it, or the transparent veil through which we glimpse, in a more or less distorted fashion, "reality"), there can be no structural connection between the two moments. This means that the social determination of the text can be formulated in a general manner, but that it "would not be extended to the *intrinsic* structure, nor therefore to the detailed scientific *analysis* of the work."[15] The text is merely set in motion by an external force, and thereafter becomes totally autonomous.

The complicated paradox by which the text is seen as a superstructural moment which itself internally reproduces the opposition of base/superstructure should perhaps be taken as an attempt to redeem the literary text from its purely derivative status. But such an attempt can never be completely successful so long as the linkage between the signifier and the signified is continually broken and the signified is displaced to a position outside the sign, where it merges with the referent. In this process the content, as a *formal* component of the text, must necessarily remain a surrogate, the sign of a reality which is *other* and which is *elsewhere*. The text can imitate this reality, can try to annihilate itself as artifice in order to draw into itself some of the properties of this nature, but it will always remain tainted by the original sin of its illusoriness. Mechanical materialism, which is never more than a reversal of idealism, reproduces a problematic which is still essentially metaphysical. The complex of forces and relations of production which constitutes the "base" takes on the overtones of a primal matter, and is set in opposition to the immateriality of the superstructure. The literary text cannot be considered a constitutive moment of the social but only a simple expression of it, the subjective reflex of a self-sufficient objectivity.[16]

The central problem of Marxist aesthetics becomes, then, that of the mediations between these two radically distinct poles. In most cases the solutions proposed have depended on a kind of alchemical transsubstantiation of economic into superstructural factors, and so, by extension, of the order of reality into the order of fiction. The text is a direct or mediated reflection of the structure of the material base, and its value is guaranteed to the extent to which it can create the illusion of substantiality. (Thus, in an extreme case, Zhdanov can claim that "socialist realism is the highest form of art known because of the reality which it paints.")[17] Mediation is effected, in other words, through a confusion of the two orders, through a sleight of hand by which reality itself permeates the literary text. But this failure to distinguish rigorously between the real and the fictive, to exclude the "real" from the order of fiction, has also been a failure to conceive of the fictive as part of the real (as a social practice with real effects). Even where a relation, not of direct determination but of homology between the base and the superstructure, is proposed, this still fails to take account of the function of discursive practices within social relations of production, and still subordinates textual structure to an originary structure of which it is the expression. Nor is it a sufficient solution to have recourse to the marked card of an unspecified interaction between base and superstructure (with the "determination in the last instance by the economic" always hidden in the deck). This formula remains empty as long as it is merely concessionary, as long as literary discourse is still theorized within the framework of a substantialist ontology.

The further consequence of the base/superstructure metaphor which is of particular relevance here is that it is necessarily linked with a particular conception of history and historical time; synchronic and diachronic metaphors are rigorously interdependent. To put this in its simplest form, the separation of the superstructure from the production process means that one of these distinct levels is conceived as the autonomous motive force of history. Both Hegelian Marxism and orthodox materialism postulate a simple historical dynamic, and one which is therefore continuous: the structure is expressive of its center (of whichever moment is determinant of the other and therefore carries history within itself), and this center generates a set of homogeneous relations between the moments of this structure, informing them with a single mode of historicity.

But it is not only in the case of historicist versions of Marxism that synchronic and diachronic conceptions are mutually implicated. Every metaphorics of the social structure generates a corresponding model of historical change, which in turn has consequences for the conceptualization of the system of literary discourse and literary history. In what follows I shall isolate three moments of Marxist literary theory that I take to be of particular significance for the construction of these categories and try to describe their different methodological problematics. They can be designated in shorthand form as "historicist," "structuralist," and "post-structuralist" phases of Marxist literary theory. In the rest of this chapter I look at the historicist aesthetics of Georg Lukács.

LUKÁCS'S WRITINGS on literary theory, from *Die Seele und die Formen* to *Die Eigenart des Ästhetischen,* are knotted together by a small number of concepts and conceptual patterns which stretch continuously beneath the series of breaks marking off the different "phases" of his production. The crucial pattern is that which crystallizes around the notion of mediation between consciousness and totality.[18] For a literary-theoretical study, the best angle of approach is through Lukács's conception of genre.[19] This is for Lukács the essential unit of literary discourse, and he remained constantly indebted for his conception of it to idealist aesthetics; that is, "he remained faithful to the view that a small number of genres, each determined by a set of recognizable laws of its own, constitute the realm of literature,"[20] and that the development of these genres reflects or expresses successive stages in the self-realization of the "world-spirit" or of mankind. *The Theory of the Novel* takes as its starting point the coincidence of the structural categories of the novel with those of the modern world,[21] the total analogy of literary genre and spirit. As late as 1952, Lukács reaffirmed, in an approving summary of Hegel's theory of genre, his belief in the organic connection between the institution of genre and history:

> The forms of the artistic genres are not arbitrary. On the contrary, they grow out of the concrete determinacy of the particular social and historical conditions. Their character, their peculiarity is determined by their capacity to give expression to the essential features of the given socio-historical phase. Hence the different genres arise at particular stages of historical development, they change their character radically (the epic is transformed into the novel), sometimes they disappear completely, and sometimes in the course of history they rise to the surface again with certain modifications.[22]

Two kinds of historical movement are implied in this account: a continuous development passing through a series of phases, and a movement of disappearance followed by re-emergence in a modified form. These two modalities are not exclusive: a form of cyclical repetition is being overlaid on a linear sequence, and what this means is that Lukács is thinking in terms of a spiraling historical movement. Thus each phase is at once progressive and yet runs parallel to a previous phase or series of phases. This translates, in practice, into the notion of rising and falling periods, corresponding to the organic development and decline (on successively higher stages) of a social class and of the literary form through which that class most appropriately expresses itself. This may go some way toward explaining what is apparently a failure of historical awareness in Lukács's work, his absolutization of a particular form of the novel as an ahistorical model of realism. The logic of his position lies in the necessary correspondence between two "rising" periods (that of the bourgeoisie and that of the proletariat), and hence between the media chosen by the parallel ascending classes to express their situation.[23] The absolute identification of the social and aesthetic levels means, furthermore, that the literary forms employed in a period of class decline are, *a fortiori*, to be seen as "decadent," and that conversely a writer's choice of a decadent form is an indication of class position.[24]

The literary genre thus stands in a privileged relation to the historical period, but it also expresses the tension between the given historical "form" (the structure of social life) and an ideal form laid down in the genre as an absolute possibility. The archetype of this realized ideal form is the epic, and the epistemological superiority of the epic to the other genres lies in its capacity for aesthetic realization of totality;[25] it is its absolute content which makes epic narrative the norm against which all narrative forms are to be measured. It *discovers* (copies) an immanent meaningfulness, whereas modern art can only *create* (construct) a pseudototality which is a substitute for "the natural unity of the metaphysical spheres."[26] The novel, then, is a necessarily degraded form of epic narrative; in it, the discontinuity between the subject and the social structure is interiorized, becoming (above all through irony) a formal component of the text, and "the immanence of meaning required by the form is attained precisely when the author goes all the way, ruthlessly, towards expressing its absence."[27]

But if the novel is a degraded form of the epic, it is also a figure of this lost possibility of realization of totality. In the later Lukács the notion of historical recurrence seems increasingly to have led him to ignore the moment of negativity he had recognized in the novel. History itself loses its uncertainty and its formlessness, and the notion of a historical teleology, leading to a return to a harmonious and hierarchized world, makes possible again (and retrospectively) an aesthetic of discovery, of imitation of the "immanence of meaning required by the form." An ethical-aesthetic valuation (realism/decadence) replaces the morally neutral categories of *The Theory of the Novel,* and the bourgeois historical novel becomes the type of a new manifestation of wholeness.

In a central passage of "Narrate or Describe," the content of genuinely epic art ("and of course the art of the novel") is described "as something that emerges and grows naturally, as something not invented, but simply discovered,"[28] and this opposition is then related to that of description and narration. The historical necessity for the decline of the bourgeois novel is adduced: "Description, as we have discussed it, becomes the dominant mode of composition in a period in which, for social reasons, the sense of what is primary in epic construction has been lost. Description is the writer's substitute for the epic significance that has been lost."[29]

But—and here the moment of antihistorical wish fulfillment in Lukács's later thought, and the real contrast to *The Theory of the Novel,* becomes apparent—if novelists can no longer *discover* meaning, this is nevertheless primarily a moral failing on their part, not the result of an objective social process: "The predominance of description is not only a result but also and simultaneously a cause, the cause of a further divorce of literature from epic significance . . . The poetic level of life decays—and literature intensifies the decay."[30]

It is in this context that we can understand Lukács's constant opposition to literary modernism and his celebration in *Wider den missverstandenen Realismus* of "normality." Already in *Die Seele und die Formen* Lukács had demanded a new realization of the great literary forms, and had failed to foresee the movement toward negation or destruction of form in modernism (later Lukács saw this process only to repress and condemn it). His response to modernism is a reactionary movement of defense. Recognizing the crisis, he is unable to draw the consequences from it. In 1911 *"he stands on the threshold of the crisis* and sees all the warning signs, but still he believes in the possibility of opposing to it a law and an attitude which by its very absoluteness could heal all the wounds and fissures of existence."[31] *The Theory of the Novel* begins that quest for a reintegration which is taken as accomplished in the essays and books of the 1930s.[32]

The dichotomy of discovery/invention is carried over into the epistemological theory of reflection. It seems correct to say that the abstract rigidity of Lukács's later theoretical framework needs to be understood as a response to the antirepresentational impetus of modernism.[33] The two complementary poles of "decadent" modern art—naturalism and symbolism—in fact correspond to the reflection theories of mechanical materialism and idealism from which he attempts to demarcate his own (orthodox Leninist) theory. On the one hand Diderot, for example, takes reflection to mean a direct registration of matter on consciousness,[34] just as Zola is concerned with surface detail in abstraction from essence or typicality; on the other hand Schiller (according to Lukács's reading) makes a radical separation between the truth reflected by art and the illusory surface *(Schein)* of the empirical world,[35] just as symbolism separates essence from appearance. On the one hand the category of singularity *(Einzelheit)* is overstressed and on the other hand that of generality *(Allgemeinheit)*, whereas a dialectical theory operates in terms of a movement backwards and forwards between three categories, with the dominant and mediating role played by the category of particularity *(Besonderheit)*.[36] The goal of artistic reflection is a picture of reality in which there is a unity of essence and appearance, individual case and general principle, immediacy and concept.[37] The "concrete artistic embodiment" of particularity is the *typical;* this involves the reproduction both of the typical features of people, feelings, thoughts, objects, institutions, situations, and so on, and of the system of relations into which these typifications are inserted. Through this reproduction, "in the whole of the work a typicality of a higher order arises: the aspect of a typical stage of development of human life, of its essence, its destiny, its perspectives."[38] But this "typicality of a higher order" is only ambivalently a product of the text, because the typical, "like all elements of artistic content, is a category of life."[39] Thus the text possesses its own autonomy only insofar as it is a correct reflection of the structure of objective reality, only insofar as it establishes an exact correspondence with the immanent meaningfulness of historical life.[40]

If history is inherently and objectively meaningful, and if the task of the writer is to reflect this structure of the historical process, then the writer performs no independent productive activity: "The requirement that realism reflect '*with objective correctness* the total objective process of life' means in actuality the reconciliation of the artist with society; through his obligation towards 'reality' it directs him to a precisely determined function in this society and it subordinates the work of art to a purposeful design [*einem Planwillen*] located outside of art."[41]

This "purposeful design" is the autonomous historical Necessity working to bring about the inevitable progress of capitalism into communism. Lukács develops this conception of the objective movement of social development in the 1932 essay "Tendenz oder Parteilichkeit." The socialist writer has no need to make "tendentious" demands of reality—that is, to intervene in the movement of history: "No 'tendency' can and must be opposed to this objective reality as a 'demand,' since the demands which the writer represents [*vertritt*] are integral parts of the self-movement of this reality itself, at once consequences and preconditions of its self-movement."[42]

The author is merely the medium through which the laws of history come to expression; as Helga Gallas puts it, "The demand for 'realistic construction' and for closed forms is a demand for the *mimetic representation* of that '*self-movement of reality*' which occurs independently of author and public."[43] History moves toward a predetermined goal, and this goal is the realization of an "objective rationality": the process is rational, and the writer must reflect this rationality in the harmonious nature of his form. The attack on modernism, then, can be seen primarily as an attack on formal distortions which deny the rationality of the historical process. The organic and cyclical rise-and-decline schema is subordinated to this concept, and indeed Lukács's refusal to consider the notion of modernist art as a reflection of bourgeois decadence suggests that, except for polemical purposes, his concern is not, as Brecht implies in a paragraph of one of his workbooks,[44] an apocalyptic vision of decline but rather a constant belief in the upward spiral of history through its rising and falling cycles.

The many references in Lukács's work to the "spontaneity," the "instinctual" or "naive" nature of artistic production must be linked to this notion that the author acts merely as a medium for the transmission of a shaped reality. Ultimately, as Hans Robert Jauss notes, this notion "endows hypostasized reality—similar to Hegel's 'cunning of reason'—with the power itself indirectly to produce literature."[45] That this charge is not an exaggeration can be extensively demonstrated. In an essay on Thomas Mann, for example, Lukács writes at one point of "the corrective which the process of reproducing reality, the passionate pursuit of this process to its very end, *in fine* [*letzten Endes*] which reality itself applies to the false thinking of the writer"[46] (one of the central ambiguities of his thought is concentrated in that *in fine*). Later he writes: "The style of the novel . . . is determined by the character of the relations between being and consciousness, between man and the environment. The more comprehensive and complete these relationships, the more realistic in scope and the more truthful in particulars [*Je umfassender . . . diese Wechselbeziehungen geraten*], the more significant the novel."[47]

Here he omits completely the transition from reality to its formal construction by the novelist: the ambiguity of *geraten,* which implies that reality organizes itself in ways favorable or unfavorable to the novel form, that in effect "reality" writes the novel, is not accidental but rather points to a failure or refusal to make the basic structural distinction between the order of fiction and the order of the real. This blurring means that the criteria we bring to bear upon the text are entirely external to it: "The work of art must . . . reflect correctly and in proper proportion all important factors objectively determining the area of life it represents," and "the objective character of the area of life represented determines the quantity, quality, proportion, etc., of the factors that emerge in interaction with the specific laws of the literary form appropriate for the representation of this portion of life."[48]

If the "portion of life" is "represented" (*gestaltet*—"given shape"), this is nevertheless not a process which modifies its nonaesthetic otherness: it goes into the work *as* a piece of life, and the mere fact that the laws of the genre which "interact" in the determination of its features are the laws "of the literary form *appropriate* for [its] representation" indicates that what is at issue here is simply an effaced presentation, the choice of a medium which will interfere as little as possible with the direct reproduction (duplication) of a purified piece of reality. This magical translation without change of substance occurs because of the absolute correspondence between the order of reality and the parallel system of aesthetic, and especially generic, canons.[49] In the writings of Lukács's Marxist period, the genre which most fully permits the shining through of an unmediated content is the historical novel, which becomes virtually identical with the novel form itself.[50] The chance it offers is for the critic to read *through* the text to an undisplaced reality which can be analyzed in conventionally political terms. To this end the novel's world must appear unbroken, an object of immediate perception.[51] The text must be closed, rounded, a totality in itself; the "organically developing work of art" must function as a piece of nature:

> The more "artless" a work of art, the more it gives the effect of life and nature [*je mehr es bloss als Leben, als Natur wirkt*], the more clearly it exemplifies an actual concentrated reflection of its times and the more clearly it demonstrates that the only function of its form is to express this objectivity, this reflection of life in the greatest concreteness and clarity and with all its motivating contradictions.[52]

Since the function of form is to negate itself, to be totally transparent, any laying bare of the form principle, any disjunction between world and fictional "world," must destroy, along with the illusion of nonfictionality, the appearance of objective historical laws.[53] Hence the "peculiar hankering after the idyllic"[54] which Brecht saw in Lukács's "formalist"[55] hypostatization of the categories of nineteenth-century realism: preteriteness ("the preterite character of the epic is . . . a fundamental medium prescribed by reality for the achievement of artistic structuration"),[56] the creation of "typical" and "living" characters,[57] the use of identification and catharsis,[58] and so on. The genre and the historical form of this genre which most fully embody the ideal of nonfictionality, of "naturalness," become representative of the total functions of literature. The central weakness in Lukács's thought, then (a weakness embedded precisely in the "mediating" category of genre), is a failure of mediation. Literature is not a conventional order of discourse; rather, literary reality is immediately identical with reality itself.[59] Or more precisely, literature is based on the iconic sign: it is natural, motivated, mirroring a sense which is independent of its interpretation. The continuity with the Lukács of *The Theory of the Novel* is provided by the continuing appeal to a metaphysics of presence in which discursive mediations fall away.

This is not, of course, simply a conceptual failure, and it cannot be explained solely in terms of Lukács's intellectual career. Several recent studies[60] have stressed that, despite Lukács's own later justification of his role in the "Expressionism debate" as having been directed against the worst features of socialist realism—a rescuing of tradition in the face of a *wrong* tradition—in fact his attack on "left-sectarian" and formally innovative writers was not directed *against* an official party line but was part of a right-wing offensive and was a formative influence in the elaboration of an official aesthetic theory. Mittenzwei, Gallas, and Cases have all followed Brecht in indicating the connection between Lukács's conservative aesthetic views and his espousal of the Popular Front policy of the 1930s, and more generally his approval of the dismantling of revolutionary socialism under Stalin.[61] In Lukács's activity in defense of the German Communist Party's disastrous attempt to ally itself with the "progressive" bourgeoisie, "the connection between anti-fascism and the cultural inheritance is immediately transmuted into an idealized struggle between Humanism and Barbarism";[62] and, as Brecht noted several times, the notion of class struggle either vanishes completely or is universalized: "In the long run everything is class struggle."[63]

But the important question is not only that of the *tactical* position within which Lukács's thought is to be situated, but that of the relation between the contradictions in his thought and the increasingly contradictory development of communism in the Soviet Union. Here I can do no better than follow Mészáros's sketch of this relationship. He isolates three central factors: (1) Lukács's personal political ineffectiveness (culminating in the defeat of the "Blum Theses" in 1928); (2) his idealization of the party as an instrument of political mediation;[64] and (3) "the practical disintegration of all forms of effective political mediation, from the Workers' Councils to the Trade Unions . . . In *History and Class Consciousness* the institution of the Workers' Councils still appeared as a necessary form of mediation and its effective instrumentality. Now, however, its place had to be left empty, as indeed all other forms of political mediation too had to leave a vacuum behind them."[65] Because of this disjunction between "the limited immediacy of political perspectives and the universality of a socialist programme," and because of the destruction of the "instrumental guarantees" of mediation,[66] the role of mediation is assigned, in Lukács's conception, to ethics. Lukács "finds himself in this respect in the position of 'ethical utopianism,' "[67] and this "abstractness of the political dimension in [his] conception of this dialectical system of mediations leaves its marks on the various complexes of problems, whether in Aesthetics or in Ontology, in Epistemology or indeed in Ethics itself to which that problematical role of 'should-be mediation' is assigned."[68] This utopianism, and this displacement of political into ethical activity, is surely to be related to the similarly utopian hope expressed in *Die Seele und die Formen* of opposing to the crisis in the world of forms "a law and an attitude which by its very absoluteness could heal all the wounds and fissures of existence;"[69] and to the advocacy of an absolute generic form which would realize an integration between subject and object which had not occurred in reality.

2

Marxism and Structuralism

THE WORK OF LUKÁCS—like that of Adorno and Marcuse, Goldmann, Della Volpe, and many others—has been dominated by the urge to construct a Marxist aesthetics—that is, a comprehensive ontology of literary discourse. This is no longer, or at least not in the same way and on the same ground, the case with the "structuralist" phase represented by Pierre Macherey's *Pour une théorie de la production littéraire (A Theory of Literary Production)* and Terry Eagleton's *Criticism and Ideology*.[1] The initial impetus of Macherey and Eagleton is to question the status of the literary text as an object "factually given, spontaneously isolated for inspection" (Macherey, 13), and of the field within which this object is constituted. If this field is a more or less fixed domain, then the only option available to Marxist theory is a different form of description of the same object, a change of terminology on the same terrain as traditional aesthetics.[2] Such a purely procedural change would rest on the empiricist presupposition that the object of knowledge exists independently of the discourse within which it is constructed. But this is clearly not true of the concept of Literature, which designates not the given totality of all writings but rather a privileged order of values, defined and realized within various institutional discourses. What is at issue is not a particular form of definition of this order but precisely "the ideological significance of that process whereby certain historical texts are severed from their social formations, defined as 'literary,' bound and ranked together to constitute a series of 'literary traditions' and interrogated to yield a set of ideologically presupposed responses" (Eagleton, 57). Put this way, the task of Marxist critical analysis can no longer be the hermeneutic release of a meaning concealed beneath the textual surface. Where the procedures of interpretation work from a preconstituted field (Literature) to the discovery of particular values within that field, Marxist criticism will take this relationship itself as its object, defining it as a socially specific structure of production. It "will no longer be satisfied with describing the finished product, preparing it to be transmitted and consumed; rather it will elaborate this product, explaining rather than describing. In a radical departure from all the active tendencies of previous criticism, a new critical question is proposed: What are the laws of literary production?" (Macherey, 12).

This question can, however, be posed in two quite distinct ways: either as the question of specific historical systems of production or as the question of the productive activity of texts. In the first case the relevant theoretical problems are those of the determinate conditions and relations under which certain texts, and certain kinds of text, are given a specific authority and articulation within the discursive economy of a social formation. Interest is directed, for example, to the relative subordination of literary to religious discourse in the feudal period, and to the conditions under which different literary genres were able to confirm or problematize this relationship by incorporating a range of other genres of discourse. The general theoretical basis for this would be a sociology of literary functions—that is, a study of the determination of systems and practices of signification within a particular set of relations of literary production. Eagleton's chapter "Categories for a Materialist Criticism" (44–63) may serve as an example of this perspective. Its defects are immediately apparent: it proceeds by deducing the status of the text from the interplay of a schematic set of categories of which the text is the concrete result. The methodology is inherently reductionist and is incapable of explaining how it is that the text is so constituted by a specific conjuncture of elements "as to actively determine its own determinants" (63).

In order to come to terms with this dialectical relation between text and system both Macherey and Eagleton tend to shift the question of the "laws of literary production" toward the problematic of the productive activity of the text, understood as a labor of transformation carried out on a raw material of ideological values, including the aesthetic ideology which governs the limits of textual productivity. Literature is thus conceptualized both as an institution which is within ideology and as a practice which distances itself from ideology by working it and changing its function. It lacks the unity of a merely expressive practice. The values produced by literary discourse can neither be equated with ideological values nor be seen as a transcendence of ideology. The text is rather a process of internal rupture and contradiction, defined in terms of the transformation of one order of signification into another. The specificity of literary discourse consists in the epistemological ambivalence of its enunciation of the ideological discourses which are both its object and its limiting conditions. According to Macherey, it is marked by "the inscription of an *otherness* in the work, through which it maintains a relationship with that which it is not, that which happens at its margins" (79). The ideological frame which constitutes the status of the text is at the same time internalized, challenged, subjected to the operations of a reflexive metadiscourse in such a way that ideology "begins to speak of its own absences because of its presence in the novel, its visible and determinate form. By means of the text it becomes possible to escape from the domain of spontaneous ideology, to escape from the false consciousness of self, of history, and of time. The text constructs a determinate image of the ideological, revealing it as an object rather than living it from within as though it were an inner conscience; the text explores ideology" (132). The key questions then become those of the cognitive status of this internal dissociation of ideology from itself as it moves to a level of partial and incomplete self-signification.

Macherey's reified syntax tends to present this process as a universal ontology of the text. Eagleton is rather more careful to talk about a range of possible operations: the analogy between the relations of text/ideology and dramatic production/dramatic text allows him to suggest the variability of the text's production of ideology, the fact that the logic of the text may work either with or against the logic of ideology (68), and the internal dissonance of the text is not seen as a conflict between two distinct poles, two incompatible discourses. In Eagleton's formulation, "the problem-solving process of the text is never merely a matter of its reference outwards to certain pre-existent ideological cruxes. It is, rather, a matter of the 'ideological' presenting itself in the form of the 'aesthetic' and vice versa" (88). This is more properly dialectical than Macherey's neat separation of text and ideology, which results in his theorizing literary discourse as at once the whole and a part of the text ("There is a conflict within the text between the text and its ideological content," 124) and, conversely, theorizing ideology both as an active presence and as that which is absent from and unenunciated in the text.

But if Macherey's theory is ambiguous at a number of crucial points, it nevertheless marks an important break with the dominant assumptions of previous Marxist literary theory. The tradition is a complex one, but Posada's description is a useful simplification:

Important sectors of Marxist criticism considered art an ideal "translation" of the real conditions of the historical process. Its task consisted in reflecting these more or less faithfully, and hence the interpretation of art should be an *analogon* of the (one hopes previous) interpretation of the given reality. On the one hand, mechanical materialism postulated a correlation between the evolution of the base and of art; on the other, explicit or concealed Hegelianism made it into a direct "expression" of the "spirit" of a class, or the integrating element of a world view seen as a social group's framework of representation of reality.[3]

This has the advantage of indicating the unity of these two tendencies in a presupposition that the text reproduces a truth which precedes it and which is situated on a different ontological plane. Macherey's theoretical innovation consists above all in his displacement of the problematic of an expressive or representational relation between two disparate realms. The conception of literary production as a process implies that on the one hand, as a produced object, the text is seen as a component of the general system of social production, that the "real" is not its object but its institutional conditions of existence; and on the other hand, as a productive activity, the text is seen as a distinct practice of signification which is related not to a nondiscursive truth but to other practices of signification. In both cases literary discourse is treated as a reality in its own right, a practice which cannot be subordinated to an external reality which in the last instance determines its own representation or expression in discourse. It is not just that literary discourse mediates the real through a specific and conventional structure of logical categories, for this is true of all language. Macherey's point is that "the autonomy of the writer's discourse is established from its relationship with the other uses of language," that it is "a contestation of language rather than a representation of reality" (59, 61).

Here too there is a danger of reifying literary discourse as a fixed function, defining it in terms of its absolute difference from "everyday speech [and] scientific propositions" (Macherey, 59) rather than as a social institution. But there is a clear advantage in shifting away from that metaphysics of the referent which acts in orthodox Marxist theory as an ultimate epistemological guarantee. Rather than being the transposition of a reality posited as absolute and absolutely known (but which is in fact a construct of other texts), the text is seen as "the production of certain produced representations of the real into an imaginary object. If it distantiates history, it is not because it transmutes it to fantasy, shifting from one on-tological gear to another, but because the significations it works into fiction are already representations of reality rather than reality itself. The text is a tissue of meanings, perceptions and responses which inhere in the first place in that imaginary production of the real which is ideology" (Eagleton, 75). This has major implications for the criteria on which a text is judged: it ensures that relations will be established between phenomena of the same logical order. But what is perhaps the most important implication is not spelled out until a later paper by Macherey and Balibar: if literary discourse "cannot define itself simply as a figuration, an appearance of reality," then it cannot be thought of as "fiction, a fictive image of the real"; it is rather a production of "fiction-effects," and therefore also of "reality-effects." And this means that "fiction and realism are not *the concepts for* the production of literature but on the contrary the notions produced by literature. But this leads to remarkable consequences for it means that the *model,* the real referent 'outside' the discourse which both fiction and realism presuppose, has no function here as a non-literary, non-discursive anchoring point predating the text . . . But it does function as an effect of the discourse."[4] And this in turn opens the way for the analysis of specific types of discourse as social institutions producing specific "realities" on the basis of definite (and historically variable) systems of rules and within determinate systems of discursive production.

The directions taken by Eagleton, Macherey, and others are founded in an extension of a number of Althusserian concepts to cover the definition of literary practice. This extension occurs in four main areas. The first concerns the conception of social totality. In opposition to the hierarchical and unilinear determinism implicit in the base/superstructure metaphor, Althusser posits a more complex model of causality in which there is an interaction between one level of the structured whole which is dominant but which is not a sole or final cause, and other levels which are dominated but which are not merely secondary effects. "Overdetermination" is the name Althusser gives to this process in which the general contradiction at the economic level is radically affected by the other levels which are its conditions of existence, and which are both determined by and in turn determine the dominant level.[5] There is no "determination in the last instance by the economic" because the last instance never comes.[6] Rather, determination is exercised "by permutations, displacements and conden-sations,"[7] and this means that the social formation is characterized by the uneven and nonteleological play of its elements, since the invariant structure of the complex whole exists only through the discrete variations for which it is the precondition. This is not a pluralism, but it allows an understanding of the effect of a plurality of determinations within a structure where one instance is dominant as a necessary condition of complexity. It is therefore distinct both from the Weberian conception of an indeterminate totality and from the economistic and Hegelian conceptions of a monocausal expressive totality—that is, "a totality all of whose parts are so many *total parts,* each expressing the others, and each expressing the social totality that contains them."[8] Althusser therefore conceives of the social whole as being constituted by distinct and relatively autonomous levels or instances which at any time are articulated in particular relations of domination and subordination and which are subject to a structural causality (97). Each level is the site of specific practices (economic, political, ideological, technical, and theoretical).

> We think the content of these different practices by thinking their peculiar structure, which, in all these cases, is the structure of a production; by thinking what distinguishes between these different structures, i.e., the different natures of the objects to which they apply, of their means of production and of the relations within which they produce . . . We think the relations establishing and articulating these different practices one with another by thinking their *degree of independence* and their type of "relative" *autonomy,* which are themselves fixed by their *type of dependence* with respect to the practice which is "determinant in the last instance": economic practice.   (58)

This model of a structure which is neither an aggregate nor the realization of a simple essence then provides the conditions for defining the specific effectiveness of distinct "superstructural" practices.

The second area of extension is derived more specifically from the concept of theoretical practice, which Althusser defines as a structure of *production* which elaborates its object of knowledge in accordance with its own laws, and which is therefore not the *representation* of an anterior real object. This definition is directed against the metaphysical presuppositions of empiricist epistemology, for which "to know is to abstract from the real object its essence, the possession of which by the subject is then called knowledge" (35–36). Knowledge is thus *"inscribed in the structure of the real object,* in the form of the difference between the inessential and the essence, between surface and depth, between outside and inside" (38). Empiricism, that is to say, simultaneously proposes and denegates the difference between the real object and the object of knowledge, reducing this difference "to a mere distinction between the parts of a single object: the real object" (40). In drawing from Marx a radical distinction between the real object (the concrete) and the object of knowledge (the concrete in thought), Althusser posits that "the production process of the object of knowledge takes place entirely in knowledge and is carried out according to *a different order* [from that of the real], in which the thought categories which 'reproduce' the real categories do *not* occupy the *same* place as they do in the order of real historical genesis, but quite different places assigned to them by their function in the production process of the object of knowledge" (41). To say that the production of knowledge occurs wholly "within thought" does not mean that thought is "a faculty of a transcendental subject or absolute consciousness confronted by the real world as *matter*," nor that it is "a faculty of a psychological subject"; rather it is "the historically constituted system of an *apparatus of thought*, founded on and articulated to natural and social reality. It is defined by the system of real conditions which make it . . . a determinate *mode of production* of knowledges" (41). Its determinate conditions include the state of the raw material it works, and this is always "an *ever-already* complex raw material, a structure of 'intuition' or 'representation' which combines together in a peculiar *'Verbindung'* sensuous, technical and ideological elements" (43). Knowledge therefore never confronts a "pure" (real) object; it is neither a reflection nor a representation of the real but a structure of discourse which *constructs* its object through an ordered transformation of pre-theoretical values.

Macherey's concept of literary production as the working of an ideological raw material clearly draws directly on this definition of theoretical practice. The third area of extension, however, is related both to literary discourse and to literary theory. This is the concept of the epistemological break which marks the transition from an ideological to a scientific form of theorization, and of the particular form of this transition, the *symptomatic reading* by which a theoretical text interrogates not the problems raised but the horizon of the problems, the "problematic," implicit in the texts which are its raw materials. This theory implies that theoretical production is based on an intertextual relation, not a relation to the extratextual real; it, as Althusser and Balibar put it, "divulges the undivulged event in the text it reads, and in the same movement relates it to *a different text*, present as a necessary absence in the first" (28). But it is not simply a reading of that which is missing from the prior text: it is rather a reading of the necessity of this absence, of the *relation* between the "seen" and the "unseen" which is constitutive of the limits of a problematic (21–22). It is therefore concerned with the dialectic between the answers inscribed within an ideological problematic and the questions which this problematic cannot pose. An epistemological break emerges from within a given horizon as a construction of the invisible questions of this horizon, not as a new set of questions or a new set of answers to old questions.

Macherey's adaptation of this concept tends to refer ambivalently both to the activity of the literary text, which foregrounds (but cannot "speak") the silences inherent in the material it works, and to the critical reading of literary texts, which is capable of posing the questions of these silences. This ambivalence is directly related to the fourth area of Althusserian theory which has influenced literary criticism: his situating literary discourse midway between theory and ideology. For Althusser, "real," "authentic" art is not to be classed as ideological; it "does not quite give us a knowledge in the *strict sense*"—that is, "in the modern sense: scientific knowledge"—but it does let us "see," "perceive," or "feel" the ideology to which it "alludes," through an *"internal distantiation."*[9] As Eagleton comments:

> This is a suggestive, radically unsatisfactory statement . . . Althusser and Macherey appear to want to *rescue* and *redeem* the text from the shame of the sheerly ideological; yet in these passages they can do so only by resorting to a nebulously figurative language ("allude," "see," "retreat") which lends a merely rhetorical quality to the distinction between "internal distantiation" and received notions of art's "transcendence" of ideology. (83–84)

The question of the epistemological status of literary discourse is, then, the crucial theoretical problem for writers in the Althusserian tradition. For Macherey the answer to it is formulated in terms of a distinction between three universal "forms" which give "three different uses of language: illusion, fiction, theory. These three discourses use more or less the same words, but the relations between these words are so different that there is no bridge, no unbroken path, from one order of discourse to another" (65). This absolute difference establishes "the distance which separates the work of art from true knowledge (a scientific knowledge) but which also unites them in their common distance from ideology. Science does away with ideology, obliterates it; literature challenges ideology by using it" (133). Implicit in this definition are two assumptions. The first is that literature can be described as a distinct ontological realm with a specific difference from the realm of ideology and an invariant function, the demystification of illusion through its parodic formal reproduction (64). Macherey later retracts this conclusion, but only to replace it with a Bernsteinian reduction of literary discourse to the single undifferentiated function of being an "imaginary solution" to the masked conflict of linguistic codes produced by the schooling system.[10] The second assumption is that the epistemological status of literary discourse can in fact be defined only *negatively:* the literary work, says Macherey, "is both the analogy of a knowledge and a caricature of customary ideology" (59). That is, it is neither knowledge nor ideology; it "is not *truer* than illusion: indeed, it cannot usurp the place of knowledge" but is rather its "substitute"; and if it is not ideology, it is also not outside ideology, since its critique of ideology is only "implicit" (64), and its function "is to present ideology in a non-ideological form" (133).

Form is the key word here: the language of illusion is "formless," and it is only in the process of "formation" of this language that the literary text can "transform" our relationship to ideology (Macherey, 64). The suggestion is that formal structures are in some sense a neutral tool applied from outside ideology, and it is with this "quasi-formalist position" that Eagleton takes issue. He does so in the first place by refusing the absoluteness of the distinction between (scientific) knowledge and (illusory) ideology. "If ideology is not knowledge, it is not pure fantasy either" (Eagleton, 84), and this means that the kind of knowledge produced by the text is the result of the working of an ideological material by tools which are themselves ideologically determined. The literary production process "is the process whereby ideology produces the forms which produce it, thus determining in general both the instruments and devices which work it, and the nature of the work-process itself" (84). It is therefore essential to examine both "the nature of the ideology worked by the text and the aesthetic modes of that working" (85).

But if Eagleton is concerned with avoiding the absolute epistemological distinctions by means of which Macherey preserves both the cognitive value of literary discourse and its subordination to the transcendental authority of theory, he is nevertheless still caught within a normative epistemological problematic. The text is able to "invert itself back into an analogue of knowledge" (85), to "yield us a sort of historical knowledge" which, however, "is not, to be sure, knowledge in the strict scientific sense" (71). This "sort of historical knowledge" is located in the space of a concession which nevertheless does nothing to modify the general distribution of discourse between the true and the false: "Epistemology does not divide neatly down the middle between strict science and sheer illusion" (71), and it is in this middle ground that the literary text produces itself as *"ideology to the second power"* (70). In a remarkable passage on Jane Austen, Eagleton's quotation marks, double negations, and parenthetical qualifications display to the full the theoretical embarrassment caused by the absence of concepts adequate to define the specificity of this episte-mological no man's land:

> The value of Austen's fiction thrives quite as much on its ignorance as on its insight; it is because there is so much the novels cannot possibly know that they know what they do, and in the *form* they do. It is true that Austen, because she does not *know*, only "knows"; but what she knows is not thereby nothing at all, cancelled to a cypher by the exclusion of the real.   (71)

This reality which is excluded is "the real as it is known to historical materialism"—an ambiguous formulation which may be read to mean either "the form in which historical materialism defines reality" or "reality, which historical materialism knows." The same ambivalence attaches to the ontological categories specifying the mode of signification of ideology: "It is because the ideological is 'real' (if not in the strongest sense) that it is not always essential for it to submit to a formal, quasi-scientific self-distantiation for it to hint at history" (71).

What happens here and in similar passages—perhaps surprisingly—is the reestablishment of a hierarchy in which one level (reality "in the strong-est sense") is located outside of discourse, as its source and its ultimate referent. As Catherine Gallagher argues, the postulation of "history" as an absolute point of origin "belies the most radical implications of se-miology," because "just as in reflection theory, the meaning of the text is located outside of it in some more 'substantial' reality."[11] Eagleton has in fact expressly attacked the semiotic conception of signification as a self-contained relational process, arguing that "History, in this schema, seems effectively to have evaporated. It is not only a question of the signi-fied . . . it is also a question of the referent, which we all long ago bracketed out of being. In re-materializing the sign, we are in imminent danger of de-materializing its referent."[12] The gestural appeal to the "materiality" of history, and its definition as "the real" in opposition to the "less real" of ideology, are indicative of the theological function the concept plays in the book's argument. The absolute existence of the referent outside any semiotic framework is the tautological guarantee of a truth which transcends ideology.

The attempt in *Criticism and Ideology* to avoid the normativeness of both reflection theory and Althusser's theoreticism is only a limited strategy, a deferral rather than a break. If Eagleton refuses to define literary discourse as mimesis, this is not because of any recognition that history is itself a textual construct (history in the sense of writing), nor therefore because he rejects the possibility of a correspondence between discourse and a pregiven, really existing structure. His refusal stems rather from a very traditional distinction between fictional and referential modes of signification, and this means that certain discourses are indeed potentially transparent to the real. Historiography, for example, "conventionally organizes its significations so as to yield an 'objective' account of the real; that it does not typically do so is because of an ideological construction of that real which is *contingent* to its character as a discourse" (73). By implication, what is contingent is precisely the structure of production of historiography; its essence as a discourse is not to construct the real but to reflect the categories which are somehow inherent in the real itself. By contrast, it is "intrinsic to the character of literary discourse that it does not take history itself as its immediate object, but works instead upon ideological forms and materials of which history is, as it were, the concealed underside" (73–74). Its "lack of a real direct referent constitutes the most salient fact about it: its fictiveness" (78). Historiography is thus directly subject to an absolute standard of measurement, whereas literary discourse is only indirectly so. But the crucial point is that "it does, nevertheless, *have* history as its object in the last instance, in ways apparent not to the text itself but to criticism" (74). And if this is apparent only to criticism, it is because the "last instance" is, in fact, the privileged order of Theory.

The solutions offered by Macherey and Eagleton in this phase of their work to the essentialism of orthodox Marxist literary theory are, then, only partial and imperfect; they are the solutions to a problem wrongly posed in epistemological terms. Tony Bennett has argued that these theorists ultimately share with Lukács a concern with "the distinguishing of the aesthetic from the non-aesthetic, of the 'literary' from the 'non-literary.' They both constitute 'literature' as a particular form of cognition which, if its specific nature is to be understood, requires the development of an autonomous level of theorizing within Marxism—a theory of 'literature' as a specialist sub-region within a general theory of ideology."[13] And insofar as "science," "literature," and "ideology" are conceived as fixed and universal forms of cognition, they are "not the result of materially conditioned practices so much as the mere manifestations of invariant structures."[14] What is valuable in the work of Macherey and Eagleton, we might say, is that their theorization of literary discourse as a process of transformation of ideological discourses gets at the complexity of the mediations between "real" and "symbolic" social practices. Because of this it is able to do away with the positivist claim to a privileged situation with direct access to the truth, and to reinscribe literary theory within a political process of judgment based in the situated assessment of what constitutes ideology.

But while Althusserian theory opens up this possibility of building the situation of the analyst into the process of judgment, it simultaneously negates this position. Despite his recognition that knowledge is produced within a determinate "mode of production of knowledges," defined by a network of material and economic, social, and ideological relations, and that the state of the (ideological) "raw material" which knowledge works is a part of the conditions of production of knowledge, and therefore sets its possible limits (*Reading Capital,* 42–43), Althusser consistently withdraws knowledge ("science") from its social determinations. The assertion of the synchronic "eternity" of the concept (107) is not merely a logical assertion; it is also a historical assertion. Knowledge is in no way relative to its (mediated) object, and the theory of history (*"as theory"*) is in no way "subject to the 'concrete' determinations of 'historical' time" (105): it remains frozen and undifferentiated, unaffected by the nature of the raw material it works or the historical conjuncture within which it is produced. Thus, logically, "science can no more be ranged within the category 'superstructure' than can language, which as Stalin showed escapes it" (133). Knowledge is *indeterminate.* In positing that there is no "practice-in-general," only distinct practices, including theoretical practice which has its own criteria of validity and its own mechanisms of appropriation (58–59), Althusser is therefore implicitly using a model of *indeterminate structure* (a series of contiguous systems unstructured by relations of dominance and subordination) rather than the effectively dialectical model of overdetermined structure. By drawing an absolute distinction between science and ideology (a distinction unaffected by his later self-criticism) and by placing science resolutely outside and above history, Althusser burdens Marxist theory with an inability to come to terms with its own political status as knowledge.

THE COLLAPSE of the Althusserian paradigm, which can in part be ascribed to an internal theoretical and political dynamic, is at the same time a moment of the larger passage from a structuralist to a post-structuralist problematic. Yet this model of a "before" and an "after" is of dubious value unless we have a clear idea of where the limits of structuralism may be drawn and of the degree of discontinuity involved in the breaking of these limits. (In the final section of this chapter, I shall examine two books that struggle with the political implications of these questions: Fredric Jameson's *The Political Unconscious* and Terry Eagleton's *Walter Benjamin, Or, Towards a Revolutionary Criticism*.)

One way of defining the limits of structuralism might be in terms of a certain positivism that accompanied the adoption of epistemological models from mathematics and the natural sciences. Philip Lewis has characterized this aspect of structuralism as "a reinforced form of critical mastery, a kind of technological control over texts, that understands—makes them intelligible, representable—as manifestations of a logical structure."[15] Its weakness is its inability to conceptualize the multiple frames within which structure is constituted. But to formulate this criticism is still to adopt a structuralist perspective insofar as structuralism is concerned primarily "not with knowledge or truth *per se*" but with the conditions of possibility of the production of meaning.[16] The difference that works itself out *within* structuralism refers above all to these conditions, and in particular to the status of the analytic metadiscourse. This is the paradox that confronts the discourse of deconstruction: that it is forced to recognize the inability of language to ground itself, and is forced to *say so* in language (as though it were grounded and authorized).[17] Thus late structuralism, focusing on the politics of its own "critical mastery," repeatedly rejects the possibility of *beginning* that would be given by a fixed relation of authority between object discourse and metadiscourse: no signifier without a signified, but no signified that cannot in its turn function as a signifier; no interpretation without a text that is itself an interpretation, a moment in an endless intertextual chain; no rhetoric without the possibility of literalness, but no such thing as the literal; no identity that is not always preceded by otherness and difference. The structuralist concept of signifying system radically undermines the traditional dichotomized categories of being and representation, object and subject—and the relations of priority or hierarchy between them—insofar as being must be thought of as deferred or mediated or even constituted by structures which are purely relational and differential; and representation must be thought of not as the echoing of a primal presence nor as the manifestation of an originary act of consciousness but as a construct of the signifying chain. There is no starting point, no point of metadiscursive authority (either the Real or Truth) which is not already caught within the play of discursive codes.

In this rejection of an order of ontological priority, in its temporalization of the spatial, and in its rounding on its own enunciative positions, deconstruction is effectively (if these things can be quantified) more dialectical than any current Marxist theory. But such a statement then needs to be moderated in two ways: first, the concept of dialectic is rejected by most post-structuralist writers as being a form of that logic of identity which reduces otherness to sameness in the very process of recognizing and incorporating the Other;[18] second, the politics of deconstruction tends to be a version of Nietzschean romanticism, and so refuses, finally, the possibility both of situating itself in relation to definite social determinations and of taking part in concerted action to change them.

Hence the provocation to Marxism. Jameson's and Eagleton's books are both preoccupied with it, directly or indirectly; both defend Marxist theory by means of a partial identification with the aggressor. The task is in many ways easier for Jameson, who has recourse to a Hegelian tradition capable of raiding, embracing, and subsuming a wide range of other theoretical positions. Indeed, this is built into the project: the concept that comes closest to defining his method—"metacommentary"—emphasizes that Jameson's path is not that of the object, "the historical origins of the things themselves," but that of the subject, "that more intangible historicity of the concepts and categories by which we attempt to understand those things."[19] The opposition is a sleight of hand, of course, that affirms by presupposing the possibility of the first alternative. But the choice of the second path allows Jameson to take as his object "less the text itself than the interpretations through which we attempt to confront and to appropriate it. Interpretation is here construed as an essentially allegorical act, which consists in rewriting a given text in terms of a particular interpretive master code" (9–10). Instead of naively adding its reading to the general stock of readings, instead of subjecting the text to an allegorizing reduction of one narrative line to another which is taken to be "the ultimate hidden or unconscious *meaning* of the first one" (22), a Marxist hermeneutic will question the function of the text in relation to its interpretations. Its concern will be with the mediations of the text rather than with its inherent sense.

From this position Jameson suggests that each "local" interpretive system valorizes a particular "master code," and that these valorizations are historically explicable (they can be subordinated to the narrative master code of History). Thus structuralism tends to take language as its key category; existentialism, the concepts of anxiety and the fear of freedom; phenomenology, the experience and thematics of temporality; psychoanalysis, the dynamics of sexuality; and the amorphous "ethical" criticism which is the untheorized mainstay of current institutional practice relies upon a humanist ideology and its attendant categories of self, identity, and so on. Despite their heterogeneity, all of these categories can be traced back to, and are the expression of, a real historical experience. The master code of psychoanalysis, for example, is to be situated not merely in terms of the institution of the nuclear family but, more important, in terms of a process of "psychic fragmentation since the beginnings of capitalism, with its systematic quantification and rationalization of experience, its instrumental reorganization of the subject just as much as of the outside world" (62): that is, in terms of a dynamic that Weber termed *rationalization* and that Lukács translated into the concept of *reification*. The nature of the subject itself has changed, and the psychoanalytic revolution, ultimately epiphenomenal, reflects this change on another plane. In the same way, the attention paid by structuralism to the mediating codes of language "is at one with its [language's] structural abstraction from concrete experience, with its hypostasis as an autonomous object, power, or activity" (63). It is the category of (concrete) experience that stands out in this context: everything depends upon its unproblematic acceptability, and yet it is posited as being *prior* to symbolic codes or the structure of the psyche— a difficult proposition that is never properly thematized.

On one level this strategy represents no more than a sophistication of the traditional Marxist tropology (leaving intact the structure of ontological opposition while complicating the forms of passage between the primary and derived poles). But it also has real advantages. Stylistically it generates structures of digression and incorporation similar to what Jameson once described as Adorno's use of the footnote as a "lyrical form" allowing him "a momentary release from the inexorable logic of the material under study in the main text, permitting him to shift to other dimensions, to the infrastructure as well as to the wider horizons of historical speculation."[20] Jameson's cumulative, integrative sentences allusively build up totalities out of multifarious discursive material, displaying in the process the breadth and generosity of his learning. And in part what is at issue here—in the performance as well as methodologically—is the category of totality. The struggle is most centrally worked out during the course of an attempted recuperation of Althusser.

Jameson follows Althusser in isolating three possible models of effectivity: those of mechanical, expressive, and structural causality. For Althusser these are mutually exclusive categories of social totality, forms of explanation of the linkage between instances of the social whole. What Jameson does is provisionally refuse any single *general* form of totality and so situate these models of causality as categories with a local and historical validity. Thus the central category of expressive causality (which he assimilates to the concept of allegory) is located "within the object"; expressive or "allegorical" interpretation has become inscribed "in the texts as well as in our thinking about them" (34), and is to that extent a necessary tool. Paradoxically, then, Jameson has shifted from the "path of the subject" to the "path of the object." The historical objectivity of structure predetermines the appropriate categories of its representation.

From this rewriting (which is intended to redeem not only an expressive model of interpretation but also the narrative unities of historicism) Jameson moves to put Althusser's concept of structural causality to unaccustomed work salvaging the objectivity of History (or rather its simultaneous externality and internality to the textual). What is problematic in Althusser's "antiteleological formula for history" (34) is that "it can readily be assimilated to the polemic themes of a host of contemporary post-structuralisms and post-Marxisms, for which History, in the bad sense—the reference to a 'context' or a 'ground,' an external real world of some kind, the reference, in other words, to the much maligned 'referent' itself—is simply one more text among others" (35). Against such an assimilation— but also in contrast to his own condemnation, in *The Prison-House of Language,* of the distinction between the concrete and the concrete-in-thought as "essentially a replay of the Kantian dilemma of the unknowability of the thing-in-itself"[21]—Jameson now welds together two seemingly incompatible propositions in a "revised formulation" of Althusser's thesis: on the one hand there is an insistence "that history is *not* a text, not a narrative, 'master' or otherwise"; on the other the concession "that, as an absent cause, it is inaccessible to us except in textual form, and that our approach to it and to the Real itself [in Lacan's sense] necessarily passes through its prior textualization, its narrativization in the political unconscious" (35). Here the Spinozan concept of an absent cause does double duty: Jameson takes it to be equivalent to the *hors-texte* of History, whereas Althusser uses it rather to designate the mode of existence of structure within the concept of structural causality. The semantic slide allows the question of History to become (again) the question of totality.

In a properly (and rare) political account of Althusser's stress on the "relative autonomy" of levels in the social formation, Jameson recognizes (what E. P. Thompson, for one, wilfully distorts) that this "may now be understood as a coded battle waged within the framework of the French Communist Party against Stalinism" (37), where the concept of expressive causality stands for that "productionist ideology of Soviet Marxism" according to which social relations constitute the more or less direct expression, the unilinear consequence, of the forces of production (so that changes in the form, and the form of ownership, of the latter will not only produce but will guarantee the real existence of a fully socialist society). The effect of Althusser's argument is to theorize social instances (the State, for example, or the institution of literature) as the sites of specific and contradictory political practices, rather than as the simple reproductions of a single central instance. The price paid for this is the possibility of dropping the "relative" from in front of "autonomy," failing to theorize the network of determinations of any level or instance (most notoriously that of Theory). But the conception of such a network is of course ultimately the point of Althusser's work. By the notion of semiautonomy he "means to underscore some ultimate structural interdependency of the levels, but . . . he grasps this interdependency in terms of a mediation that passes through the structure, rather than a more *immediate* mediation in which one level folds into another directly." His real object of attack is "unreflected immediacy" or the immediate identities of homology (here Lucien Goldmann is thrown to the wolves), and it thus becomes apparent that his "polemic target is at one with that of Hegel" (41). This in a very broad sense may be true, but the proposition writes out some not insubstantial differences.

From another direction, finally, Althusser is wheeled in to do battle against the post-structuralist problematization of the concept of totality. Here again, and characteristically, Jameson begins with a celebration of the negative, of the adversary position. Part of what is usually suggested by the concept of totality is an aesthetic of organic form, whereas the concept of structural causality stresses that "the appropriate object of study emerges only when the appearance of formal unification is unmasked as a failure or an ideological mirage"; it would then stage this object "as an *interference* between levels, as a subversion of one level by another." Nevertheless, the priority granted in Althusserian theory to the concept of mode of production means that "the current post-structural celebration of discontinuity and heterogeneity is therefore only an initial moment in Althusserian exegesis, which then requires the fragments, the incommensurable levels, the heterogeneous impulses, of the text to be once again related, but in the mode of structural difference and determinate contradiction" (56).

Many of the book's major themes are announced in this confrontation. Its limits may be suggested by Eagleton's remark that "the passage through and beyond Althusser is never really effected,"[22] that Jameson has never urgently felt the need to come to terms with the most radical aspects of Althusser's challenge to the humanist and historicist traditions in Marxism. Thus it is that the hermeneutic described as Althusser's (a progression from disruption to closure, from the text to its encompassing horizons) in fact resembles rather more closely Jameson's own practice. This practice is codified in the long opening essay "On Interpretation." To put it very schematically: Jameson suggests an interpretive progression passing through three concentric frameworks or horizons, modeled on those of patristic exegesis and reproducing the effects of the "libidinal apparatus" by which the text generates different levels of ideological investment. The first phase (the terminological influence of Frye is not accidental) governs the construction of the text within the horizon of "political history, in the narrow sense of punctual event and a chroniclelike sequence of happenings in time" (75); here the object of analysis coincides more or less with the individual work, understood as a strategic act within this political arena. The second phase covers the more broadly extended tensions of the class struggle, and the object of analysis is now "reconstituted in the form of the great collective and class discourses of which a text is little more than an individual *parole* or utterance." Jameson calls this object of study "the *ideologeme,* that is, the smallest intelligible unit of the essentially antagonistic collective discourses of social classes" (76). It is worth noting that, insofar as these discourses are apparently internally homogeneous, we are concerned at this level not with the play of heterogeneous discourses *within* the text but with the expressive function of the text in the play of class ideologies. The third framework is that "of history now conceived in its vastest sense of the sequence of modes of production and the succession and destiny of the various human social formations" (75). Within this ultimate horizon texts are read in terms of "the *ideology of form,* that is, the symbolic messages transmitted to us by the coexistence of various sign systems which are themselves traces or anticipations of modes of production" (76).

The concept of genre would, I think, constitute one such sign system; and it is to an analysis of the romance genre that the brilliant second chapter, "Magical Narratives," is dedicated. The reasons for the decision to concentrate on romance can be found in the phrase I last quoted: "traces or anticipations of modes of production." If the Marxist vision of history is marked by its "salvational or redemptive perspective of some secure future" (103), then its usual "negative" hermeneutic (which discovers the traces of violence and oppression in cultural artifacts) must be supplemented by a "positive" hermeneutic directed toward that imagery of libidinal energy which prefigures "the renewed organic identity of associative or collective life" (74). Such a hermeneutic, which is something like "a generalization of Durkheim's theory of religion to cultural production as a whole" (292), sets against the "instrumental" or "functional" forms of analysis of Jameson's second phase a "communal" and "anticipatory" methodology (296). Its strength lies perhaps in its ability to explore the forms of gratification offered by even the most repressive ideologies. But for all the passion of Jameson's commitment to the utopian impulse,[23] there seem to me good grounds for the reserve with which it is usually treated. The concept through which Jameson attempts to theorize the collective projection of desire is that of the Asiatic mode of production, with its consolidation of a dispersed collective unity in the image of the body of the despot (295). But even if we concede the validity of this concept, what Jameson glosses over is precisely its historical specificity. His strategy is first to postulate, on the basis of a rather dubious passage in the *Grundrisse,* a set of "cultural fantasies which cluster around the notion of 'Oriental despotism' in the political unconscious" (295, n. 16), and then anachronistically to project these fantasies as a general type of that fusion of desire with power which the concept of political unconscious never in fact adequately theorizes. Granted, revolutionary (and counterrevolutionary) activity channels desire; but in a culture already saturated with the falsely utopian, can the "dialectical" extraction of revolutionary hope from even the most degraded of ideologies be anything other than a blunting of Marxism's negative, suspicious, critical force? To do him justice, Jameson is fully aware of the problem, and his discussion of the methodological balancing of "ideology" with "utopia" returns finally to the dark side of Benjamin's thesis on cultural transmission, "reasserting the undiminished power of ideological distortion that persists even within the restored Utopian meaning of cultural artifacts and reminding us that within the symbolic power of art and culture the will to domination perseveres intact" (299).

A similiar use of precapitalist models informs Jameson's view of the relation between text and ideology. The unity of the times of "trace" and "anticipation" is grounded in the Lévi-Straussian notion that texts (all texts, with varying degrees of success) work as "the imaginary resolution of a real contradiction" (77): they work *with* ideology (as "anticipation") to overcome the traces of the real sedimented within the text as a contradictory formal patterning. The model is derived from the study of tribal societies; but it must *a fortiori* be true, Jameson argues, of the much more contradictory class societies of the capitalist era. The conception of literary production generated from this model is explicitly directed against that of modernism: for the "formal history" of successive breaks or deviations from a constantly reestablished norm Jameson substitutes the notion of stylistic production as "a projected solution, on the aesthetic or imaginary level, to a genuinely contradictory situation in the concrete world of everyday social life" (225). The criteria of analysis thus cease to be immanent in the literary text or system; the yardstick is now the real itself, external and prior to the text even if it is visible and knowable only as formal structure. "Style" is thus still epiphenomenal and incapable of producing knowledge. It works at "the aesthetic or imaginary level": the two are equivalent, and "imaginary" presumably carries, at least in part, its Lacanian overtones. And yet Jameson wants to have it both ways: what the text responds to is *both* this concrete reality of social contradiction *and* the "symptomatic expression and conceptual reflex" (83) of this reality, taking the form of a "subtext" which "is not immediately present as such, not some common-sense external reality, nor even the conventional narratives of history manuals, but rather must itself always be (re)constructed after the fact" (81). This distinction between two levels of contradiction then makes it possible for Jameson to use a Greimassian semiotics of binary opposition to construct the system of ideological closure which the text works and transforms. The active and critical function of literary discourse is thereby redeemed, but at the expense, I think, of contradicting the initial model of imaginary—that is, ideological—resolution.

What is at issue here—if I may worry at the problem a little longer—is the ontological distinction between levels of the real and the forms of mediation between them. Jameson's formulations are consistently double edged. The literary text is an active production of that history to which it is a reaction: "It articulates its own situation and textualizes it, thereby encouraging and perpetuating the illusion that the situation itself did not exist before it, that there is nothing but text." This illusion conceals the reality that history "is *not* a text, for it is fundamentally non-narrative and nonrepresentational" (82). History "is what hurts, it is what refuses desire and sets inexorable limits to individual as well as collective praxis" (102). But then again what can be added "is the proviso that history is inaccessible to us except in textual form, or in other words, that it can be approached only by way of its prior (re)textualization" (82). This is surely a case of having one's referent and eating it too. If history is accessible only through discursive or epistemological categories, is there not a real sense in which it therefore has only a discursive existence? In which its very otherness, its excess over the textual, is still a textual construct? But the really important question, I think, is why there should be any *necessity* for Marxism to ground its politics in an appeal to a transcendental realm prior to any mediation, an appeal to the unifying cause behind the effects of power it deals with. In Jameson's case there seem to be two reasons for this (both ultimately a function of his Hegelian location of structure in the real). The first is that in the final analysis he believes in the recoverability of the "absent cause" (so that it is in fact not properly absent but rather a lost or concealed presence). Thus the function of the concept of a political unconscious is said to lie "in detecting the traces of that uninterrupted narrative, in restoring to the surface of the text the repressed and buried reality of this fundamental history" (20). This reality is, surprisingly, defined not as that of class struggle but, in purely humanist terms, as "the collective struggle to wrest a realm of Freedom from a realm of Necessity." Within the framework of this totalization of antagonistic social classes into a homogeneous human race, the unitary "human adventure" must then be "retold within the unity of a single great collective story" (19).

The second reason for this appeal is that, for all his insistence on mediation, Jameson characteristically conflates the real object with the object of knowledge. Discursive categories are not so much the products of institutional practices functionally interrelated with other social realms as they are effects of the structure of that reality which they thematize and put into circulation. Thus "the possibility of performing . . . a conceptual abstraction subjectively is dependent on the preliminary objective realization of such a process within the raw materials or objects of study. We can think abstractly about the world only to the degree to which the world itself has already become abstract" (66). This then affects the category of mediation insofar as it necessarily presupposes a structure of binary opposition in which one pole is given ontological priority over the other— precisely the structure that Derrida identifies as characteristic of metaphysical thinking. Certainly Jameson insists that a model based on isomorphism between levels needs to be replaced by "a hierarchical model in which the various levels stand in determinate relations of domination or subordination to one another" and by the categories of "production, projection, compensation, repression, displacement, and the like" (44); and certainly he refuses flatly to affirm that superstructural phenomena "are mere reflexes, epiphenomenal projections of infrastructural realities." Nevertheless, "at some level this is certainly true, and modernism and reification are parts of the same immense process which expresses the contradictory inner logic and dynamics of late capitalism" (42).

The book's major development of a practice of mediation comes in the chapter on Conrad's *Lord Jim*. The central operation is described as "the invention of an analytic terminology or code which can be applied equally to two or more structurally distinct objects or sectors of being" (225). The metalanguage employed should be one that is capable of respecting the relative autonomy of the multiple realms to which it is applied (here they are Conrad's style, impressionist painting, and "the organization and experience of daily life during the imperialist heyday of industrial capitalism"), and yet must be capable of restoring, "at least methodologically, the lost unity of social life" (226). At some level distinct social instances can be reduced to an identity which is not that of a differential totality or, in Foucault's phrase, a "system of dispersion." Any one of a number of mediatory codes could have been chosen, including "social class, mode of production, the alienation of labour, commodification, the various ideologies of Otherness (sex or race), and political domination" (226). The one Jameson chooses to work with (almost arbitrarily, it would—wrongly—seem) is reification or rationalization. The concept is predicated on a notion of the organic unity of precapitalist social forms and modes of experience, and then the disintegration or fragmentation of these traditional solidarities in a process of quantification and (re)functionalization. Thus, to take one of Jameson's privileged instances, the faculty of sight becomes in the capitalist period relatively separate and specialized, and it thereby "acquires new objects that are themselves the products of a process of abstraction and rationalization which strips the experience of the concrete of such attributes as colour, spatial depth, texture and the like, which in their turn undergo reification." This is hardly open to falsification; but what I want to stress here is the corollary Jameson draws from it: that "the history of forms evidently reflects this process" (63). Impressionism, for example, is discussed not in terms of the development of painterly conventions, the relative autonomy of a practice, but in terms of its direct intervention in the process of perception, its offer of "the exercise of perception and the perceptual recombination of sense data as an end in itself" (230). The mediation of the *system* of painting is simply ignored.

Similarly, changes in the status of the subject can be read off more or less directly from the process of reification (153–154), and new monadic forms of the ego in turn give rise to specific narrative devices: to the Jamesian codification of point of view, for instance, which, coming into being "as a protest and a defence against reification, ends up furnishing a powerful ideological instrument in the perpetuation of an increasingly subjectivized and psychologized world" (221). In Conrad's hands, point of view tends to become dissociated from the expressive categories of "consciousness" and "psychology" (224) and to develop into a practice of *écriture*, an exercise of style which is allied on the one hand to impressionism and on the other to positivist doctrines of perception. What unites all these things is a historical "autonomization of the quantifying functions" which "permits an immense leap in the production of new kinds of formalization and is the precondition for the coming into existence of hitherto unimaginable levels of abstraction" (228), particularly in relation to the senses themselves. The structure of capitalist production, that is to say, produces deep-structural categories which shape the organization of lived "experience"; and modernist art functions as both a realization of these categories and, at the same time, a restoration of the archaic and libidinal elements which have been stripped away. But the price Jameson pays for this establishment of a dialectically expressive and reactive identity between disparate realms is a blurring of the specific differences between them. Consider the use of the concept of abstraction in this passage:

> The increasing abstraction of visual art thus proves not only to express the abstraction of daily life and to presuppose fragmentation and reification; it also constitutes a Utopian compensation for everything lost in the process of the development of capitalism—the place of quality in an increasingly quantified world, the place of the archaic and of feeling amid the desacralization of the market system, the place of sheer colour and intensity within the greyness of measurable extension and geometrical abstraction.   (236–237)

The "abstraction of visual art," "the abstraction of daily life," and "geometrical abstraction" are in fact quite distinct concepts, two of them technical terms referring to specific processes (nonrepresentationality; mathematical formalization), and the other a vague metaphor which gestures at a broad definition of "experience." The act of mediation is brought about only by means of a pun which conflates distinct and irreducible domains.

In *Marxism and Form* Jameson had written of Benjamin's attention to "invention and technique as the primary cause of historical change," that "such theories . . . function as a substitute for Marxist historiography in the way they offer a feeling of concreteness comparable to economic subject matter, at the same time that they dispense with any consideration of the human factors of classes and of the social organization of production."[24] It is true that Benjamin's technologism is not a temptation for Jameson, but in many ways the conceptual terrain he works remains akin to the post-Lukácsian problematic of the Frankfurt School, of which Jameson has been one of the leading proponents in English. Terry Eagleton's book on Benjamin pays some attention to questions of mediation, arguing that the violent and semi-ironic metaphors through which Benjamin thinks the relations between base and superstructure "signify not just an individual theoretical lapse, but an objective lacuna within modern Marxism: the absence of a theory of the relations in question that would be at once non-mechanistic and non-historicist."[25] But these questions are never really as central as they are for Jameson. Eagleton's concerns are much more directly political; in particular he is concerned to come to terms with the politics of post-structuralist theory.

One of the ways in which Eagleton approaches this is by infiltrating Benjamin into the enemy ranks: his work "seems to me strikingly to prefigure many of the current motifs of post-structuralism, and to do so, unusually, in a committedly Marxist context" (xii); and "as a collector of the contingent, of that which escapes the censoring glance of history in its sober yet potent unremarkability, Benjamin in some sense prefigures the contemporary critical practice of deconstruction" (131). As might be expected, this identification is not always without its difficulties. Consider, for example, the dense and suggestive discussion of the concepts of trace and aura. On the one hand the trace is a moment or aspect of the aura, "whether as its petrified physical residue or . . . the unconscious track, fraying or *Bahnung* which psychoanalytically speaking is the aura's very mechanism" (31). But on the other hand the trace is also subversive of aura insofar as it constantly refers (like the print of the potter's thumb) to those elements of the production process that mark the object's historicity, scar it with the signs of its accumulated historical functions. Either to erase the trace or to bring it to light is thus a political practice, in which "the object may need to be treated as a palimpsest, its existent traces expunged by an overwriting, or it may secrete blurred traces that can be productively retrieved." But the metaphor is misleading insofar as it suggests a surface inscription rather than the constitutive "writtenness" of the object in the text of social relations (32). From this point Eagleton moves to develop an analogy with the constitution of the subject: the illusory self-identity of the ego is matched by the object's " 'aura,' 'authority,' 'authenticity'—names which designate the object's persistence in its originary mode of being, its carving out of an organic identity for itself over time" (32). It is this myth of origin that is destroyed by mechanical reproduction; but this destruction cannot be taken for granted, for "just as the psychoanalytic subject is able to designate itself as a homogeneous entity over time only by repressing the traces of its unconscious desires, so the auratic object, whether it be cultural artifact or state apparatus, continually rewrites its own history to expel the traces of its ruptured, heterogeneous past. The political task of 'liberating' an object, then, takes the form of opening up its unconscious—detecting within it those chips of heterogeneity that it has been unable quite to dissolve" (53). Benjamin's use of the metapsychology of *Beyond the Pleasure Principle* allows him to extend this parallel between object and subject. The trace is incompatible both with lived experience *(Erlebnis)*, which rebuffs the perceptual stimulus, and with the more "authentic" experience of *Erfahrung*, where there is a complete disjunction between consciousness and the unconscious; in both cases "writing has rudely invaded the inmost sanctum of experience itself, whose productive mechanism lies exposed as nothing more than a set of inscriptions" (35).

Eagleton concludes this argument by asserting that "what we have here is an adumbration of the contemporary theme of the non-coincidence of signification and being, whether in the form of Michel Foucault's flamboyant assertion that Man and language can never be coterminous, or in Jacques Lacan's reflections on the 'fading' of the subject in language, its Hobson's choice between meaning and being" (35). But it is just here that the difficulties arise. Neither Foucault nor Lacan would argue for an *opposition* between meaning and being, because "being" is not thinkable outside of language. Although there is in Lacan a nostalgia for a lost authenticity, there is also a commitment to the constitution of being in the symbolic. It is perhaps partly because of the residual and ineradicable essentialism of the concept of aura that Eagleton is here led to force the comparison; and it is also true that what is "adumbrated" is in fact Derrida's rather different and apparently less politicized concept of trace.

A similar strategy of infiltration is employed with regard to Bakhtin, of whom Eagleton says that he "recapitulates *avant la lettre* many of the leading motifs of contemporary deconstruction, and does so, scandalously, in a firmly social context" (150). In particular, Bakhtin's *Rabelais and His World* stands as something like the model of a political criticism. In a "devious" gesture that creates "a lethal constellation between that re-deemed Renaissance moment and the trajectory of the Soviet state," Bakh-tin "pits against that 'official, formalistic and logical authoritarianism' whose unspoken name is Stalinism the explosive politics of the body, the erotic, the licentious and semiotic" (144). The order of discourse, hegemonic structures of power are inverted, perverted, subverted in the semiotic riot of carnival which, ambivalently destructive and liberatory, gives birth to the promise of utopia. While stressing the power of Bakhtin's categories, Eagleton is also careful—unlike so many others in the current flush of rediscovery—to make the necessary political criticism of the corporatist and populist dimensions of Bakhtin's thought: carnival is "a *licensed* affair" (148), a specular reversal which may in some ways serve as an example of "that mutual complicity of law and liberation, power and desire, that has become a dominant theme of contemporary post-Marxist pessimism." But insofar as it is "a kind of fiction," coming to life only through its oppo-sitional relation to ruling-class culture, it seems in fact to avoid "the double-bind that all utopianism sets for the unwary: the fact that its affirmative images of transcendence rest upon a potentially crippling sublimation of the drives necessary to achieve it in practice" (149). It has the further advantage that it sets in relief the chiliastic and relatively "empty" Utopia of Benjamin, which is related only as negation to historical time—a neg-ativity that has its historical basis in the absence of the revolutionary party (148). It would also seem possible to counterpose Bakhtin's socio-semiotic theory of discourse to Benjamin's belief in the prelapsarian unity of word and body and the cratylic immediacy of the sign to its referent (151–152). But Eagleton courageously argues that matters are rather more complex than this, for "the Judaic belief in the expressive unity of word and body, given a dialectical twist, can just as easily reappear as the ground for a materialist re-location of discourse within the social practices from which, as Benjamin shrewdly sees, modern semiotic ideologies have stra-tegically isolated it" (152). "At the very least, 'onomatopoeic' and mate-rialist notions of language join hands in common opposition to what Benjamin sees to be the idealism of Saussure" (153, n. 75).

This raises the question of what is meant by a "materialist" theory of language, and indeed the question of what force the concept of the material itself has. The issue is first joined in the confrontation set up between Benjamin's meditation on baroque allegory and Leavis's commitment to the aesthetic ideology of the symbol. What Benjamin discovers in allegory is an excess of signification over the signified, a surplus of "the materiality of the letter itself" (4) over meaning (the example Eagleton cites is the baroque echo game). Whereas "the allegorical object has undergone a kind of haemorrhage of spirit" and lies "drained of all immanent meaning," the "ineluctably idealizing" *symbol* "subdues the material object to a surge of spirit that illuminates and redeems it from within" (6). The equation between signified and spirit is established by way of Derrida's account of phonocentrism (the proximity of voice to the ideality of meaning). In attempting to combat the "idealism" or the "spirituality" of the symbol, Eagleton appeals to the double "materiality" of the signifier and of the referent. But this is not only bad linguistics; it also invokes the fruitlessly metaphysical opposition of matter to spirit in a context which calls rather for properly Marxist categories. The damage this does is evidenced in a subsequent and related discussion of the commodity.

The commodity can be thought of as "the baroque emblem pressed to an extreme." In this form "the materiality of the signifier has on the one hand degenerated to esoteric self-reference, and on the other hand has been evacuated by exchange-value to mere abstraction. The commodity is the 'bad side' of the emblem, grossly swelling its material density at the same time as it robs it of its referential value." That is to say that the excessive materiality of the signifier, which would seem to guarantee the concreteness of the referent, brings about a closed autoreferentiality, a collapsing of the object "back upon itself as a monstrous tautology" (30). Despite a surface appearance of substantiality, the essence of the commodity, the "secret" of its "truly tautological status," is its "virulent anti-materialism" (29); each commodity "presents to the other a mirror which reflects no more than its own mirroring" (21). And this contradiction is reflected in contemporary semiotics, which tends to "reproduce at the level of the sign that blend of formalistic idealism and vulgar materialism that Marxism locates in the very structure of the commodity." Semiotics "may valuably re-materialize the signifier—but only at the risk of collapsing history into it and conflating all materialisms into one." The "bad" materialism of semiotics succumbs to the "sex appeal" of the sign-as-commodity, its combination of "the fleshiness of the stripper with her elusiveness," whereas the Marxist critic will refuse the substitution of "strip-shows" for "genuine sexuality" (30).

The sign conceptualized in the form of the commodity is like the subject caught in the Imaginary closure of the mirror phase. But what Eagleton seems to want to oppose to this is not so much the Symbolic (a concept coextensive with that of language) as that most brittle of Lacanian categories, the Real. It is only in this way that I can take the nostalgic references to the referent and the hostility to tautology. But tautology is the condition and the precondition of all signification. Only insofar as language is a (hypothetically) closed system can it be thought as a system of differences articulating the semantic continuum rather than as a system of correspondences, of nomenclature, predetermined by the structure of the real or, in effect, by a conceptuality "given" in nature. What is suppressed in the commodity form is not referentiality but the semiotic frame of the system of relations of production. Reference is an operation distinct from and posterior to signification, a "supplement" which can in no way introduce substance into the sign. Even granted that much contemporary theory fetishizes the materiality of the signifier, the answer is not to oppose a good to a bad materialism of the signifier, and then to set this against the "idealism" of Saussure. For the signifier is not material; the signifier is necessarily realized in phonic or graphic material but is not identical with this material. Its "identity" is that immaterial mode of existence of the trace defined and constituted by a system of differential relations. And the relevant opposition here is not that between idealism and materialism but between an empiricist and a structuralist conception of the sign.

In its polemical oscillations Eagleton's book frequently (and often rewardingly) lacks the unscarred smoothness of an academic monologue. Key questions are not "settled" but are taken up from different angles of attack. The possibility of a political semiotics is elsewhere approached through a brief history of the science of rhetoric, which in its classical form Eagleton describes as a type of " 'discourse theory', devoted to analyzing the material effects of particular uses of language in particular social conjunctures. It was a highly elaborate theory of specific signifying practices—above all, of the discursive practices of the juridical, political and religious apparatuses of the state. Its intention, quite consciously, was systematically to theorize the articulations of discourse and power, and to do so in the name of political practice: to enrich the political effectivity of signification" (101). After a sketch of the decline of rhetoric through its splitting off from dialectic, from science, and finally from an autonomized Literature (a circular process in which "an initially logocentric rhetoric had passed into the pernicious falsities of print, to be opposed by an equally logocentric anti-rhetoric") (106), we encounter a figure looking like Paul de Man but named Nietzsche. The radicalism of Nietzsche's project lay in his exposure of "the covertly rhetorical nature of all discourse" and his turning of the "technical" aspects of rhetoric against a conception of language as essentially a form of communication. As a result, "rhetoric was undermined on its own ground: if all language worked by figure and trope, all language was consequently a form of fiction, and its cognitive or representational power problematized at a stroke." The political implications of this were at once critical and evasive: in unmasking the will to knowledge as a form of the will to power, the Nietzschean genealogy effectively denied its own authority and the possibility of any stable position from which the *dominant* ideology could be denounced (to the extent that any denunciation would be complicit, in its will to power, with that ideology). Thus "in retreat from market-place to study, politics to philology, social practice to semiotics, rhetoric was to end up as that vigorous demystifier of all ideology that itself provided a final ideological rationale for political inertia" (108).

A Marxist response to this would presumably both recognize (as Eagleton does) that Marxism is itself a rhetoric, and then stress the distinction between dominant and subordinate cultures and the fact that effective power and authority are located in the former, even though subordinate cultures are always more or less incorporated into the hegemonic culture. Eagleton's argument is that ambiguity is reactionary under all circumstances (110) and that a materialist understands the "self-molesting discourse" of, for example, politics "by referring it back to a more fundamental realm, that of historical contradictions themselves" (109). This may be the same answer, but it is problematic, I think, in its apparent assertion of a general and stable criterion against which to evaluate the political effects of language. As he writes elsewhere, "we cannot think ourselves back beyond language, for we need language in order to do so in the first place . . . An origin is nothing to speak of" (69). The question at issue is, again, that of the possibility of grounding Marxist politics in a category of History which would be external to its discursive mediations.

The question is addressed directly in an attack on Colin MacCabe's use of Benjamin to dispute the contention that "the past has its own order independently of its present enunciation" (in the book's pantomime of disguises, "MacCabe" means "Hindess and Hirst"). On the one hand MacCabe is right "to insist that the past is a discursive construct of the present"; but on the other the past "is not, of course, merely an imaginary back-projection of [the present]. Materialism must insist on the irreducibility of the real to discourse; it must also remind historical idealism that if the past itself—by definition—no longer exists, its effects certainly do" (51). And he proceeds to attack that "epistemological imperialism" which, in fetishizing the situation of utterance as the point of genesis of the historically Other which it has itself created, abolishes the difference and distance of the past. In part what is at issue is the Foucauldean and post-structuralist emphasis on discontinuity (60); and, while it may be doubted whether Benjamin's essay "The Story-Teller," with its narrative of the decline of "experience," is the best corrective to this, it is certainly true that Benjamin's meditations on history go to the core of the questions facing "a contemporary Marxism once more pondering the 'alternatives' of continuity and rupture, caught as it is between a discredited historicism on the one side and an unacceptable synchronicity on the other" (63).

In direct contrast to a Jamesonian construction of Marxism as a "mighty world-historical plot of humankind's primordial unity, subsequent alien-ation, revolutionary redemption and ultimate self-recovery in the realm of communism" (64), Eagleton indicates both the ways in which Marx's 1857 "Introduction" breaks with a historicist teleology and the ways in which it remains trapped within an evolutionist framework (65). It is Nietzsche who "presses Marx's transitional formulations to a boldly affirmative point," a fully "structural" conception of the disjunction between genesis and function and of the political (re)functionalization of the past. In so doing, Nietzsche prefigures Benjamin's "anti-historicist insistence on the ruptures, recyclings and re-insertions that underlie the bland ideology of 'cultural history.' " But then comes the refusal of sympathy that closes off so much that is valuable in Nietzsche. His conception of history "is equally ideo-logical: by spurning all continuity as metaphysical, he threatens to subvert much of what Benjamin designates by 'tradition.' If Marx wishes to sublate the 'earlier meaning,' Nietzsche desires to suppress it"; he is himself the "creator" of "historical rubble" (66).

This is nonsense, of course: a case of shooting the messenger. Its purpose is in fact to produce a further metamorphosis of Benjamin, this time into what is probably the incongruous figure of E. P. Thompson. Although the socialist movement derives its poetry not from the past but from the future and stands "in ironic relation to the historical 'text' it exists to produce, and whose emergence will finally signify its own demise" (69), it also works to foster, "across the structurally discontinuous social for-mations identified by Marxism, that 'fiction' of a coherent, continuous struggle which is Benjamin's 'tradition' " (and which is a key motif in the work of the English "left-organicist" historians). Indeed, "that fiction is not a *lie* . . . For there *are* real historical continuities, and it is a dismal index of our theoretical befuddlements that one needs to assert anything so obvious in the first place" (73). But these assertions surely answer the wrong kind of question. In Benjamin's thinking, tradition is not a question of existence but of political work; in Eagleton's words, it is "the practice of ceaselessly excavating, safeguarding, violating, discarding and reinscribing the past" (59). It is not the essence of history, nor an alternative to it (48), and it bears no resemblance to any historicist hermeneutic (labor history, cultural history, literary history); the emancipatory force of the past "is to be always elsewhere. It is only through the radical discontinuity of past and present, through the space hollowed by their mutual eccentricity, that the former may be brought to bear explosively upon the latter. Any attempt to recuperate the past directly, non-violently, will result only in paralyzing complicity with it" (44).

The emphasis on the violence needed to salvage history for its victims is characteristic not only of Benjamin's rhetoric but of Eagleton's. There is a comment at one point on the aesthetic of anxiety that generates the sexual violence of the image of "blast[ing] open the continuum of history," where "continuum" signifies both the whore of history's "endless, meaningless amenability, but also the hymen—the smooth membrane that prohibits penetration, and which must be ruptured in an act of rape" (46). And yet this vocabulary of violence is Eagleton's own: things are "blasted apart," "exploded," "detonated," "penetrated," and Benjamin's work is, in the book's last sentence, "blast[ed] . . . out of its historical continuum, so that it may fertilize the present" (179). The linguistic celebration of violence is strangely at odds with a work that takes the project of feminist criticism as in many ways the paradigm of a textual politics. And part of the difficulty lies precisely in the fact that the politics is textual, that it is felt to be a substitute for the real thing. Hence the attack on Macherey's supposed assumption that ideology will "be unhinged by theory and literature sooner than by such traditional devices as class struggle" (90); or the assertion that deconstruction exemplifies a sort of "reformism of the text" (as though the alternative were to storm the text at the barricades) (134). Indeed, this overpoliticization of textual analysis informs much of the discussion of deconstruction.

Despite a wonderful "Oedipal Fragment" addressed in fear and awe and hatred to Derrida ("Die derider!"), the section devoted to deconstruction refuses almost completely to identify its target(s). But unless Eagleton is supposing a homogeneous movement with a unitary political position, it seems fair to assume that he intends less the master in Paris than the epigones at Yale. In a first moment of the argument the confrontation between deconstruction and Marxism is set up in terms of an epistemological opposition: "Either the subject is wholly on the 'inside' of its world of discourse, locked into its philosophico-grammatical forms, its very struggles to distantiate them 'theoretically' themselves the mere ruses of power and desire; or it can catapult itself free from this formation to a point of transcendental leverage from which it can discern absolute truth" (131). This opposition of inside to outside is of course a double bind; but the double bind can be described in such a way as to provide an appropriate political metaphor for the position of deconstruction: that of the complementarity of reformism and ultraleftism (134). At this level of logical typing, it is not a particular intellectual practice but the revolutionary working class that will deconstruct the inside/outside dichotomy. It is important to note here that everything is staked on a sort of revolutionary monism: the transformation of capitalism can be brought about only under the leadership of the industrial proletariat—not by "peasants, guerrillas, blacks, women or intellectuals" (133). In the England of the eighties this rejection of the possibility of a dispersed, plural, decentered politics is close to Benjamin's messianism. This is not to say that Eagleton is wrong in drawing parallels between deconstruction's privileging of plurality, heterogeneity, and indeterminacy, and the traditional thematics of liberalism. But this is no more than a possible conjuncture; it does not justify the functionalization of the parallel as a direct manifestation of the class struggle ("Deconstructionism, then, can salvage some of the dominant themes of traditional bourgeois liberalism by a desperate last-ditch strategy") (138). Nor does it justify either the criticism that deconstruction rejects any "transcendental vantage-point from which definitive judgements could be delivered"—as I wrote earlier, this seems to me part of the strength of much post-structuralist theory—or the heavy appeal to authority in the claim that "objectivity is suspect, for we know, do we not, that it must rest upon metaphysical notions of absolute truth? (At least we know if we have not read Lenin)" (140). If the Lenin that we have not read includes, for example, those passages in *Materialism and Empirio-Criticism* in which the "base" is redefined as "matter," or in which we are assured of the existence of a truth which is absolute, suprahistorical, and independent of any social determinations,[26] then we must perhaps despair of the Marxist dialectic.

The repeated appeal to an ontological grounding of structures of power in some extrasemiotic realm, however qualified, tends to distract attention from the more important issues of the constitution of the Real in and the dispersal of power through discursive systems. (It is notable that a more recent book by Eagleton, *The Rape of Clarissa,* while sharply critical of specific deconstructive readings, is nevertheless methodologically much closer to a Derridean account of textuality).[27] But at its best Eagleton's work is able to offer what is precisely a dialectical conceptualization of the politics of discourse and of metadiscourse. In an elegant foreshadowing of a Marxist theory of comedy, for example, he writes that Brecht teaches us "the deep comedy of meta-language, which in distantiating its object displays just where it is itself most vulnerable"—namely, in the fact "that any place is reversible, any signified may become a signifier, any discourse may be without warning rapped over the knuckles by some meta-discourse which may then suffer such rapping in its turn" (160). Where Jameson ascribes history to the romance paradigm, Eagleton sees it as comic in form; and Marxism itself "has the humour of dialectics because it reckons itself into the historical equations it writes" (161). The way forward, for Eagleton and for Marxist cultural theory, lies neither in a rejection nor in a complete accommodation of those varied languages called post-structuralism but in an acceptance of the challenge they offer to Marxism to rethink the status of the dialectic and to build a semiotic politics on the ruins of a metaphysics.

3

Discourse and Power

A T THE HEART of such a politics, at the heart of any Marxist theorization of culture, is the concept of ideology. In this chapter I seek to construe the concept in semiotic terms. Without a fully formulated conception of ideology it becomes impossible to theorize the linkages between social relations of production, social power, and systems of discourse. And yet it is, I think—because of the force of the arguments against the current usage of the concept—a gamble as to whether this redefinition is possible.

This is so in the first place because the concept is traditionally defined within a relation between truth and error, as the designation of error. The theorization of error or false consciousness is not possible without establishing a position of authority which would be external to the ideological; but to the extent that this position claims an epistemological and so a political authority, it reveals itself to be complicitous with power, with the will to knowledge which is a form of the will to power. Such a criticism is not in itself conclusive, since it can be shown to derive from the same claim to mastery, and because it naively supposes the possibility of an exemption from the field of power. It is a criticism which fails to account for its own conditions of possibility. Nevertheless it has the effect of denying the universality of that standard of rationality that Marxism has ascribed to itself and against which deviation is measured, and of enforcing the paradox that the critique of ideology must itself be relativized to the position of power from which it is enunciated.

In the second place, the concept of ideology is predicated upon a distinction between the symbolic and the real, and hence an exclusion of the symbolic from the real. However much the "last instance" is, in classical Marxism, mediated and deferred, its eventual finality relegates the symbolic to an epiphenomenal status. The problem that is posed is that of the working through of a further paradox, in which the real would be thought not as substance but as a texture of symbolic systems, and the symbolic would be thought as having a real effectivity. There are additional problems here which have to do with the generality and inclusiveness of the concept of the symbolic, and with the postulation of a single general form of causality.

In the third place, the concept of ideology seems necessarily to presuppose a relation between knowledge and a knowing subject. The relation may apply at the level of individuals, but is more generally a relation at the level of social class. In the simplest formulation, class is conceived as an expressive unity; more complex formulations for the most part merely qualify this model. In particular, it is not clear that the concepts of hegemony and the "relative autonomy" of ideology do not repeat the metaphysical framework that defines the orthodox theorization of ideology.

Since these questions cannot properly be answered in abstraction from particular textual constructions of the category of ideology, I have chosen to examine briefly one particularly lucid account, in one of the great texts of classical Marxism, of the working of ideology. This account is Engels's reading of the city of Manchester, a reading which is doubly instructive: first, in that the semiotic system Engels reads is at once superstructural and directly functional, and second, in that Engels's reading can be understood in terms of quite contradictory methodologies.

Manchester in 1844, Engels writes, is built in such a way that "a person may live in it for years, and go in and out daily, without coming into contact with a working-people's quarter or even with workers," on condition that he is not seeking to *know* the structure of the city—"so long as he confines himself to his business or to pleasure walks."[1] This restriction of knowledge is made possible above all by the fact that "the working-people's quarters are sharply separated from the sections of the city reserved for the middle class" (348).

This quasiuniversal "person" (part of the text's political ambiguity lies in the status of its inscribed reader) is then specified as "the members of the money aristocracy," who

> can take the shortest road through the middle of all the labouring districts to their places of business, without ever seeing that they are in the midst of the grimy misery that lurks to the right and the left. For the thoroughfares leading from the Exchange in all directions out of the city are lined, on both sides, with an almost unbroken series of shops, and so are kept in the hands of the middle and lower

bourgeoisie, which, out of self-interest, cares for a decent and cleanly
external appearance, and *can* care for it.   (348)

The effect of this structure is a "concealment of everything which might
affront the eyes and the nerves of the bourgeoisie" (349); and this concealment is at the same time *motivated:* there is a relation of distorted
representation, of simultaneous concealment and manifestation, between
the façade and the districts behind it.

> True, these shops have some affinity [*Verwandtschaft*—Stephen Mar-
> cus translates this well as "concordant relation"[2]] with the districts
> which lie behind them, and are more elegant in the commercial and
> residential quarters than when they hide grimy working-man's dwell-
> ings; but they suffice to conceal from the eyes of the wealthy men
> and women of strong stomachs and weak nerves the misery and grime
> which form the complement of their wealth.   (348–349)

Engels seems to be using the model of a truth which is hidden beneath
an "external appearance" and which is nevertheless revealed on the surface
in an alienated form. One can *infer (schliessen)* what lies beneath appearances ("Anyone who knows Manchester can infer the adjoining districts,
from the appearance of the thoroughfare"), but it is nevertheless *invisible*
("But one is seldom in a position to catch from the street a glimpse of
the real labouring districts," 349). The "separation" between working-
class and middle-class districts would therefore be the bar between a signifier (the thoroughfares) and its repressed signified (the working-class
districts); the "concordant relation" would be a relation of signification,
or rather of (mis)representation.

But it is not only the middle-class thoroughfares that Engels reads;
elsewhere the text reads, with great thoroughness, the working-class districts themselves. The whole city is a semiotic system. The separation,
then, is not between a signifier and a signified but between two sets of
signifiers, one of which (the thoroughfares) stands synecdochically for the
whole and one of which is repressed. The working-class districts are not
the *truth* of the city, nor are they the deep structure which generates an
illusory surface structure. They are that part of a semiotic system which
is significantly invisible to "the eyes and the nerves of the bourgeoisie"
(349).

What is produced by this asymmetrical relation between two sets of
architectural signifiers is not so much a single and necessary structure of
illusion (since "anyone" can read the city, by using his feet) as a structure
of *positions of reading* through which individuals inscribe themselves within

the semiotic system. There are two main positions (two types of reader): (1) the bourgeois reader who is affirmed by the city as a universal subject (the text confirms this universality: the bourgeois reader is "anyone"); and (2) the proletarian reader who is a nonsubject (the text confirms this, at least at this point, by excluding this position). A third, synthetic position is that of the theoretical reader who, in speaking the repressed discourse of the working-class districts and relating it to the discourse of the middle-class enclaves, produces a structural reading of the relation between the parts of the signifying system, and relates this system to the system of class relationships within which it is overdetermined.[3] These positions are not *imposed* on agents; they are merely *potential* positions. The position of a theoretical reading, in particular, is not a fixed class position (Engels is a middle-class businessman); and although it has the potential to be translated into revolutionary practice, it can also be used (this is suggested by the fact that the text is addressed to an implied bourgeois reader, who is warned of the consequences of capitalist oppression) to defuse revolutionary action (for example, 581).

This is one sense in which we can speak of the "relative autonomy" of ideology; another sense is discussed in terms of the origin of this "peculiar" structure. Here the text grapples with the problem, which it cannot adequately theorize, of a causality which is structural and yet corresponds to the objective intentions of the bourgeoisie. The construction of the city is "hypocritical" *(heuchlerisch),* although it is based on straightforward economic considerations: "I know . . . that the retail dealers are forced by the nature of their business to take possession of the great highways; I know that there are more good buildings than bad ones upon such streets everywhere, and that the value of land is greater near them than in remoter districts" (349). Nevertheless the exclusion *(Absperrung)* of the working class is "systematic." But immediately Engels concedes that "Manchester is less built according to a plan, after official regulations, is more an outgrowth of accident, than any other city" (349). However, even if its construction is not controlled by the bourgeoisie, the effect of this random construction is that it can be translated directly into a propagandistic metadiscourse: "When I consider in this connection the eager assurances of the middle-class, that the working-class is doing famously, I cannot help feeling that the liberal manufacturers, the 'Big Wigs' of Manchester, are not so innocent after all, in the matter of this shameful method of construction" (349).

One sentence crystallizes these contradictions and suggests a possible resolution: the sharp separation between working-class and middle-class quarters comes about "by unconscious tacit agreement, as well as with outspoken conscious determination" (*durch unbewusste, stillschweigende Übereinkunft wie durch bewusste ausgesprochene Absicht;* 348). "Determination" may refer only to the control exercised by one class; but "agreement" indicates the unconscious concurrence of both classes in the exclusion operated on the proletariat. As Marcus notes, "this astonishing and outrageous arrangement cannot be fully understood as the result of a plot, or even a deliberate design, although those in whose interests it works also control it. It is indeed too huge and too complex a state of organized affairs ever to have been *thought up* in advance, to have pre-existed as an idea."[4]

ENGELS'S ANALYSIS mobilizes the classical tropes of an empiricist reading: the relation between the surface and the hidden, between seeing and not seeing, between will and accident. At the same time it can be read as putting into play a possible contradiction between two distinct strategies of reading: the one he deploys, which we could call "interpretation," and which is partly blind to Engels's own inscription as a reader in the text of Manchester; and a second strategy which reads the determinants of reading, the system that makes possible both those interpretations based directly in class interest and those directed against it. The concept of ideology produced by this second strategy would concern not the translation of an originary class position but the effects of an objective and conventional system of signification—that is, the allocation of a differential structure of interpretation. Any semiotic system will generate specific possibilities of reception: it will construct both a semantic structure and a limited set of formal positions from which this structure can be interpreted.

At one level the contradiction between these two strategies can be referred simply to conflicting epistemological presuppositions. If structure is located in the real, then ideology will be seen to be generated directly by this real structure. The theory of commodity fetishism in *Capital* is close to this position: the structure of commodity production involves as a necessary effect the production of surface forms which are illusory and opaque. Misrecognition of the structure is a consequence of the distinction within the real between deep structure and surface structure. In a similar manner, capitalist production directly produces the illusions of the contractual equality of socioeconomic agents, or of the givenness and ahistoricality of the social order. Ideology is *imposed* by reality in the sense that limits are set to the immediacy of "experience": a worker, for example, will draw a finite set of possible deductions from the hierarchical and serial organization of the work process according to the position that they occupy within that process. "Reality (the object) determines the place of the subject within it and, therefore, the conditions of its experience of it. Reality determines the *content* of ideology; it generates false recognitions of itself by subjecting subjects to circumstances in which their experience is distorted."[5] What is assumed in the thesis of ideology as a representation of an alienated reality is, first of all, preconstituted subjects who represent to themselves an objectivity which presents meaning directly to them; and second, that there is a necessary congruence between the subjects' position in the production process and their ideological position. Ideology is a simple effect of an autoeffective process. Thus "it is not that the subject is mistaken [*se trompe*] but that *reality deceives him* [*le trompe*], and the appearances in which the structure of the production process are concealed are the starting point for the way individuals conceive of reality."[6]

Althusser's critique of this empiricist position, and indeed his general critique of economism and historicism, seem to me to remain more powerful than any countervailing response; I shall not argue the case for them here. Their consequence is that, if structure is located, conversely, in the systems of signification through which the real is constituted as an object of knowledge, then ideology can be seen as an unmotivated system which is a product of social determinations but is discontinuous with the structure of production. It is not the expression or the transformation of a concealed deep structure (the structure of production which would be its secret truth). Rather, it represents the intrication of relatively self-contained semiotic systems in the field of antagonistic class relations rooted in relations of production.

The counterpart of this rejection of an expressive conception of ideology is a critique of the epistemological problematic of the possibility of a correspondence between representation and the real, and the consequent move toward a nonepistemological conceptualization of knowledge and its objects. This shift is perhaps most dramatically exemplified in Hindess and Hirst's argument that theoretical objects are constituted "within definite ideologies and discourses,"[7] whereas the "distinction and the correlation characteristic of epistemology depend on objects which exist independently of knowledge, and yet in forms appropriate to knowledge itself."[8] Epistemology works by presenting an appropriate form of order to theoretical discourse which will guarantee the fit between the theoretical grid and the order of the real. The bases for this closure of discourse are: (1) the construction of privileged and tautological criteria of validity; (2) normative requirements concerning the mode of operation of discourse; and (3) an aprioristic conception of the process of production of knowledge.[9] But discourse in fact remains stubbornly *unlimited*, because "the forms of closure of discourse promised in epistemological criteria do not work. They are silent before the continued discourse of theories which they can never correspond to or appropriate."[10]

The occasion of this critique is a rejection of the definition of ideology as "false consciousness" (and of the scientism that accompanies it). If ideology is defined—as Althusser, for example, defines it, in Lacanian terms—as the "imaginary," then

> the forms of the "imaginary" cannot arise spontaneously from the subject (that would convert recognition into *imagination* and restore the constitutive subject), equally, they cannot be given by "reality" (that would restore a simple reflection theory). The forms of the imaginary should, if these positions were to be avoided, have the status of *significations*, representations which are reducible neither to a represented which is beyond them, nor to an origin in a subject, but which are effects of the action of means of representation.[11]

The signifieds of discourse (including the "referential" discourses of science or history) are generated not from an extradiscursive real to which we may appeal as a final authority but within specific processes and practices of signification. The decisive criterion of analysis can thus no longer be the relation between discourse and a reality which is external to it, since discourses are "interpretable and intelligible only in terms of their own and other discourses' constructions and the categories of adequacy which they apply to them."[12] Instead, the relevant criterion is that of the relations between discourse and *power*, the intrication of power in discourse. We would be specifically concerned with the institutions, the forms of transmission and diffusion, and the pedagogical forms which impose and maintain discourses and which contain dissenting or marginal positions within certain limits. It would still be possible to apply specific local criteria of adequacy and appropriateness (although not of validity), but there could be no appeal to the epistemological unity of a knowledge process in general.

The danger here is that of simply reversing the empiricist argument by postulating the autoeffectivity of discursive systems and reducing all signification to the single model of highly autonomous symbolic systems which produce a uniform mode of being of the subject. But ideological systems work in very disparate ways and through very different forms of constitution of their subjects. There can be no single model of ideological structure because there is no hard and fast line between the "real" and the "symbolic." The distinction between the real and symbolic realms is not ontologically given but is a social and historical result. The discursive is a socially constructed reality which constructs the categories of the real and the symbolic and this distinction between them. It assigns structure to the real at the same time as it is a product and a moment of real structures. It therefore covers a spectrum of semiotic systems from both realms. Thus "material" structures—for example specific work processes—are also immediately symbolic structures (structures of power—that is, the meaningful position of individuals within these processes). Conversely, symbolic systems cannot be conceived only on the model of intellectual formations transmitted through special institutions to empty subjects. They involve varying degrees of motivation, explicitness, and systematization; they are directly or indirectly linked to the process of material production; and they are appropriated by agents (and by different classes of agents) in different ways.

THE POLITICAL IMPLICATIONS of the abandonment of Marxism's epistemological certainties are of course bitterly disputed, and much recent work seeks to reclaim the Real and the Material as sources of epistemological (and hence political) authority for Marxism. Perry Anderson, who played so important a role in opening up English Marxism to European philosophy, has attacked structuralist theory in a rhetoric reminiscent of nothing so much as a religious denunciation of atheism. Structuralism's "speculative aggrandizement of language" and "free-wheeling nescience" have brought about an "attenuation of truth" and a dismissal of the "referential axis."[13] In the "abyss of Parisian relativism" (65) the imperialism of the linguistic model has destroyed the possibility of causal explanation and so of "history proper" (50), and brought about the disappearance both of the historical theme of man and of the subject or agent of knowledge (52). Derrida is said to have "liquidated" the "last vestige" of the "autonomy" of structures: the subject; to have "freed" structures from subjects; and so to have brought about the reign of "absolute chance," "a subjectivism without a subject," indeed "a finally unbridled subjectivity" (54). In short, the linguistic model "strafed meaning, over-ran truth, outflanked ethics and politics, and wiped out history" (64). In a similar vein Terry Lovell argues that in a "relativist" and "conventionalist" problematic, theoretical terminology is defined systemically rather than referentially; but this model "is not open to Marxist materialism. Signs cannot be permitted [sic] to swallow up their referents in a never-ending chain of signification, in which one sign always points on to another, and the circle is never broken by the intrusion of that to which the sign refers":[14] somewhere there must be an end to signification, an ultimate nonsignifying ground. At one point Lovell finds it in the Holocaust, which she mobilizes as the sign of the ultimately Real; but that of course is precisely the ideological function of the Holocaust, to act as a *sign* of the real, as an argument. Elsewhere she devastates the heretics with splendid metaphors: while Althusser "sails dangerously close to the wind," the post-Althusserians "abandon caution and openly embrace conventionalism."[15] For Lovell everything turns on the category of the material, as the object of experience and as the solid ground against which to measure the symbolic. But in this kind of context (where it is set against the ideal or spiritual) the concept is a metaphysical one and is only contingently related to Marxism. More important, it ensures that the distinctive criterion of Marxist analysis becomes the materiality of the commodity rather than the inscription within it of the process and the relations of production which determine its value and which are not, strictly speaking, material.

Against any such dichotomous conception of a "material" economic base and an "immaterial" superstructure, it seems important to argue that all social systems are semiotic systems producing significations realized in material sign-vehicles. The system of natural and physical objects is necessarily always a system of social values also; and the materiality of the body is a support of the complex gender systems through which sexual difference is constituted. The economic system is concerned precisely with the transformation of quantities of matter-energy into information: at one level into use values, at a second level into the complex signification of exchange value, which endows qualitatively different commodities with a symbolic equivalence and so permits their circulation as signs within a generalized equation.[16] The political-juridical system articulates and consolidates class positions on a secondary and self-contained plane of power relations and categories of subject which is constrained by, but not necessarily fully congruent with, the structure of relations of production, and which in turn is functionalized in the struggle to secure the appropriation of surplus value. The ideological system, which mediates the categories of the other systems and allows individuals (as "subjects") to construct their relation to these constraining structures, works as a system of signification only through its embedding in material forms.

There can therefore be no absolute ontological distinction (of the order material/immaterial or real/symbolic) between the systems whose complex intrication constitutes the social structure. Rather, social structure can be thought in terms of a play of constraints, determinations, and restrictions exercised upon each other by a range of semiotic practices and institutions. This play will result in particular states of balanced tension which will shift as the complex convergence of forces at any one point shifts; there are no necessary outcomes or stages of struggle, and there can be no *general* model of the relation between components of social structure. To substitute in this manner an overdetermined series of semiotic formations for an ontological dichotomy is not to argue that each formation is equally determinant of every other formation, or that any one formation is the expression of others, or that a social structure is no more than a system of symbolic systems. Any of these arguments would ignore the fact that value systems have the particular function of realizing relations of *power*. Power is equally a symbolic value, but it has direct material effects. It involves "need, work, and exploitation, that is . . . factors which brutally beset the human body of man in its psycho-physical materiality and not just the sign systems practiced by him."[17] Power is realized in all formations (possession of economic, political, and ideological values, and optimally also of the means of producing them), but this realization is asymmetrical. In class societies control at the level of relations of production tends to be realized in terms of hegemony in other formations; but these relations of control and determination are fought out within each formation in terms, and within formal constraints, which are peculiar to each formation.

One of the effects of this asymmetry of social systems is a disjunction between semiotic formations, such that one formation cannot be seen as the direct translation of the production of values in another. This "relative autonomy" of practices—the historical result of the uneven realization of power at different levels by the hegemonic class in complex and dynamic social systems—renders invalid an expressive model which reduces social systems to a central deep structure of which each level would be the isomorphic transformation. Further, economic practice is not a "last instance," a final and therefore absolute determinant of social structure imposing a necessary teleology on the development of this structure. Rather, the specific structure and temporality of each formation produce a limited range of possible developments; the actual course of development is realized in the play of the class struggle, where the limited teleology of class goals is worked out.

I TAKE THE FOLLOWING to be the general requirements of a working theory of ideology. First, that it not assert a relationship of truth to falsity (and so its own mastery over error) but concern rather the production and the conditions of production of categories and entities within the field of discourse. Second, that it not deduce the ideological from the structure of economic forces or, directly, from the class positions of real subjects of utterance; that it theorize the category of subject not as the origin of utterance but as its effect. Third, that it not be an ontology of discourse, deriving effects of meaning from formal structure, but rather theorize the multiple and variable limits within which relations of power and knowledge are produced.

These requirements are largely negative, and there is perhaps a strong argument to be made against the normativeness of any conception of ideology—an argument that one should more properly attempt a description of the determinations according to which discourses have historically been distributed between the true and the false.[18] But that would still leave unproblematized the position from which this description would be made. Marxist theory is inescapably involved in making political judgments about discourse, on the basis of categories which are necessarily provisional and are themselves positionally constituted. This political force of the concept of ideology must be retained. But if the ideological is not to be ontologized, it should be regarded as a *state* of discourse or of semiotic systems in relation to the class struggle. Rather than being thought through an opposition to theory (a space external to the determinations of ideological production), it would be thought as a differential relation to power. Given that all discourse is informed by power, is constituted *as discourse* in relation to unequal patterns of power, then political judgments can be made in terms of particular historically specific appropriations of discourse by dominant social forces.[19] Note that this involves two distinct theses: first, that of the productivity of power; second, that of the inequality of powers. This means that power is not simply on one "side," and hence that the "sides" in any situation may be mobile and tactically constituted; they are not necessarily pregiven (except in the limit case of simple social contradiction) and cannot necessarily be specified in advance, since ideology is both constituted by and involved in the constitution of social contradictions. But it also means that power is never monolithic, stable, or uniform in its effects. Every use of discourse is at once a judgment about its relation to dominant forms of power and either an assent or a resistance to this relation.

Insofar as power invests all discourse, the category of ideology is a way of referring to systems of value in which all speakers are enclosed and which is the productive basis of all speech. Insofar as power is always asymmetrically split, the category refers to a particular political function-alization of speech. It is both a "universal" category and a category that refers to the tactical appropriation of particular positions by a dominant social class (in Engels's text, the "universalizing" capture of the thorough-fares on behalf of the bourgeoisie). But it does not refer to specific "class ideologies" or class cultures. Here I follow Nicos Poulantzas's argument against a "number-plate" theory of ideology, according to which each class would possess its own distinct and characteristic view of the world, and his contention that "the dominant ideology does not simply reflect the conditions of existence of the dominant class, the pure and simple subject, but rather the concrete political relation between the dominant and the dominated classes in a social formation."[20] The hegemonic practice of the ruling class attempts to ensure that subordinate classes operate within limits defined by the dominant ideology. "Subaltern groups are always subject to the activity of ruling groups, even when they rebel and rise up; only 'permanent' victory breaks their subordination, and that not immedi-ately."[21]

This is not an argument that subordinate classes accept the tenets of a distinctly defined and externally imposed "dominant ideology," nor is it an argument for the necessary effectivity of such an ideology in integrating a social formation and securing the reproduction of the relations of pro-duction. Nicholas Abercrombie, Stephen Hill, and Bryan S. Turner have mounted what I think is a correct critique of functionalist conceptions of ideology (including a large part of recent Marxist theory) which assume that there *is* social coherence and that ideology is instrumental in securing it. But my argument concerns not "an" ideology which would be separately specifiable, but rather the differential, and differentially effective, invest-ment of discourse by power, and in particular ruling-class power. What is at stake in this process is the consolidation of class power (through the integration, in the first instance, of the disparate fractions of the ruling class and then, insofar as possible, of other classes) and the reproduction of the conditions for the extraction of surplus value (conditions which are always a combination of economic structures, the juridical and political relations buttressing them, judicial and military force or its potential, and the "consent" of the working classes). But to describe what is at stake is not to describe an actual and necessary effectivity. Hegemonic strategies establish a shifting and tense balance between contradictory powers and concede greater or lesser degrees of autonomy to discursive positions occupied by subordinate classes (although even in yielding ground, such hegemonic strategies tend to define the terrain of struggle: to set the agenda of the thinkable and to close off alternative discursive possibilities). Hegemony is a fragile and difficult process of containment. Further, there are historically quite distinct degrees of coherence of the "dominant ideology." It may be the case either that one discursive domain (for example, religion in the feudal period) is so heavily invested as to constitute in itself the "dominant ideology," or that the investment of power may range across a number of domains, no single one of which is dominant. It may be the total structure of a discursive domain which is appropriated because of its high correlation with a social function, or it may be one particular set of categories within a domain or across several discursive domains (the concepts of nation or individual, for example, which draw upon and pull together quite different discourses and practices); and it may be the case that the resulting stresses are neither coherent nor noncontradictory. It is quite true to say, then, that "the functional relation of ideology and economy is . . . a contingent one, specifiable only at the level of concrete societies. There cannot be a general theory of ideology."[22] Here, however, I attempt no a priori specification of which discursive domains were most heavily invested or appropriated in particular periods, since this is precisely a matter for reconstruction from textual analysis.

If the function of ideological investment (in Freud's sense of *Besetzung*) is to bring about an acceptance or a tolerance of the hegemonic position of a dominant class, resistance is nevertheless written into the structure of all discourse. If power is no longer thought of simply as a negative and repressive force but as the condition of production of all speech, and if power is conceived of as polar rather than monolithic, as an asymmetrical dispersion, then all utterances are potentially splintered, formally open to contradictory uses. Utterance is in principle dialogic. Both ideology and resistance are *uses* of discourse, and both are "within" power. Ideological utterance is marked by redundancy, by an automatization which appears as a kind of semantic crust proclaiming its authority and its status as second nature.[23] Resistance is the possibility of fracturing the ideological from within or of turning it against itself (as in children's language games) or of reappropriating it for counterhegemonic purposes. This turning is an application of force. In both cases the conditions of possibility are given in the structure of discourse (although they are not necessarily grammatically marked), but they are not intrinsic qualities of the language; they take the form of enunciative acts, and of judgments about the status of those acts.

THE CONCEPT of ideology is still predominantly reserved for systematic and immediately political or propositional conceptualization—for "opinion" or "world view." But by ascribing political value only to what openly claims the status of political or philosophical discourse, this restriction of the ideological sphere impoverishes our understanding of the area in which class conflicts are fought out. In class societies, where the production and circulation of meaning function as a determined and determinant level within antagonistic social relations of production, all meaning is, in the fullest sense of the word, political. The concept of ideological system therefore needs to comprise not only explicitly conceptual systems but the totality of codes and values through which speakers make investments in the construction of realities. A theory of ideology is a theory of semiotic value, because within the symbolic order the position and intensity of values are the index of a mediated tactical assertion, the site of a struggle for symbolic power, and are charged with the traces of that struggle. The ideological structure is coextensive with the semiotic field—with the totality of signifying systems. Bakhtin/Vološinov makes this point when he writes that "the domain of ideology coincides with the domain of signs. They equate with one another. Wherever a sign is present, ideology is present too. *Everything ideological possesses semiotic value,*" and "without signs there is no ideology."[24] This is not to claim the falsity of all signifying systems but to stress the arbitrariness of the sign—the fact that it signifies only by virtue of a social consensus, and that where this consensus is founded on social relations which are contradictory, the symbolic order is necessarily involved in this contradiction.

Bakhtin/Vološinov's conception of the sign as an entity which "reflects and refracts another reality outside itself, i.e. possesses meaning, represents something other than itself,"[25] however, ignores the extent to which meaning is produced by structural interrelationships within the signifying system, and instead locates the process of semiosis in the isolated act of representation, the relation between the sign and its referent. But ideological value does not reside in the falseness of a particular act of representation. It is only at the level of the articulation of the sign in a particular structure of signification that we can speak of a production of meaning, and here "meaning" must be conceived strictly as a function of the diacritical coherence of the structure. Signification depends not on the correlation of signs with bits of reality but on the order of signs among themselves. A meaning is not the sign of something irreducible to which it points as its essence but a sign of its own position in a differential system.

Within the semiotic order language holds a privileged position insofar as the values generated in all other signifying systems can be translated into linguistic form: "The field of linguistic value corresponds entirely to the field of meaning."[26] At the lowest level of semantic structure the semiotic order could thus be defined as a collection of abstract positional units formed within a number of distinct systems of differential relations but corresponding to the signifieds of the language system.

At this level of definition the axioms of structural linguistics are crucial. Saussure's conception of the purely relational character both of the signifier and of the signified destroys the traditional empiricist notion of signification as a relation between a material signifier, an abstract concept, and a "thing" for which the word "stands."[27] Language is no longer a secondary formation, an accretion superimposed on a naturally articulated reality, but rather it actively articulates our representations of reality.[28] The assumption that the sign simply associates a word with the thing it names presupposes "that ready-made ideas exist before words;"[29] whereas Saussure's conception of the closedness of the sign stresses just this gap which founds the *systematic* structure of language and the dependent independence of thought. It establishes that relative arbitrariness which enables us to grasp systems of representation as particular kinds of games rather than as a reflection of the real; and it demolishes the privileged position that substantives enjoy in any empiricist typology, making it possible to think of relations, processes, and qualities, as well as entities, as objects of signification.

Language thus, in Eco's words, establishes "a 'cultural' world which is neither actual nor possible in the ontological sense; its existence is limited to a cultural order, which is the way in which a society thinks, speaks and, while speaking, explains the 'purport' of its thought through other thoughts."[30] The referent cannot therefore be understood as a transcendental signified external to the order of language, since "the so-called 'thing itself' is always already a *representamen* shielded from the simplicity of intuitive evidence. The *representamen* functions only by giving rise to an *interpretant* that itself becomes a sign and so on to infinity. The self-identity of the signified conceals itself unceasingly and is always on the move."[31] Meaning is an endless chain of semiosis,[32] a movement between units which are virtual, positional, and therefore irreducible.

The articulation of the semantic realm into pure differential values depends, however, on an implicit hypostatization of the signified (or more correctly of the empty content-form) as a position defined outside of particular systems of signification. It deals in atomized units and rests on something like the lexicographer's convenient fiction of the existence of stable lexemes. In fact, the *double* relationality of the levels of form and content means that the correlation of signifier to signified, and so the production of meaning, takes place only within specific relations of signification. The system of these relations I shall refer to as discourse (I include in this term nonverbal semiotic systems). If we follow Foucault's terminology, the mode of existence of language in discourse is the statement *(énoncé),* whereas the sentence is the relevant unit of analysis at the level of grammar or language system *(langue).* What distinguishes the statement from the sentence, the speech act, or the proposition is not an *addition* of meaning (since isolated sentences and propositions can be meaningful) but the mobilization of the complex of rules and conventions of the language games that constitute meaning in use. The statement is not a *unit* of discourse but rather a function cutting across the other domains of structure such as grammar and acting as the condition of possibility of linguistic manifestation in these domains. Statements are by definition contextual, but they are not the direct projection of an actual situation. Rather, the statement is always a component of "an enunciative field in which it has a place and a status." It belongs to textual and intertextual systems, so that "if one can speak of a statement, it is because a sentence (a proposition) figures at a definite point, with a specific position, in an enunciative network that extends beyond it."[33]

On this definition, discourse cannot be equivalent to speech in the linguistic sense of *parole* (it is closer to the extended sense that Derrida gives to *écriture*). Here again it is Bakhtin who has done the pioneering theoretical work. Michael Holquist summarizes it this way:

Utterance, as Bakhtin uses it, is *not* . . . unfettered speech, the individual ability to combine *langue* elements with freely chosen combinations. As he says, "Saussure ignores the fact that besides the forms of language there exist as well forms of combination of these forms." If we take into account the determining role of the other in actual speech communication, it becomes clear that there is not only system in language independent of any particular articulation of it, but there is as well a determining system that governs any actual utterance. We might say the world of *parole,* like the sphere of *langue,* is controlled by laws; but to say so would be to change completely the definition of *parole* as used by Saussure.[34]

Recent linguistic analysis, however, has largely failed to move beyond the *langue/parole* opposition. It has been dominated on the one hand by a formalism which treats the text as an extension of the syntactic and logical structuring of the sentence, and on the other hand by an embarrassed empiricism which, in attempting to take into account the role of context and enunciation in the shaping of text, finds itself unable to formalize the infinity of possible speech situations.[35] In both cases the result is a renewal of the traditional dichotomy between text and context or between *énoncé* and *énonciation,* in which only the former is seen as properly linguistic,[36] and the situation of utterance is conceived as contingent, circumstantial, "subjective," nonsystematic.

In seeking to displace this opposition I shall be drawing on the work of four theorists—Bakhtin/Vološinov, Foucault, Pêcheux, and Halliday. I propose in the first instance that utterances are produced within the framework of a number of distinct *universes of discourse* (or discursive formations)—the religious, scientific, pragmatic, technical, everyday, literary, legal, philosophical, magical, and so on—and that it is not possible to assign a cognitive privilege to any one of these universes (even, paradoxically, to that within which this statement is made): each must be regarded as having equal epistemological validity, but as performing different *functions;* that is, each has a different mode of authority within the discursive economy as a whole and in relation to the distribution of social power. These formations govern the production of relatively autonomous semantic realms, forms of referentiality and figurality which are specific to each realm, and the production and reproduction of the subject as subject of signification through its positional inscription within these overlapping and often contradictory semiotic horizons.

At a more specific level—the level of the situation of utterance—the production of meaning is a function of the *genres of discourse,* which Bakhtin/Vološinov defined as normatively structured clusters of formal, contextual, and thematic features, "ways of speaking" in a particular situation.[37]

Each genre is stratified as a social practice through the importance of "language-etiquette, speech-tact, and other forms of adjusting an utterance to the hierarchical organization of society."[38] The production of meaning is thus always highly specified by the rules of the discourse structure in which it occurs, and the structure of the genres of discourse is directly correlated with the semiotic constraints of the speech situation.

The concept of discourse genre has been given greater precision through M. A. K. Halliday's development of the concept of register (in what follows I shall use the terms *register* and *genre* interchangeably; the musical term *register* has the disadvantage of suggesting a scale on a single plane, whereas Bakhtin/Vološinov's term *genre,* which is taken from poetics, implies the unity of multiple convergent planes). Register is the semantic potential associated with a given type of situation.[39] It may be marked by formal characteristics, but "the distinction between one register and another is a distinction of *what* is said as much as of *how* it is said, without any enforced separation between the two" (34). According to this theory the speech situation is conceived not spatiotemporally but semiotically, as a situation *type*—that is, a "constellation of meanings deriving from the semiotic system that constitutes the culture" (109); and this constellation can be analyzed in terms of the three variables of field, tenor, and mode.

Field is an ambivalent concept in Halliday, referring both to a specific semantic domain or "subject matter" and to the ongoing social process in which participants are involved and of which this semantic domain is one manifestation (110). Halliday never directly addresses the problem of disjunction between the two. *Tenor* refers to the relations of power and solidarity between speakers (Halliday refers to these, more blandly, as "status and role relationships," 122). Tenor includes choice of an appropriate degree of formality, and the assignation of a particular truth status to the text. *Mode* refers to the semiotic medium, the rhetorical channels, and the forms of textual cohesion adopted. It is important to note that field, tenor, and mode are not empirical categories; they "are not kinds of language use, nor are they simply components of the speech setting. They are a conceptual framework for representing the social context as the semiotic environment in which people exchange meanings" (110), and "they represent the situation in its generative aspect" (62).

Registers, or discourse genres, are systems of rules governing the production, transmission, and reception of "appropriate" meanings by "appropriate" users in "appropriate" forms in particular social contexts. That is, they are normative systems (whose rules can be broken or changed or parodied) specifying what can and cannot properly be said at a given time and place. The concept refers to the relation between discursive practices and the *systematic* structuring of discourse. Tzvetan Todorov remarks that "any verbal property whatsoever which is optional at the level of the language system can be made obligatory in discourse; the choice that a society makes between all the possible codifications of discourse determines its *system of genres*."[40] Discourse is therefore not the random product of a free subject operating "outside" or "above" the language system, and it is not "an aggregate of conventional forms of expression superposed on some underlying content by 'social factors' of one kind or another" (Halliday, 111). It is the production of a unified cluster of semantic, structural, and contextual meanings in accordance with generic norms. Discourse is not *parole;* a theory of the systematic structure of discourse renders invalid the Saussurean dualism on which modern linguistics is founded. Pêcheux has proposed that the opposition *langue/parole* be replaced by the couple *langue/processus discursifs*, intending by this an opposition not of the abstract to the concrete, the necessary to the contingent, the objective to the subjective, but of two types of system.[41] It follows from this that, although the categories of field, tenor, and mode have linguistic consequences (field governs lexis; tenor mood, modality, and intonation patterns; and mode forms of cohesion, patterns of voice and theme, and forms of deixis), they are not themselves linguistic features. In this model discourse is the crucial level at which meaning is produced, and the lexical and morphosyntactic levels are subordinated to their functionalization within discourse; they represent category options whose uses and effects are indeterminate until they are subsumed within a higher level of codification.

In terms of this model a genre such as prayer is unified by a specific pattern of address (second-person oral to an absent but omnipresent superhuman superior), by grammatical and syntactic structures (vocatives, subjunctives, request structures) corresponding to this authority situation, and by an appropriate decorum, including, in many varieties of prayer, an archaicized vocabulary and a reliance on formulaic constructions.[42] Legal discourse is characterized by an elaborated, "written" vocabulary and syntax defining personal and impersonal modes of property and propriety and putting into play a double set of formalized relationships: that between subjects-in-law whose contractual equality is determined by their free possession of their own person,[43] and that between expert and layman. David Crystal and Derek Davy have described the language of legal documents in terms of a strongly hypotactic subordination of clauses; anaphoric poverty and a concomitant repetition of lexical items; frequent use of conditional and concessive structures; frequency and mobility of adverbials; frequency of nominal group structures, with a marked preference for postmodification; a high proportion of nonfinite verbal groups; and the use of archaisms, of a specialized lexis including synonymic or near-synonymic lexical pairs ("goods and chattels"), of a higher proportion of Romance-derived than of Germanic-derived items, and of a "studied interplay of precise with flexible terminology."[44] To this should be added the characteristic incorporation of a metadiscursive specification of the categories at work in the discourse proper, and in particular of their conditions of validity and applicability. Literary genres, to take a final example, can be thought of as secondary stylizations of primary registers, with a stressed distinction between actual and implied speaker and a special kind of closure—but in this their function is not distinct from other nonliterary ironic or figurative modifications of primary registers.[45]

An important problem in categorizing the kinds of genre is their heterogeneity. Some sociolects, such as political argument or the anecdote, are relatively autonomous of a particular situation type;[46] others, such as ceremonial discourse (church rituals, laments, investitures, and so on), are closely tied to the form of their occasion. But this heterogeneity can be seen as the result of the constitutively unequal fusion of the functions associated with field, tenor, and mode in the complex structure of genre, and this means that genres can be categorized according to the dominance of one of these variables over the others. Conversely, we can identify genres by the fact that, within this structure-in-dominance, they will possess a characteristic constellation in each of the three areas. This will allow us to distinguish them from organizations of discourse which are *more* general (for example, from style and dialect, and from the discursive formations which subsume sets of genres) and *less* general (for example, from speech acts in Searle's sense, from formal structures such as the pun or the aphorism, or from highly situational acts such as telling off a superior).

The table below gives a very rough categorization of the kinds of discourse genres that we might posit as structuring the field of discourse. The complex intrication of field, tenor, and mode means that assigning dominance is often somewhat arbitrary: jokes and sermons are strongly marked by tenor as well as mode; prayer and military commands are strongly marked by mode; the language of commercial transactions is strongly marked by field. And some of the genres listed—scientific and professional jargon, conversation, literary genres—need to be broken down much further into their constitutive subgenres. The more difficult problem, however, is the impossibility of any such closed taxonomic system. This is so for two reasons. The first is a methodological difficulty: an empirical listing of genres would depend in advance upon criteria of definition and discrimination which presuppose that the field is already known, and which, being logical axioms rather than historical regularities, could never yield an exhaustive account of discourse. This means that it is in principle only ever possible to work with the category of genre as a hypothesis projected from texts which never quite conform to these models, but which must be read *as though* a master list of genres existed. The second reason is that "as soon as the word 'genre' is sounded, as soon as it is heard, as soon as one attempts to conceive it, a limit is drawn. And when a limit is established, norms and interdictions are not far behind."[47] Derrida suggests that the law of genre is a taboo on miscegenation, but that the condition of this taboo is the counterlaw of the impossibility of *not* mixing genres and genders.[48] The model of closure operated by any system of classification tends to reinforce "an idealist position whereby 'discourse' or 'culture' become grammatical unities rather than the *locus* of contradictory prac-

Dominance of field	*Dominance of tenor*	*Dominance of mode*
Languages of science and professional jargons (e.g., juridical or medical discourse)	Face-to-face conversation	Oratory
		Sermon
	Invective and boasting	Cant
	Gossip	Natural narratives
Administrative discourse	Greetings	Sacred or scriptural discourse
Political debate/discussion	Language of publicity	
	Language of commercial transactions	Parody and impersonation
Journalese (and subgenres)	Prayer	Jokes
Sports commentary	Military commands	Graffiti
Newscasting	Ceremonial discourse	Riddles and word games
Historiography	Pedagogic language	Literary and dramatic genres and subgenres
Philosophical dialogue	In-group jargon	
Language of technical analysis	Epistolary style	
	Language of showmanship	
	Amatory discourse	
	Labels and notices	

tices";[49] whereas the possibility, the *inevitability* of the mixing of genres
gives rise to a paradox which Derrida applies only to literary discourse
but which must, I think, be extended to all discourse. This is that, on the
one hand, "a text cannot belong to no genre, it cannot be without or less
a genre. Every text participates in one or several genres, there is no genreless
text; there is always a genre and genres"; yet, on the other hand, "such
participation never amounts to belonging,"[50] because "the trait that marks
membership inevitably divides, the boundary of the set comes to form,
by invagination, an internal pocket larger than the whole; and the outcome
of this division and of this abounding remains as singular as it is limitless."[51]
I will come back later to the question of how we are to live with this
paradox.

IF MEANING is produced in accordance with generic discursive norms,
it is therefore not an abstract potential but is closely tied to the structure
of the context of utterance.[52] Foucault argues, in *The Archaeology of Knowledge,* that relations of signification can be assigned only within "a specific,
well-stabilized enunciative relation" (90), because language is based on a
principle of thrift which gives rise to homonymy and synonymy, and
therefore to an unsteady sliding between signifier and signified which is
eliminated only in a higher order of contextual codification where the
fixing of signifiers to signifieds, and the selection from the complex network
of implied predicates attached to a cultural unit, takes place. Pêcheux
similarly claims that words receive their meaning from the discursive formation in which they are produced: "The meaning [*le sens*] of a word, an
expression, a proposition, etc., doesn't exist 'in itself' (that is to say in its
transparent relation to the literalness of the signifier), but is determined
by the ideological positions brought into play in the socio-historical process in which words, expressions, and propositions are produced."[53] Polyvalence is a function of the semantic shift that occurs in the passage from
one discursive formation to another. To put this slightly differently: linguistic *value* is produced within particular generic constellations of field,
tenor, and mode, and the lexical "core" of a word is no more than an
aggregate or average produced by the interlocking and overlapping of
genres of discourse at any point in time. The particular enunciative frame
taken as applying in any particular situation determines the probability
and the conditions of appearance of discursive objects, their possible functions, and whether and to what extent they are to be assigned the status
of referentiality and truth.

Questions of semiosis and epistemology are thus not separable from questions of modality—that is, of the truth status, the degree of seriousness, and the degree of authority carried by an utterance.[54] Speakers enter discourse by way of subject positions inscribed in the structure of genre. These positions are modes of relation to authority, but, as Foucault argues, "the subject of the statement should not be regarded as identical with the *author* of the formulation—either in substance or in function . . . To describe a formulation *qua* statement does not consist in analyzing the relations between the author and what he says (or wanted to say, or said without wanting to); but in determining what position can and must be occupied by an individual if he is to be the subject of it" (95–96). The formalization of registers over time means that there is not necessarily a direct correspondence between the social position of speakers and the positions they occupy in discourse. Rather there tends to be a simple binary structuration of most genres, specifying a dominant (unmarked) position as that of a ruling-class adult male and a repressed position as that appropriate to members of dominated classes, females, or children. In the case of those registers reserved to dominated groups, this coding is reversed. In practice this binary codification into appropriate and inappropriate users means the excodification of certain classes of user whose status as nonsubjects is then concealed by the pseudouniversality of dominant registers.

The crucially important factor here is the discontinuity between discursive positions and the actual social position of a speaker. The positions of utterance and reception which are specified as appropriate are empty and normative positions which may be filled, or rejected, or ironized, or parodied, or replaced with alternative positions; the speaker may fill them consciously or unconsciously, or may fuse them with other positions, or may simply be unaware of them or incompetent to fill them. There is thus a complex network of subject positions available to the speakers of a language (enabling the transformation of existing registers and the generation of new ones), and this means, in Foucault's words, that "the subject of the statement is a particular function, but is not necessarily the same from one statement to another; in so far as it is an empty function that can be filled by virtually any individual when he formulates the statement; and in so far as one and the same individual may occupy in turn, in the same series of statements, different positions, and assume the role of different subjects" (93–94). Paul Henry makes a similar distinction between a speaker's (discursive) *position* and (actual socioeconomic) *locus,* and exemplifies this by two statements made by a mother to her son: "Johnny, come home," and "John James Smith, come home." In both cases the structure of her utterance is defined by her adoption of positions specified by a genre of discourse (conventionalized situations of command); but in the first statement there is a correspondence between her social *locus* and the position she occupies, whereas in the second, in which she shifts to adopt a position within a different register—a position carrying a different mode of authority, perhaps that of a headmaster—there is no correspondence.[55]

The possibility of register shift, and of discontinuity between class positions and discursive position, produces several important effects. One is that individuals deprived of social power are able to subvert official modes of authority on the symbolic level. This can work through a refusal of "appropriate" positions of reception (for example, a refusal to be "talked down to"); through the formation of closed counterregisters (argot or thieves' cant is an extreme example); through parody of official discourse (such as through mimicry, a deliberate stress on the incongruity between real social position and discourse position);[56] or through a fusion of positions in an ambiguous utterance (this possibility tends to be characteristic of literary discourse). The other major effect of register shift involves a loss of control by agents over the positions they occupy. The "Freudian slip" is an example of the uncontrolled displacement of one register onto another. And since register is a contextual category, this displacement involves the intrusion of another context of situation (the "other scene") into the manifestly defined context.

The concept of subject positions encoded in the structure of the genres of discourse has a certain affinity with Basil Bernstein's conception of the binary codification of discourse[57] and with Pierre Bourdieu's theorization of the unequal distribution of cultural capital through the legitimating institutions of the educational apparatus.[58] Halliday and his colleagues in fact directly adopt from Bernstein the categories of restricted and elaborated code in order to formulate the inscription of the production of meaning within social contradictions. Discursive competence is a symbolic capital acquired in the process of socialization, and the class structure determines relations of possession or dispossession of this capital: "The distribution of speech forms is equally a realization of the distribution of power."[59] Thus the codes governing discursive competence "can be seen to embody a range of meanings access to which is determined by the place the individual occupies in the social structure,"[60] and they therefore govern the probable positions and moves of the speaker in a given context. As Halliday writes in *Language as Social Semiotic*, "The codes act as determinants of register, operating on the selection of meanings within situation types: when the systemics of language . . . are activated by the situational determinants of text (the field, tenor and mode . . .), this process is regulated by the codes" (67).

There are, however, important weaknesses in the theorization of the relation between code and register. It is unclear whether code, which is both "above" the system of discourse and yet is realized *through* register (Halliday, 111), functions as a semiotic differentiation which is internal to the structure of register, or whether, insofar as it is a "principle of semiotic organization governing the choice of meanings by a speaker and their interpretation by a hearer" (111), it is rather a differential mode of *access* to register: a sociopsychological *disposition* rather than a structure of potential meanings. This ambivalence results from the fact that Bernstein, in particular, ties the socioeconomic position of agents directly to the mode of semiotic organization corresponding to that position: "The speech form is taken as a consequence of the form of the social relation or, put more generally, is a quality of a social structure."[61] Despite the qualifications, this conception leads Bernstein to view the elaborated and restricted codes as essentially class languages, and so to reify the polarization of the linguistic order.

The theory of codes is also essentially a theory of the unequal distribution of discursive competence: "Only a tiny percentage of the population [that is, the ruling class] has been socialized into knowledge at the level of the meta-languages of control and innovation, whereas the mass of the population has been socialized into knowledge at the level of context-tied operations,"[62] and "one of the effects of the class system is to limit access to elaborated codes."[63] The symbolic order is thus a secondary effect of the order of power, and the formation of subjects takes place through the filtering of the power order through the codes.

The distributionist theory—especially in the more sophisticated version elaborated by Bourdieu—has considerable explanatory power as a theory of the contradictory coding of genre and the ways in which the dominated classes are, as a consequence, largely excluded from the use of an important range of genres. But insofar as it causally equates socioeconomic position with the subject positions encoded in discourse, it is inadequate to theorize the process in which agents are produced and reproduced as subjects in the very act of producing significations.

In the same way, in Althusser's account of the construction of the subject through the process of interpellation, the result of the linkage of the concept of subject to the question of social reproduction is to reduce individuals to functional supports of the system: "The concrete individual and the subject of 'interpellation' tend to be identified. But, as a result, Althusser's subject becomes identical with the unitary self-possessed subject of 'consciousness.' "[64] Insofar as this process exactly defines the function of ideology, Althusser can thus argue that "the eternity of the unconscious is not unrelated to the eternity of ideology in general."[65] *All* individuals, without distinction or differentiation, are "subjected" to this process, and the process is purely negative: the imaginary is pure illusion, and every individual is necessarily and inescapably trapped in it. Furthermore, the decentering of the subject in Althusser takes place in the split between ego and superego rather than in relation to the primary processes of the unconscious. Commenting on Althusser's identification of the Subject with Lacan's Other, Colin MacCabe points out that

> instead of Lacan's insistence on the impossibility of a consciousness transparent to itself, Althusser produces an omnipotent subject who is master both of language and desire. The consequence of this mastery is that there is no *theoretical* perspective for ideological struggle in the face of dominant ideologies for there is nothing which escapes or is left over from the original production of the subject by the Subject (this political pessimism coincides with the functionalism of the concept of the Ideological State Apparatus).[66]

Or rather, the only possible transcendence of ideology occurs in theory, which is a process without a subject.[67] As Stephen Heath writes in an argument against the reduction of the ideological to the Imaginary and to the question of the formation of the subject, the Althusserian account of interpellation "effectively takes the subject as given and not an effect of the signifier," whereas a materialist theory of the subject should designate "not a unity, not even a unity of division, but a construction and a process, a heterogeneity, an intersection."[68]

Such a theory must be predicated on the nonidentity of the subject with itself and the possible discontinuity between positions occupied within the economic, political, and symbolic orders. Discourse, according to Foucault, is therefore a space "in which the dispersion of the subject and his discontinuity with himself may be determined" (*Archaeology of Knowledge*, 55). The subject is not an entity existing prior to the positions which it fills; it is rather a process within the network of signifiers. The clearest example of this is the appropriation of those nonreferential signifiers known as "shifters": personal pronouns, adverbs of time and place, tenses of the verb, and so on, forms in which the concepts of I and you, of here and now are definable only in relation to the act of speaking. Emile Benveniste accordingly argues that "subjectivity" is founded in the linguistic category of *person*—a structural category with purely linguistic reference. "It is in and through language that man is constituted as a *subject*; because only language establishes in reality, in *its* reality which is that of being, the concept of 'ego.' "[69]

Benveniste restricts the process of the subject to the constitutive operation of formal grammatical structures (which he distinguishes sharply from the "supralinguistic" realm of discourse).[70] The subject form is constructed, however, within an order of signification which is broader and more differentiated than the order of grammar. The "I" pronounced by a judge is not equivalent to that pronounced by the accused; the "I" of the child is not that of the teacher; the male "I" is not the female "I." Different degrees of subjectivity and subjection are articulated within the contextual norms of discourse, and this articulation involves all the determinants of register. To appropriate a discursive position involves the assumption of an "appropriate" form of authority and rhetorical organization, and an appropriate ordering of the semantic field. That is, it involves the assumption of levels of meaning corresponding to field, tenor, and mode. To be the subject of a discourse is to produce this complex of meanings—that is, to take over structures of meaning which are *presupposed* in the structure of the genre.

The concept of presupposition is central to a theory of how implied subject positions are locked into implied structures of meaning in such a way that the subject understands itself as the real producer of these meanings. Bakhtin/Vološinov's conception of the *enthymematic* structure of discourse defines the logic of self-evidence which is an important consequence of generic norms.[71] Field and tenor of discourse determine the level of discursive explicitness—that is, the appropriate kind and degree of presupposition—and this in turn establishes the quality of textual cohesion, especially anaphora. Since the function of genre is to bring into play *domains* of conventionalized meaning, any text will adumbrate a range of such intertextual domains. The "free" (preconstructed, implicit) information in a statement is frequently more important than the "tied" information, insofar as it anchors the statement to a context other than the immediate one.[72] In an analysis of scientific discourse, for example, A. J. Greimas concludes that its truth statements are always linked referentially to another discourse or another system of knowledge: its authority is established by interdiscursive reference to an endlessly deferred Authority.[73] By establishing the limits of the sayable, genre allows the unsaid to be said without being uttered—that is, without the speaker's taking responsibility for the enunciation of the message.[74] Thus in the case of ellipsis, or of most rhetorical tropes, what is involved is a distribution of meaning between a foreground and a background of nonactualized meanings which fall within the scope of the semantic potential of a genre.

THE THEORY of discourse I have been elaborating is one that posits the systematic (if shifting and contradictory) unity of what have traditionally been seen as empirically separate components of discourse: that is, the codes of genre specify organized fields of semantic material, layered in depth and in complex relation to other fields; appropriate positions of enunciation, authority, and credibility, and patterns of strategic interaction; and appropriate linguistic and rhetorical options. The system of genre is that set of metalinguistic rules governing the coordination of these functions in the production of meaning for a particular semiotic environment.

My account of genre has drawn extensively on Bakhtin/Vološinov and Halliday; but there is in fact a surprisingly close correspondence between Halliday's categories and the concepts Foucault uses in *The Archaeology of Knowledge* to describe the enunciative function. Thus to *field* corresponds Foucault's *referential,* which consists of "laws of probability, rules of existence for the objects that are named, designated, or described within it, and for the relations that are affirmed or denied in it" (91): that is, both concepts designate the conditions of existence of discursive entities within a particular discursive domain; to *tenor,* the system of relations of enunciation, corresponds the set of *subject positions* determining the forms of inscription and effectivity of speaking agents in discourse; and to *mode* corresponds, somewhat less precisely, the concept of a *materiality* which determines the repeatability of the statement through different fields of use, its institutionally determined status as an object, and its possible functions and availability.

The anomalous concept in this series is what Foucault calls the *associated domain.* This is the "collateral space" or border needed to transform a sentence or a proposition into a statement. It is not equivalent to a "context," since it is rather what makes specific contextual relations possible (97). It thus seems to have the same regulative functions as the concept of genre: it determines the field of related sentences and texts (it groups modes of utterance), and it functions as "the associated field that turns a sentence or a series of signs into a statement, and which provides them with a particular context, a specific representative content" (98).

Foucault posits four levels of textuality which make up this field:

1. "The series of other formulations within which the statement appears and forms one element": that is, the unity of *text*.
2. "All the statements to which the statement refers (implicitly or not), either by repeating them, modifying them, or adapting them, or by opposing them, or by commenting on them": this we can call the *intertext*, and already it extends the enunciative field into the realm of the virtual.
3. "All the formulations whose subsequent possibility is determined by the statement, and which may follow the statement as its consequence, its natural successor, or its conversational retort": this is the constitutively dialogic structure of utterance.
4. "All the formulations whose status the statement in question shares, among which it takes its place without regard to linear order, with which it will fade away, or with which, on the contrary, it will be valued, preserved, sacralized, and offered, as a possible object, to a future discourse" (98–99).

This last, it seems to me, is almost precisely equivalent to the concept of genre or register; but there is one crucial difference. Whereas register is a generative concept formulating the restricted conditions of production of a potentially infinite number of utterances, the concept of statement refers uncertainly to a *function* which is the precondition of discursive events, and to *actual* discursive events. This ambivalence is, I think, a result of the fact that Foucault thinks of discourse in purely positive terms, and needs to fit the concept of statement both into the "structuralist" task of an analysis of the conditions of possibility of discourse, and into the positivist task of "a pure description of discursive events" (27), the definition of "a limited system of presences" (119).

In terms of this latter task, the field of these events is thought of as "a grouping that is always finite and limited at any moment to the linguistic sequences that have been formulated" (27). The actuality of these events is taken as an indication of their necessity: analysis is concerned not with the plenitude of meaning but with the determination of "the principle according to which only the 'signifying' groups that were enunciated could appear" (118). The law of this necessity is a law of *rarity,* and it allows us to establish the relation between the "relatively few things that are said" and all that could have been said. The unsaid is not, however, a *repressed* discourse which could be restored. Gaps, absences, and limits are merely that—determinate and finite moments of discourse. "There is no sub-text. And therefore no plethora. The enunciative domain is identical with its own surface" (120).

The realm of discourse is, however, also internally split by a different aspect of rarity: the scarcity of statements which is the source of their value and which makes them the object of political struggle. Statements are "duplicated not only by copy or translation, but by exegesis, commentary, and the internal proliferation of meaning. Because statements are rare, they are collected in unifying totalities, and the meanings to be found in them are multiplied" (120). Here it is possible to catch sight of a gesture of exclusion: some statements are real, meaningful, primary, whereas others are derivative. The realm of (first-order) statements is an *essential* realm. It is also, finally, a *closed* realm. The principle of the rarity of statements supposes "the incomplete, fragmented form of the enunciative field" (119). This incompleteness can be constituted as such only in relation to the possibility of totality and closure. Both as a field of events and as a field of virtualities, discourse is referred to a model of completion. It is because of this aggregative conception of discourse as a sum of actual and necessary events that the associated domain is seen as only one aspect among others of the enunciative function. By contrast, the generative concept of register, which postulates that "an infinity of variant texts can be created within any one given genre,"[75] subordinates to itself the corresponding categories of field, tenor, and mode, and it is to that extent a more powerful explanatory model.

Let me briefly sketch three further theoretical difficulties with Foucault's account of discourse. The first is that in *The Archaeology of Knowledge* the systems of the discursive formation and the enunciative function are separately described and are then taken to be homologous and are superimposed. The claim is made that "to describe statements, to describe the enunciative function of which they are the bearers . . . is to undertake to uncover what might be called the discursive formation" (115). The coincidence between these two levels is necessary in order to establish the identity of the statement as the object of description in each case. But this coincidence is never formally established; it is simply taken for granted, and there is in fact no good reason why the conditions of existence of each level should converge.[76]

The second problem is that Foucault is concerned almost exclusively with the conceptual or cognitive functions of discourse. The exclusion of "literary," "philosophical," and "political" texts is noted (178); but what passes in complete silence is the exclusion of "ordinary" language—that is, the mass of speech genres which deal in *connaissance* rather than *savoir*, and in which the keying and the transformation of more formal genres produce possibilities of resistance to power-knowledge. Like Althusser, Foucault continues to privilege the form of scientific knowledge. The multiplication of the thresholds in relation to which a science is constituted still assumes a general form of scientificity which is common to all developed bodies of knowledge (186); and mathematics, despite the cautions, remains the general model of scientific knowledge.

The third problem is that the effect of emphasizing the positivity and regularity of discursive formations is to play down the question of their disruption or of resistance to them. The strength of the politics more or less developed in Foucault's work is its sense of the complicity between the powerful and the powerless; it is much less capable of answering the question of what resistance there could be that would not reproduce the power it negates. If the dispersal and pluralization of resistances "does not mean that they are only a reaction or rebound, forming with respect to the basic domination an underside that is in the end always passive, doomed to perpetual defeat," it is nevertheless not at all clear how the "strategic codification of these points of resistance that makes a revolution possible"[77] could escape the condition of being merely the specular reversal of the state. Dana Polan notes in this respect the monolithic force of Foucault's descriptions of power-knowledge, and a totalization of the domain of power which leaves no room for its failure;[78] and Polan contrasts this with Donzelot's suggestion "that every action that a dominant power engages in is a fragile, vulnerable action, engaged in to combat (often unsuccessfully) the dangers of class and oppositional unities, and often undone by these oppositions."[79]

The crucial question for a theory of ideology must be that of the possibility of disruption of discursive authority, and the integration of this disruption into general political struggle. This possibility can be thought in terms which do not rely upon the postulation of a realm of freedom external to discourse: that is, in terms of a noncorrespondence between socioeconomic locus and discursive position and in terms of the uneven articulation of subject positions inscribed in different domains. The overlap and contradiction of genres of discourse produce at once an effect of semantic stability (an effect of the unity of Being as guarantor of the variant repetition of meaning) and an effect of semantic contradiction (realms of Being fail to correspond). David Silverman and Brian Torode write that, against the assertion "that 'members' in consensual fashion work to sustain a single social fact world, it appears to us that speakers articulate conflicting relations between voices. This occurs both within the repertoire of a single individual, and between individuals."[80] These voices, and the realities they sustain and are sustained by, are not neutral, and the relations between them do not constitute a dialogue. The clash of voices is a clash of power, and the analysis of discourse is an analysis of and an intervention in this politics.

4

Russian Formalism and the Concept of Literary System

THE DEFINITION of ideology advanced here is of course strategically oriented to the reconstruction of a Marxist literary theory, although I think it may bear a more general application. Its key features are these: ideology is thought of as a *state* of discourse rather than an inherent quality (a truth status or a particular thematic structure); it is defined in terms of its appropriation by a hegemonic class, but because language is the point of intersection of a network of power relations this involves no necessary, motivated, or stable class correlations; and utterances are thought of as being governed by the structures of the *genre* of discourse and the discursive *formation,* structures which are more or less specific and which delimit certain possibilities of use and certain semantic domains. Effects of truth, representation, and subjectivity are thought to be functions rather than causes of discourse.

The concept of discourse works here as the concept of a systemic process, and it replaces the concept of *parole,* with its suggestions of the contingent and "subjective" structuring of actual utterances. The discursive formations which regulate the production of discourse are defined neither ontologically (as the counterpart of domains of Being) nor formally (as linguistic unities) but functionally, by their variable capacity to produce particular forms of knowledge, and subjects appropriate to those forms. Discursive formations need be neither self-contained nor coherent; they may overlap with and contradict other formations, and they may generate internally contradictory codifications.

The result of these redefinitions should be that the essentialist concept "literature" is replaced by the concept of its particular historical occasions: that is, by the concept of the literary discursive formation. Let me give a provisional account of what I mean by this. The literary formation is a differential system distinguished in historically variable ways from other discursive formations and with historically distinct modes of interaction with them (which may include its complete absence or its absorption into another formation—that of religious discourse, for example). The concept designates a set of practices of signification which have been socially systematized as a unity and which in turn regulate the production, the reception, and the circulation of texts assigned to the category. It thus constitutes a common form of textuality for formally and temporally disparate texts, although this shared space may be riven by antagonistic regimes of signification corresponding to different class (or race or gender or religious) positionings and their different institutional bases.

Because it has an institutional dimension, the concept of the literary formation (or literary system) corresponds closely to Brecht and Benjamin's conception of the *Apparat:* that is, it has the form of an ensemble of norms, practices, and institutional conditions. This means that social functions need to be understood as a component of textuality. In particular, the concept of the relative autonomy of the literary system must be understood as the result of particular historical conditions and a particular articulation with other systems, not as an inherent quality of literary discourse.

The boundaries of the literary system are policed, rigorously or tolerantly, by a constant normalizing scrutiny designed to maintain their integrity. But because the system is a historical result rather than a mode of ontological or linguistic order, the unity which can be ascribed to it is neither stable nor monolithic. Furthermore, its boundaries must be maintained in time as well as space. The system exists as a tension between the level of the code and the level of messages (texts) generated by the code, and which in turn modify it. This dialectic between synchrony and process determines the specific forms of historicity of literary production at any one time, as well as the possible modes and limits of appropriation or transformation of other discursive domains.

Tied as it has been to a theory of representation, Marxist theory has failed to describe adequately the systemic conditions of signification. And tied to a theory of a nontextual history which is represented by texts, it has failed to theorize adequately textual historicity. In what follows, therefore, I concentrate on what has been, and in some ways continues to be, the most developed attempt to conceptualize that level of codification I have called the literary formation or system: the enterprise of Russian Formalism. The theoretical development of Russian Formalism, and of its structuralist successors in Prague, is the record of an exemplary attempt to fuse an immanent approach to the literary text and the literary system, which would locate significance in the structure of textual relations and not in genetic or mimetic features, with an awareness of the essential historicity of these relations. Implicit in their concept of literary evolution was a theory of the mechanism of systemic change; but this theory was never satisfactorily elaborated, both because of a refusal to postulate a direct causal connection between historical change and the apparently autonomous development of the literary system, and because of the Formalists' almost constant separation of aesthetic from extra-aesthetic functions (a separation which confirms the hiatus between the literary series and the social system into which it is inserted). Nevertheless, despite this incompleteness, and despite the extent of the Marxist critique of the Formalist school,[1] its methodological bases can provide a useful lever for overcoming the dichotomy of intrinsic (formal or literary) and extrinsic (social or thematic or ideological) values.

PARTICULARLY in its later phases, the Formalist school worked toward a dynamic conception of the temporal field in which the literary text is situated. This field is constituted by the intersection of the diachronic and synchronic systems to which the text belongs—that is, by the fact that every diachronic series is at each moment determined by the systematic configuration of elements at that moment, and that conversely "the synchronic structure of the work includes diachrony in that it carries within itself as a negated or cancelled element those dominant modes of the immediately preceding generation against which it stands as a decisive break, and in terms of which its own novelties and innovations are understood."[2] The text is seen not as an object but as a process, and our attention is directed not to the achieved finality of the text but to the transformational structure of textual production and reception. This structure integrates the text into a series of three moments: production, automatization, and defamiliarization (new production), so that the historical dimension of the text involves not only its past (the norms against which it reacts) but its future (the transformation of norm-breaking features of a text into a new norm). Thus "pure synchronism now proves to be an illusion: every synchronic system has its past and its future as inseparable structural elements of the system," and the *opposition* of the concepts of system and of evolution "loses its importance in principle as soon as we recognize that every system necessarily exists as an evolution, whereas, on the other hand, evolution is inescapably of a systemic character."[3] But perhaps even more important than this attribution of a diachronic depth to the concept of system is the Formalists' stress on deviation from the aesthetic norm as the central factor in literary evolution. (As Jurij Striedter points out, this is directly contrary to the New Criticism's emphasis on the norm itself).[4] What is immediately valuable about this is that artistic value is no longer measured by the optimal fulfillment of the norm (a notion which underlies all those theories which view the "great artist" as one who is most expressive of the consciousness of his or her class or society, who corresponds most adequately to its ideological needs); rather, the literary norm is associated with the automatized and the canonic, and "linear" succession, the maintenance of the norm, is reserved for those modes of institutionalized iteration which seek to repeat an origin.[5] The function of the reigning literary norm is thus inherently ambiguous: it is at once the recognized and sanctioned standard of literary production, and yet—precisely *because* of this—at the moment of its ascendancy it has lost much of its cognitive value.

The theory of literary evolution which was developed from the view of new production as a rupture with the canonic state of the literary system (a rupture which is always a determinate negation, insofar as the negated norm leaves its trace within the new text, so that the history of the form continues to be present as a kind of accretion of broken prohibitions) runs directly counter to the classical concept of literary history as a continuous linear process moving through the homogeneous "objective spirit" or "style" or "sensibility" of unified epochs. Writing against such an organic-teleological concept of "evolution," Jurij Tynjanov says:

> When people talk about "literary tradition" or "succession" . . . they usually imagine a kind of straight line joining a younger representative of a given literary branch with an older one. As it happens, things are much more complex than that. It is not a matter of continuing in a straight line, but rather one of setting out and pushing off from a given point—a struggle . . . Each instance of literary succession is first and foremost a struggle involving a destruction of the old unity, and a new construction out of the old elements.[6]

The notion of struggle indicates the disjointed and discontinuous nature of change within the literary system. René Wellek goes so far as to see a Hegelian element in this conception: "Dialectics replaces the principle of continuity. Sudden revolutionary changes, reversals into opposites, annulments and, simultaneously, preservations constitute the dynamics of history."[7] The comparison is interesting but probably of limited value, because the literary historiography of the Russian Formalists is marked by an absence of the Hegelian sense of teleology; if reaction and deviation are the motor force of literary change, there can be no question of a *goal*, or even necessarily of a congruence with other areas of human activity.

But even if we can posit a large degree of autonomy for the literary series, nevertheless the specifically literary processes of change within the series are still social phenomena. It is the Formalists' inability—and not only in the early stages of the school's development—to go beyond a mechanistic conceptualization of the processes of automatization and de-familiarization (*ostranenie*) which constitutes their major theoretical weakness.

These two concepts (automatization and *ostranenie*) were elaborated as part of the original attempt by the Formalists to isolate the specificity of the literary work, its "literariness" (*literaturnost*); the automatic, rigidified language of everyday speech, with its reliance on ellipsis and cliché, was opposed to the "defamiliarized" language of poetry, a language which is perceptible because of its strangeness and difficulty. Viktor Šklovskij provides a theoretical framework for this opposition by setting it in psychological terms: "If we start to examine the general laws of perception, we see that as perception becomes habitual, it becomes automatic . . . Such habituation explains the principles by which, in ordinary speech, we leave phrases unfinished and words half-expressed. In this process, ideally realized in algebra, things are replaced by symbols."[8] This assumes that literary discourse should aim at a direct "seeing" of "things," and that, therefore, the mediation of the alien material of the sign is the mark of an impaired "seeing"—of an automatized "recognition." Šklovskij, however, is unwilling to be forced into the position of regarding this signifying material as something separate from and secondary to the signified "content." The ambiguity of his attempted reconciliation of these two different conceptions becomes apparent from the vagueness of reference with which he endows his central category: as Jameson notes, "*ostranenie* can apply either to the process of perception itself, or to the mode of presentation of that perception."[9] Šklovskij's argument culminates in this passage:

> The purpose of art is to impart the sensation of things as they are perceived and not as they are known. The technique of art is to make objects "unfamiliar," to make form difficult, to increase the difficulty and length of perception because the practice of perception is an aesthetic end in itself and must be prolonged. *Art is a way of experiencing the artfulness of an object; the object is not important.*[10]

The problem here is that by equating the textual signified (that is, an image constructed wholly within the limits of its language) with a referent in the real world, Šklovskij is compelled to project the "artfulness" of art *outward*, onto the "object," and yet simultaneously to endow this empirical substance with an aesthetic quality, a quality of "form," which *preexists* the text. This hypostatized quality properly belongs neither to the text nor to the empirical world but is caught in a limbo between them.

There is thus a tension between two aspects of Šklovskij's thesis: on the one hand there is the psychological concept of the estrangement of automatized perception and the creation of a new vision of the world; on the other hand, as an incompatible alternative to this view, "perception made difficult by estrangement is directed to the estranging form itself."[11] Elsewhere Šklovskij writes that " 'artistic' perception is a perception that entails awareness of form (perhaps not only form, but invariably form)."[12] The parenthetical "not only" betrays, again, the failure to theorize clearly the relation between form and content, or rather to transcend the demarcation between the intra- and the extra-aesthetic. This later absolute stress on form is a further attempt to resolve the dichotomy by simple reduction. Thus he writes of Sterne, "By violating the form, he forces us to attend to it; and for him this awareness of the form through its violation constitutes the content of the novel."[13] But form now becomes an end in itself, and Šklovskij cannot conceive of the self-referentiality of a text as more than a "play" with technical elements; that is, he cannot see the norm and the breaking of the norm as phenomena which refer to more general modes of social authority. Šklovskij limits the concept of form to purely constructional devices; he excludes the whole range of thematic material, and the concept therefore tends to be mechanical.[14]

Similarly, the Formalist theory of the immanent dialectic of automatization and estrangement treats this dialectic as a quasiautomatic process.[15] To quote Šklovskij again:

> A work of art is perceived against a background of, and by means of association with, other works of art. The form of the work of art is determined by the relation to other forms existing before it . . .
> Not only a parody, but also in general any work of art is created as a parallel and a contradiction to some kind of model. *A new form appears not in order to express a new content, but in order to replace an old form, which has already lost its artistic value.*[16]

The accentuation of the primacy of intertextual relations and their role in motivating systemic change is important and fruitful as far as it goes, but the interesting phrase here is the last one: the word *lost* suggests a *natural* process, as though the change in artistic value were organic and not governed by changes in the work's reception. Tynjanov, despite his concern for the historical situation from which change emanates, is capable of an even more mechanistic conception of the process of literary evolution. He defines the four following stages: "(1) In connection with the automatized constructional principle a dialectically opposite constructional principle appears; (2) this constructional principle seeks out its easiest application; (3) it is extended to the largest possible number of phenomena; (4) it becomes automatized and elicits opposing constructional principles."[17] This reads almost like a parody in its stress on the objectivity of a sequence of purely technical developments. Medvedev/Bakhtin relates this notion (which, however, is not predominant in Tynjanov's best work) of the literary system as an "objective fact," independent of the subjective consciousness of the producer and recipient of literary works, to the Formalists' reaction against a psychologistic aesthetic and the naive interpretation of the work as an expression of an "inner world," a "soul"; but he observes that in the process of this reaction, "the work is cut off both from real social realization and from the entire ideological world." Ideology is identified as an individual-subjective fact rather than as a social relation of discourse, and so "while liberating the work from the subjective consciousness and psyche, the formalists at the same time estrange it from the whole ideological environment and from objective social intercourse."[18] As a consequence of this, the theoretical basis of Formalist theory remains trapped in the presuppositions of its opponents: "In severing literature from the ideological world, the formalists turned it into some kind of stimulus for relative and subjective psychophysical states and perceptions. For their basic theories—deautomatization, the perceptibility of the construction, and the others—presuppose a perceiving, subjective consciousness."[19]

THE FORMALISTS' UNDERSTANDING of literary evolution as a process which is immanent in the literary system and based primarily on intertextual relations has two consequences. The first is that the study of literary discourse is seen to require a sharp separation between literary and extraliterary factors, and that the latter are (with only apparent exceptions) rigorously excluded from consideration; Ejxenbaum, for example, in his reply to Trotsky, speaks of an absolute separation of the fields of competence of Marxism and formal analysis, since the genetic field and symbolic creation belong to two distinct orders of being which are irreducible to each other.[20] Furthermore, as long as there can be no mediation between the literary system and ideology, the phenomenon of intertextuality must be deprived of its social dimension (its relation to the "extraliterary") and regarded as a more or less self-motivating process. The second consequence, however, is a broadening and generalization of the evolutionary moment: "Since every work of art can only appropriately be perceived as form, but every form only as a 'differential quality,' as a deviation from a 'dominant canon,' then the pre-given material must always be taken into account at the same time,"[21] and therefore the literary-*historical* aspect becomes a necessary component of formal analysis.

The development of a linked conceptualization of the categories of system and history is something that happened only late in the career of the Formalist movement. Graham Pechey and Peter Steiner both isolate three successive models or metaphors structuring the growth of the movement. The first, which Steiner calls that of the *machine,* is based in an initial negative definition of literary language in relation to practical or everyday language. The concept of defamiliarization is at this stage ahistorical and unmediated insofar as it is set directly against "everyday life" rather than against the literary system.[22] Pechey's second model—that of a differential definition by which the text is understood within the historical succession and interaction of forms, and the concept of device is replaced by that of function[23]—should perhaps be seen as a preliminary moment of his and Steiner's third model. Steiner's second model is that of the *organism,* a biological model of the literary text as a complex unified whole made up of heterogeneous and hierarchically differentiated elements. The leading representative of this "morphological Formalism" is Vladimir Propp, and Steiner makes a strong case for the derivation of his "transformational morphology" of the folk tale from Goethe's morphological writings.[24] Propp was almost alone in accepting the challenge of developing an inductive poetics, and in particular in attempting to isolate the smallest constituent unit of genre. This phase of Formalism failed, however, to develop a transformational poetics; and, in replacing the mechanistic opposition of art to life with that of the regular to the accidental, it failed to develop "a systematic explanation of literary change."[25] This was the possibility established by the third Formalist model: that of the *system.* Derived from Saussure's concept of the system of *langue,* the metaphor has radically different implications once it is removed from the opposition to *parole.* Indeed, the concept is explicitly directed against Saussure's belief in "the asystemic and catastrophic nature of changes in *langue*"[26]; it "is intended precisely to theorize both the internal dynamic of distinct cultural orders and the dynamics of their correlation, their mutation in widely diverging temporalities."[27]

The development of the concept of system by Tynjanov permits a more complex understanding of the relation of formal elements to literary-historical change (and thus, eventually, to historical change). The concept is applied at three levels: first, that of the literary text, which can now be seen not (as in the early writings of Šklovskij) as an aggregate of artistic devices (with the corollary that literary evolution involves a mere substitution of devices) but as a structured and functional system, a "regularly ordered hierarchical set of artistic devices"[28] (with evolution therefore being seen as a shift in this hierarchy). Second, the text system refers to the synchronic literary system in which it is situated (and to the diachronic series from which this system was formed). The elements of the text function simultaneously within both these orders, and their intratextual function is overdetermined by their intertextual function: "An element is on the one hand interrelated with similar elements in other works in other systems, and on the other hand it is interrelated with different elements within the same work. The former may be termed the *auto-function* and the latter, the *syn-function*."[29] Central to the intertextual dimension of these elements is the literary *genre,* which mediates between the text and the total system of a period. The genre forms in effect a subsystem of the literary system; it exists only as evolution, is the immediate "dominant" of the text, and organizes the elements of the text according to both their syn- and their auto-function.[30] The third application of the concept of system is to the differential relation between the literary system and extraliterary reality conceived of as an ordered set of systems (the totality of the social formation is thus a system of systems). This relation is equally determinant of the mode of being of formal elements: "The very existence of a fact *as literary* depends on its differential quality, that is, on its interrelationship with both literary and extra-literary orders. Thus, its existence depends on its function."[31] This view of the dialectical determination of formal elements, through their simultaneous integration in disparate functional systems, allows Tynjanov to posit intersystemic influence as a moment of systemic change, and even to come close to connecting this intersystemic moment with that principle of deviation from an automatized norm which is at the heart of his theory of literary evolution: "The very concept of a continuously evolving synchronic system is contradictory," since "a literary system is first of all *a system of the functions of the literary order which are in continuous interrelationship with other orders.*"[32] Literary history is based neither on a purely immanent development, nor on a strict determination by other orders, but is a process of constant uneven modification of literary by extraliterary functions and vice versa.

In effect, the correlation of literary (constructional) function with extraliterary functions, which is achieved through the correlation of different interlocking systems, makes possible the establishment of a theoretical plane where facts of the same order can be mediated. This is evident from the fact that the concept of system is used in the same way to assess the interaction of the synchronic literary system with previous literary systems and with other systems: both enter systematically (and in ways we might guess to be connected) into the determination of the "intrinsic" function of textual elements, and it is in this sense that Tynjanov and Jakobson write that "the evolution of literature cannot be understood until the evolutionary problem ceases to be obscured by questions of episodic, non-systemic origin, whether literary (for example, so-called 'literary influences') or extraliterary. The literary and extra-literary material used in literature may be introduced into the orbit of scientific investigation only when it is considered from a functional point of view."[33] It is worth noting that "the extraliterary" is used by Tynjanov to mean not only extrinsic forces and situations influencing the function of constructional elements (for example, the genetic situation of the work) but also the thematic content of the work. Tynjanov, however, refuses to draw a sharp distinction between formal elements and "external" material: "The concept of material does not extend beyond form—it too is formal; its confusion with extra-constructional factors is a mistake."[34]

A further guarantee that it is facts of the same logical level which are being mediated is the principle that "the study of evolution must move from the literary system to the nearest correlated systems, not the distant, even though major systems,"[35] and this means in the first place a movement "from literary function to verbal function."[36] Extending this slightly, it is through verbal function that literature is related to behavioral norms: "Social conventions are correlated with literature first of all in its verbal aspect. This interrelationship is realized through language. That is, literature in relation to social conventions has a verbal function."[37] By using language as the "nearest correlated system," Tynjanov comes close to something like the notion of an intertextual relation to the extraliterary realm, a relation of like to like (and this is why the relation of form to "material" is not a stumbling block for Tynjanov as it is for Šklovskij).

When Tynjanov attempts to specify what he means by intersystemic determination, however, the examples he gives are relatively trivial. He speaks, for instance, of the interrelationship of social convention with literature as constituting the "orientation" of a text, and cites the declamatory ode (which is intended for public recitation) as having an oratorical orientation.[38] But this is to restrict intersystemic influence on literary function to extremely narrow limits, by confining it to the empirical speech situation of the text. It is virtually the kind of genetic reduction which Tynjanov deplores in his opponents, and it is "formalist" in the bad sense—that is, in its equation of the extraliterary with the work's "context" rather than with other modes of discourse, and in its exclusion of thematic factors. Even when Tynjanov thinks of the determination of literary function in terms of an appropriation of extraliterary into literary discourse (for example the incorporation of the letter form into the eighteenth-century novel), this is still only a relatively minor part of what he conceives to be the process of literary evolution: it is the "positive" side of evolution. But the fundamental dynamic of literary change occurs through an intertextual reference which is negative. The process involves not only the incorporation of noncanonic discourse but the rejection of canonized discourse. In other words, by neglecting this negative dynamic, Tynjanov shows himself to be incapable of linking together extraliterary determination with the processes of automatization and reaction against the automatized norm. We are left with a disjunction between intertextual and intersystemic relations, a final unmediated dualism: on the one hand the diachronic relationship of functional elements to elements in other literary systems, and on the other hand the relationship between literary and extraliterary functions. The reason for this failure of mediation lies in Tynjanov's inability to think of the literary norm as something which is *simultaneously* a "specifically literary" and a social fact—that is, his inability to grasp the immanence of the social order within the literary order. As long as automatization and *ostranenie* are seen as automatic processes, he cannot conceptualize norm formation and norm breaking as socially determined changes in the literary system.

One could put this differently by shifting the critique of Tynjanov's theory to his notion of the "system of systems" as a set of contiguous orders.[39] The justification of this notion is well expressed by Ehrlich: "The view of the social fabric as a 'system of systems' substituted the postulate of *correlating* various self-evolving series for the insistence on *reducing* the secondary sets of data to the primary ones."[40] But what is surprising here is that this view violates the theory, first formulated by Jakobson and adopted by Tynjanov, of the system (hence also of the system of systems) as a hierarchically ordered set of factors which is structured by a dominant.[41] If we compare this theory with Althusser's notion of the "structure in dominance" (and the similarity is such that there may well be a direct connection between the two), it becomes evident that the weakness of Tynjanov's view of a set of merely juxtaposed series is that it cannot account for the overdetermination of the total system by the structure of social power. This, of course, is not the same thing as a reduction of superstructural systems to a "primary" system. It follows logically from this that Tynjanov will be unable to account for the authority of the automatized norm in terms of the control of discursive production by the apparatuses of class power, nor to see deviation from the norm as anything more than a "specifically literary" phenomenon. Indeed, for Tynjanov the whole sphere of literary production and reception is completely isolated from any intervention by the institutions of discursive control: the School, the salon, the Church, the publishing and distribution systems—that is, the institutions which govern the reception, dissemination, and legitimation (or rejection) of the literary product. It is this which influences his choice of *language* as the "neighboring order": unlike the concept of ideology, the concept of language is relatively undifferentiated with respect to the overdetermination of the superstructure by the system of social power relations; it lends itself more readily to the division into literary/nonliterary discourse than to an articulation of values which would cut evenly across both discursive areas.

AFTER THE SILENCING of the Formalist movement in the early Stalinist period, many of its theoretical insights were taken up and modified by members of the Prague Linguistic Circle. In particular, the concept of function was further developed by Jakobson and Jan Mukarovsky. Jakobson isolated an "aesthetic function" which marks off literary language from the rest of language: "Poetry is language in its aesthetic function,"[42] and the object of a science of literature is not "literature" but literariness, the aesthetic function which constitutes a text as a literary text. The presence of this function is not a simple presence, however. The poetic text fulfills "neither an exclusively aesthetic function nor an aesthetic function along with other functions; rather, a poetic work is defined as a verbal message whose aesthetic function is its dominant."[43] While "poeticality" is only one component of a complex structure, it is "a part that necessarily transforms the other elements and determines with them the nature of the whole."[44] Jakobson defines the working of the aesthetic function against the referential and affective functions of nonliterary language. It is manifested "when the word is felt as a word and not a mere representation of the object being named or an outburst of emotion, when words and their composition, their meaning, their external and inner form acquire a weight and value of their own instead of referring indifferently to reality."[45] He insists, finally, that he, Tynjanov, Mukarovsky, and Šklovskij do not abstract art from its social context but are aware of the dialectical interrelationship between art and other sectors of the social structure. "What we stand for is not the separatism of art but the autonomy of the aesthetic function."[46]

The danger, however, with notions like those of "literariness" and of an "aesthetic function" is that, instead of referring to the historical and structural concept of the literary system (as an institutionalized set of discursive norms and practices governing the production of new texts), they can tend to hypostatize a quality which resides in the text, to treat an analytic fiction as an essential *property*. This is quite clearly evident in Mukarovsky's conception of the aesthetic function, despite his disclaimer.[47] The basis for the distinction between aesthetic and extra-aesthetic function is, again, the differentiation between the communicative and the artistic functions of language[48]—that is, "between a self-referential phenomenon (poetry) and one that is communicative (aimed at emotions)."[49] Mukarovsky is, of course, careful to stress that there can be no rigid separation between practical and poetic language. One can posit no more than the *dominance* of a particular function, side by side with other subordinated functions.[50] Hans Günther interprets Mukarovsky's theoretical standpoint here to be that "poetic language . . . is distinguished by the 'displacement of the center of gravity' from the referential function of words to their insertion in the composition of the poetic sign, although without the communicative functions being excluded."[51] But this still does not fully clarify the way in which the poetic sign manages to signify simultaneously in two different ways. The whole concept of function remains ambivalent in Mukarovsky's writings insofar as it denotes a quality inherent in language or in an artifact; when he writes, for example, of the gradual passage from nonaesthetic to aesthetic function in churches or in scientific texts,[52] he is not concerned with the social determination of this passage but treats it as the mutation of an inner dynamic in the object. Function is not conceived of as a *use* to which something is put, nor can we ask how the aesthetic function actually "functions." What is involved here is a hypostatization of the aesthetic realm, an unwillingness to explore the consequences of the notion of function. The opposition which Mukarovsky works out between "instruments" and "art works" similarly fails to grasp that the aesthetic, in its very lack of direct instrumentality, develops its own specific kinds of instrumentality. Mukarovsky cannot think of the self-referentiality of art, and the consequent semanticization of form, as in any way a relationship to reality (since the realm of art is ultimately unconnected with reality).

The relation between aesthetic and extra-aesthetic value is treated by Mukarovsky in two different theoretical contexts. The first deals with the interaction of the aesthetic series with the rest of the social formation. Following Tynjanov (and laying himself open to the same objections), Mukarovsky argues for a notion of the nondominated contiguity of autonomous social structures: "The realm of social phenomena, to which literature belongs, is made up of a number of series (structures), each of which has its own autonomous development: these would include science, politics, the economy, social stratification, language, morality, religion, etc. Despite their autonomy, however, the individual series mutually influence each other."[53] By means of this vaguely expressed "mutual influence," aesthetic value is determined both by the "immanent development of artistic structure" and by the "motion and shifts in the structure of social life";[54] the postulate of autonomy (and the fact that the "artistic structure" is apparently separate from "social life") ensures that there can be no interconnection between the two factors.

In a second context, Mukarovsky discusses the relation of aesthetic to extra-aesthetic values within the text, and draws the conclusion that the text is effectively a *collection* of extra-aesthetic values. Thus, "if we ask ourselves at this point what has happened to aesthetic value, it appears that it has dissolved into individual extra-aesthetic values, and is really nothing but a general term for the dynamic totality of their mutual interrelationships. The distinction between 'form' and 'content' as used in the investigation of an art-work is thus incorrect," because "all elements of a work are, without distinction, components of form," and "all components are equally the bearers of meaning and extra-aesthetic values, and thus components of content."[55] This apparently dialectical view, however, conceals the same dualism of internal/external, of unmediated intra- and extra-aesthetic realms, which I noted in Tynjanov, since value is not created "internally" in the process of revaluation of the literary norm but is imported into the text. Mukarovsky is in fact aware of the danger of positing the transparency of the artistic construct, and elsewhere draws a further distinction between its immediate function (the manifestation of reality directly through the text, in the form of extra-aesthetic values),[56] and its symbolic function, the self-referential opacity of the aesthetic. His difficulty then is to account for the presence of "reality" in the latter, since, just as aesthetic value dissolves into individual extra-aesthetic values, so the extra-aesthetic functions disappear in a properly "aesthetic" reception of the text. What this comes down to finally is the problem of the *transformation* of extra-aesthetic values within the text—a problem which is not resolved by Mukarovsky's reference to aesthetic value as "the dynamic totality of their mutual interrelationships"—and the problem remains constant as long as there is a question of the induction rather than the production of meaning. Ingrid Strohschneider-Kohrs, for example, uses Mukarovsky's categories to argue that it is through the subordinated, nonaesthetic functions that the work takes cognizance of the real: "What Mukarovsky calls 'functions,' relating to 'extralinguistic instances and goals,' should be understood as literary elements *intending, indicating,* or *mediating* reality. They bring about the transformation of extraliterary impulses into intraliterary struc-ture."[57] But here too it is the *content* of a verbal function, not its actual form, which is used as an indicator of the extraliterary; and this content, which is a fixed quantity, is previous and external to the aesthetic function. The contradictions in Mukarovsky's theory are emphasized, finally, by the fact that his disciple Kvetoslav Chvatik can reconcile it, without too much distortion, with vulgar-Marxist doctrine: he relates the concept of the purely organizational role of the aesthetic function to the notion, central to orthodox reflection theory, of the transparency of form (by means of which our attention is concentrated on "the thing itself . . . as it really is"):[58] the poles of formalism and mechanical materialism meet at their extremes.

ONE OTHER PATHWAY out of and beyond formalism has been followed by many Marxists in recent years.[59] This is Bakhtin's development of a "sociological poetics" with its roots both in Russian Formalism (Gary Morson would say it is a *moment* of Formalism)[60] and in a post-Saussurean theory of discourse. It is an attractive path, and it will be clear from the previous chapter how strongly I have been influenced by Bakhtin (in his various voices). But although this body of work (if it has that unity) is in many ways exemplary, there are also major theoretical problems with it, and it is not clear to me that it can be unproblematically redeemed for or incorporated into Marxist theory.

The Medvedev/Bakhtin critique of Formalism, for example, is too often dogmatic and dismissive rather than critical. Crucially, it denies that there is any evolution in "the formal method," which it treats as a "unified system."[61] By arguing that "the Formalists try to reveal the intrinsic, immanent laws of the development of forms within a closed, purely literary series," that they exclude the operation of extraliterary determinations, and that "the very category of interaction is unknown to the formalists. At best they know only the partial interaction of simultaneous lines within the literary series" (159), Medvedev/Bakhtin not only ignores Tynjanov's attempt to conceptualize intersystemic relations but also conflates Tynjanov's model of literary change with Šklovskij's, as though the two were easily compatible. His insistence that the states of automatization and perceptibility have no effect upon the intrinsic structure of the text but affect merely "something absolutely external to the work, the accidental subjective state of the perceiver" (167) is itself a bad formalism, failing to understand automatization as a process which transforms "the text" itself and as a social condition rather than a fact of consciousness. And he misses the point of Tynjanov's conception of literary evolution by claiming that "in order to reveal an evolutional connection, it is necessary to show . . . that the two phenomena are connected in substance and that the first one essentially and necessarily determines the one that follows it. This is just what Tynjanov does not show. On the contrary, he strives to show that there is no evolution in literature and that another type of succession dominates. But, then, he uncritically and illogically calls this succession evolution" (165). Apart from the pettiness about labels, this quite disregards the novelty of Tynjanov's formulation of a decentered and discontinuous dynamic of historical change.

Perhaps more damaging are the political and methodological shifts in the work of the 1930s and 1940s. Although there are real problems about the presentation of Bakhtin's work in English, it seems clear that the critical Marxism of the early books is increasingly replaced by a populist vocabulary concerned with permanent or recurrent structures of antagonism rather than with differential structures of change. This is why, for all the brilliance of its construction of the different chronotopic structures of the novel, there is no *history* of the novel in *The Dialogic Imagination* or in *Rabelais and His World*. The novel is understood on the one hand by way of a constitutive and ahistorical opposition to the genre of poetry, conceived as a realm of the self-possession and self-presence of voice;[62] and on the other hand by reference to "the authentic folkloric roots" of the novel in the culture of popular laughter (21, 50). Like the world of the epic for Lukács, the "immanent unity of folkloric time" (218) functions for Bakhtin as a constant norm against which the development of the novel is measured, and to which it continually seeks to return. Bakhtin thus either works with a static, ahistorical, and populist theory of rupture or else retains a straight-forwardly Formalist model of change (418, for example).

But even in the core of Bakhtin's work, the theory of language for-mulated in "Discourse in Life and Art," *Marxism and the Philosophy of Language, Problems of Dostoevsky's Poetics,* and "Discourse in the Novel," there are severe contradictions and confusions. These have to do partic-ularly with the question of the level at which discourse is structured (the category of the "concrete" tends to work in a naively realistic way to obscure Bakhtin's insight into the systemic situational organization of the utterance),[63] and with a psychologism which understands the dialogic by reference to a pregiven intentional consciousness[64] (although again this is contradicted by countervailing emphases in the theory, especially the con-cept of inner speech). The use that I feel able to make of Bakhtin's work is therefore eclectic rather than systematic, and it is particularly difficult to use it for the reworking of a theory of literary history and of the dynamic of the literary formation. The weakness of the Medvedev/Bakhtin critique of Formalism means that the passage out of Formalism has not been successfully achieved, and we are threatened with a repetition of the For-malist aporias unless we can learn how to put them—the problems rather than the answers—to productive use.

The crucially important thing the Formalists did was to establish the unity of the conceptual level at which extraliterary values and functions become structural moments of a text, and at which, conversely, the "spe-cifically literary" function acquires an extra-aesthetic dimension. Holding on to this principle is perhaps a question of being *sufficiently* "formalist"— that is, of being willing to relate literary discourse to other discourse (to the structured order of the semiotic field) rather than to a reality which transcends discourse; to relate literary fictions to the universe of fictions rather than to a nonfictive universe.

This is part of the reason why I have felt the need to reformulate the concept of ideology in semiotic terms. A number of consequences flow from this redefinition. First, the description of ideology as a state of dis-course rather than an intrinsic quality allows for the identification of historically differential states of the same piece of language. Rather than being seen as a unitary structure, the text is seen as having a variable relation to social power; its functions therefore are also variable. To assess a state of language is not to produce an objective description but to make a socially and historically specific judgment of the relation between texts and between modes of textual authority within a particular system (and conversely, the system is not objectively given but is reconstructed on the basis of these judgments). Second, since as much weight is given in my definition to formal linguistic and rhetorical structures and to positions of enunciation and reception as to thematic features, an analysis of textual ideology pays attention to all of the interrelated and overdetermined levels at which signification is constructed, although without assuming that textual structure is in itself ideologically significant. Third, the possibility of discursive contradiction or resistance means that literary discourse can be thought as a metadiscourse which is continuous with and yet capable of a limited reflexive distance from the discourses it works (although the conditions of this working are themselves not external to power). Finally, theorizing the relation between ideology and discourse in this way also allows us to think the movement of the literary system (its production and reception) in terms of reaction and discontinuity rather than in terms of a correspondence or homology between literary discourse and social structure. The central Formalist concept of the negative dynamic of literary evolution makes it possible to escape that historicism which can perpetuate itself only on the basis of metaphors of identity.

The decisive question then becomes that of the relation between two forms of temporality: a time of repetition which is internal to a literary series, and a differential time, that of the event, which initiates a new pattern of repetitions or deflects an existing pattern into a new course. It is on the basis of a complication of this simple polarity that the complex temporality of any actual system is constructed. Except in the simplest cases, a literary system is not internally homogeneous; it is made up of different domains of normativity between which there is no necessary correspondence. What constitutes these domains as components of a single system is a continuous overdetermination of genres and codes by a normative aesthetic regulation and by the attempt to appropriate literary discourse to more general structures of hegemony.

It is in relation to the normative regimes of reading thus established that specific judgments about ideological value can be made; indeed, the process of value judgment becomes crucial to the description of events within a literary series; there can be no *detached* account of a textual process from which the analyst would be excluded, because what is at issue is precisely the problem of what is to count as an event and a series. Criticism is a part of the literary system, and any reading either supports a normative regime of reading or disrupts it. But a judgment about the more or less ideological state of a text is at the same time a judgment about its relation to a system of power. Thinking ideology as a *state* of discourse, as the specific ways in which it is put to work, allows us to think the concept of automatization not as a purely automatic process but rather as the effect of a revaluation of the text brought about by its "inscription in social contradictions"[65]—that is, as a moment of its reception. The Formalists tend to separate the moments of canonization and automatization, but my argument implies that the two are closely related. Automatization is effectively a consequence of the appropriation or sanctioning of a text by the institutions governing literary production.

Foucault argues that "in every society the production of discourse is at once controlled, selected, organized and redistributed according to a certain number of procedures, whose role is to avert its powers and its dangers, to cope with chance events, to evade its ponderous, awesome materiality."[66] The effect of these procedures is to regulate textual production in accordance with complex sets of overlapping, juxtaposed, or contradictory literary norms which work to maintain a high degree of predictability. In the process of canon formation the text is removed from its real historical time to be situated in a time of habitual repetition,[67] the time of *habitus*,[68] where it becomes familiar and so, gradually, imperceptible.[69] But this is not simply a change in its external status or its conditions of existence, since these conditions are a component of textuality. The text is a relational process and a moment of literary change, and to suppose a fixed and objective signification is to take at face value the second nature into which the canonized text is inscribed.

As Heinz Brüggemann notes, the modes of legitimation are in each case historically variable;[70] the area of dominant normatization determines (although only negatively) the direction of new production, but in all cases the productive impulse is intertextual: either a replication which is continuous with the norm or a break with the norm on the basis of the norm (establishing a discontinuity which is never a pure "originality" and necessarily involving new possibilities of aesthetic cognition). But given that the literary norm is the effect of a broadly social determination of the "specifically literary" process of evolution, it now becomes possible to think of intertextuality as a concept which abolishes the categorical opposition of the "specifically literary" and its "context" of social power: the two are fused in the relation between discourse and literary norm.

Ferrucio Rossi-Landi uses a similar argument to redefine the concept of literary realism in relation to the categories of ideology. Predications of existence, he argues, are all referable to a particular universe of discourse and so are subject to the epistemological categories of that universe. Consequently there is not one "realism" but many in many universes of discourse.[71] Realism in literature is a question of the transmission of a message which will be easily understood and appropriated by a particular public; and this ease of reception is a function of the redundancy (the automatization) which characterizes ideological information. Thus, "a form of artistic realism is present when an artist in a given linguistic/communicative market, and so in a given society and at a given moment of history, encodes a message which is destined to be decoded by the public as representative of the dominant ideology" (229). And this message is marked by "its relatively low quantity of information" (120). It is only through some such concept of the socially specific nature of realism, Rossi-Landi argues, that we can understand why, for example, medieval mystery plays were "realistic" in their time.

To stress in this way that it is predominantly in its social appropriation—the uses to which it is put—that the extraliterary significance of the text is established is not to deny that literary production is equally a social phenomenon, nor to envisage the process of production as a private or isolated act. The point is that production and consumption are not simple opposites; the text is not produced, once and for all, at the "moment of production." Rather, as Bennett argues, "if production is completed only with consumption, then, so far as literary texts are concerned, their production is never completed. They are endlessly *re-produced,* endlessly remade with different political consequences and effects."[72]

What I have outlined here is a model in which the literary system is defined by a play of contradictory temporalities corresponding to automatized and nonautomatized states of language: a play between the more and less ideological. What this should then allow us to do is describe particular texts in terms of their specific historical status and their historically changing ideological value. It should mean that we can theorize the relation of the literary to extraliterary series as a concentration of social value within the former; and that we can develop a mode of analysis which, rather than isolating the text in its "specifically literary" autonomy or moving outward from the text to its nonliterary "context," can identify the movement of power in the variant forms of literary textuality.

5

For a Literary History

THE CONCEPT of a break which disrupts the time of an established literary series is both a historical and an epistemological category;[1] it describes the possibility of the production of new forms of knowledge within a discursive formation. But to speak of a break with the literary norm (or the variable *complex* of norms) suggests a single and isolated event. It would be truer to say that what is involved is a disseminated process of challenge and critique occurring at various textual levels, from the smallest unit of formal structure to the institutional apparatus governing relations of literary production. This process is founded on difference, either overt, as in parody, or implicit: that is, the new structure forces the recognition of its differential quality with respect to the old; it is not an absolute newness but an otherness, a determinate negation. Every moment in a text represents a point of tension between more and less probable choices, lower and higher degrees of information.

There are two consequences of this. The first is the repeated trace of the past order in the new text, endowing it with a temporal depth which is the basis of its variant historicity; the second is a manifest or latent reference to its differential quality (although this element of self-reflexivity will have different historical modalities, ranging from implicit reference to the canon to the programmatic foregrounding characteristic of the modern and the techniques of pastiche and quotation of the postmodern). But the historicity of the text extends beyond this trace of the past as a constitutive moment of the present, to the possibility and the particular historical modalities of the text's assimilation and repetition.[2] This relation to the future is not a teleology as long as the direction of the break is thought of as being indeterminate, unpredictable, and open ended. Although the break is structured to a certain extent by the norms against which it reacts, it is never a simple reversal of these norms; rather, the fact that it is always a breakthrough out of a seemingly closed system guarantees the unexpectedness of its solution (however "natural" it may appear later: distance in time makes it increasingly less possible to understand the difficulty with which Stendhal broke with the novel of Scott, or Kleist and Büchner with Weimar classicism, or Vallejo with Modernist lyricism). A theory of literary evolution, then, must reject the conception of historical movement as an evenly unfolding and integrated continuum, and stress instead the relatively arbitrary nature of change. It should move away from thinking in terms of the directly meaningful nature of cultural material, and seek to understand, historically and concretely, the mediations through which it both corresponds and fails to correspond to more general structures of social development.[3] An understanding of this ambivalent status of new production, somewhere between sociocultural motivation and arbitrariness, can lead us beyond a further weakness in Formalist theory. Just as structural linguistics has often been accused of seeing speech as a purely accidental and spontaneous act, the opposite of the "system" which is the sole bearer of history,[4] so the Formalists tend to view the act of defamiliarization as an isolated, spontaneous, and therefore ahistorical occurrence in relation to the regularity and social congruence of the literary system. The alternative to this view is not necessarily to correlate the break with a contradictory social force (as, for example, in the theory of the "ascending class" as a force which shatters the ruling ideology) but to locate its historicity in its unity with the transcended norm and its integration in a speech situation which is always, indirectly, a power situation.

The choice of constructional elements (including thematic material) is always a choice within or against ideology, since all available devices are preinvested with ideological value: they are rational/irrational, poetic/prosaic, orderly/disorderly, harmonious/inharmonious, in good/bad taste, archaic/modern, moral/immoral, high/low, and so on (the traditional discrimination of styles provides a good example of the investiture of purely formal options with prescriptive value vis-à-vis their ideological content). The act of writing is thus political to the extent that it involves a repetition or a deconstruction of forms which have become ideologically assimilated and motivated, and which reflect the authority of a social order; and any reading of a text, simply as a sequential reconstruction of choices made, is directed to the level of automatization or defamiliarization which the text manifests, and so, ultimately, to its degree of integration in a system of discursive authority. This comes fairly close to Jauss's concept of aesthetic distance, whereby the space between the new text and the horizon of expectations (the system of discursive norms) is used as a measure of aesthetic value; and the notion of the gradual appropriation and auto-matization of the new text by regulative institutions corresponds to Jauss's theory of the inevitable disappearance of aesthetic distance, as the original negativity of the text becomes self-evident and predictable in the horizon of future aesthetic experience.[5] Such a theory need not be simply linear, and it need not exclude the concept of the simultaneity of past and present texts: it merely historicizes the way we can think of this simultaneity. The synchronic literary field is made up of elements of different "ages," of a noncontemporaneity of the simultaneous; but the dominant force within this field is usually the sets of norms established by the immediately pre-ceding literary generation.

THE PROCESS of literary evolution occurs in two contradictory ways: discontinuously, through the production of deviant forms of textuality, and continuously, through the reproduction of the literary norm. But the categories of production and reproduction also have a broader sense, which includes the technical basis of literary activity and its integration into the general structure of material and mental production. This distinction be-tween material and mental production overlaps, but does not coincide with, that between productive and unproductive labor, which Marxism conceives as a historically specific distinction grounded not in the structure of the produced object but in "the social relations embodied in the la-bour."[6] Whereas unproductive labor is exchanged with revenue, productive labor is exchanged with capital in such a way as to produce surplus value. In late capitalism, however, these relations of production have altered dramatically, and the conceptual value of the distinction has become doubt-ful. The fact that scientific and cultural capital have become integral to the organic composition of capital in the form of fixed outlays for research and advertising makes it difficult to exclude certain forms of unproductive labor, and in particular unsalaried intellectual labor, from the production of surplus value.

These changes have been theorized by Jean Baudrillard in terms of a revolution in the structure of value, giving rise to a shift from the order of signification which he calls "production" to that free-floating order of the simulacrum he calls "simulation."[7] In very similar terms, Jacques Attali speaks of a transition from a "mode of representation," in which the product "stands for" the labor it embodies, to a "mode of repetition," in which labor is serially organized and bears no direct signifying relation to the product.[8] Both of these schemes are rendered problematical by their neo-Hegelian emphasis on the succession of self-contained semiotic stages; but they have the value of seeking to come to theoretical terms with the integration of cultural or scientific capital in the process of commodity production, as well as in the process of circulation and revalorization of the commodity. Like any good Hegelian theory, they make possible a retrospective reworking of the categories of a "previous" order. In this case they make possible a conception of capital not just as stored-up labor but as stored information: or, more precisely, a conception of labor itself as a form of information. They make possible a semiotic conception of the "material" production process.

In more conventionally Marxist terms, Brecht long ago stressed the integration of literary production into the system of commodity production, through changes in market conditions and through the development of new technologies of signification which have a decisive indirect effect upon literary work.[9] The system of commodity production of literature differs radically from that of precapitalist systems,[10] perhaps most importantly in the separation which it introduces between writer and audience—the fact "that 'writing to someone' has become 'writing.'"[11] The complexity of the moments intervening between writer and reader—the publishing and publicity industries, the apparatus of distribution, and so on—confirms the abstractness of the relationship. In the face of this phenomenon, romantic-conservative distinctions between "technical" and "creative" (commercial and noncommercial) art become untenable, a reactionary assertion of the privileged and exclusive character of the work of art.[12] The relation of "high" to "low" art is a relation *within* the total system of aesthetic production, and it is into an analysis of this totality of production, with its "normal" and "exceptional" modes, that we must insert the analysis of any particular text. Further, we can better understand the technical aspects of literary development if we take into account not only the literary formation, with its subgenres and survivals and its own history of changing relations of dominance between genres, but also the range of other genres of discourse and the other semiotic formations with which the literary system is interrelated. This makes it possible to consider the influence on literary development of technical developments in other areas (for example the interconnection between pictorial perspective and the Renaissance stage, or between the printing process and the secular romance of the late Middle Ages). Historically, literary development has occurred above all through the evolution of genres and the displacement of established genres by newer genres; but "in the age of mechanical reproduction," this intraliterary evolution has been profoundly modified by the development of nonliterary media, especially film.[13] The various semiotic modes of artistic production are more interdependent now than ever before, and this has radically altered both the hierarchy of aesthetic modes and the internal structure of traditional genres (for example by the incorporation of montage techniques into the novel, or, conversely, by the rapid obsolescence of traditionally literary genres like the family saga as a result of their reworking in television serials). Technical innovation shares many of the features of the kind of ideological break which I have up till now discussed solely in terms of the contestation of normative generic features. The drama, in which the function of a technical apparatus has always had greater importance than in other literary modes, provides the clearest examples: Aeschylus' introduction of the second actor; the development of the medieval stage and, later, the proscenium arch; the agit-prop techniques of the early Soviet theater; and Piscator's use of film projection all amount to effective "defamiliarizations."

In the broadest sense, then, the literary system is a mode of production, a structure of functional relations in which there exists a hierarchy of genres,[14] a constant modification of relations to other modes of artistic production—which in turn modifies the hierarchy—and a specific relationship to an audience. But in the twentieth century the literary system has undergone a restructuring of unparalleled rapidity, caused by the profusion of new artistic and communicative modes developed around the turn of the century; in addition to film, the list would include radio, mass-circulation daily newspapers, the advertising industry, and new distribution techniques for popular fiction. More recently, television, video systems, new film technologies such as super-8, and microcomputer technologies have radically altered the interrelation of semiotic formations and the hierarchies of value associated with previous literary formations. The new information technologies are a direct result of the extension of the communications network by the expanding capitalist system, but their effect on literature takes place through their expansion of the number of modes of "literary" and narrative discourse, against the background of the "extraordinary persistence through the centuries, in European literature of a limited number of generic models . . . and of the places which these models occupied within generic systems."[15] The systematic crisis caused by new modes of literary and quasiliterary production is in part no more than a quantitative effect—the enlargement of the cultural system to include new audiences—but this necessarily becomes a qualitative problem.

One persuasive account of the effects of this crisis is given by Baudrillard, who describes a world of pure mediations, a world in which the simulacra precede and give rise to the models, in which the real is what is constructed to guarantee the authenticity of representations.[16] But Baudrillard totalizes this world, allowing no unevennesses, no gap between the intermeshed systems of simulation; and he is persistently nostalgic for a "lost" referentiality, a lost world of real objects and the *pleine parole*.[17] There never was a nonmediated world; but the mediations are more visible and more powerful now because they are industrially constructed in systems of prolonged repetition. As Walter Benjamin pointed out, art has always been reproducible, but the new technologies of repetition constitute a radical change in the system of dissemination of aesthetic information.[18] On the one hand, as forces of production, they offer the possibility of a total desacralization of the artwork; on the other hand, as the concept of cliché, stereotype, *Schablone* indicates (the terms all refer to the printing process), they speed up and expand the process of automatization so that, as long as the apparatus is not radically transformed, they become a powerful tool for the appropriation and neutralization of divergent new texts, and for the reinforcement of the authority of the canon (or rather of multiple official and nonofficial canons).

Insofar as technical innovations contribute to production rather than reproduction, their effect is, according to Benjamin, threefold: they transform mechanical techniques (for example the nickelodeon) into aesthetic forms; they produce effects which had been imperfectly achieved by the traditional forms; and they change the nature of our reception of traditional forms.[19] Unlike the essentially negative process of normbreaking through which literary evolution usually takes place, they have an additional positive constructional function with respect to the genre: that is, technical innovation seems to represent a real *progress* in the development of literary forces of production, rather than simply a change in direction. The temptation this offers is to equate material and immaterial production, to see literary evolution in terms of the development of the general productive forces. Ultimately this can lead, as I think is the case with Benjamin, to a fetishization of technology. An understanding of technique as an autonomously developing force which is in itself progressive is only the obverse of the romantic-reactionary rejection of the mechanical. More specifically, by assuming such an autonomous process, Benjamin ignores the social functions served by the technical apparatus—that is, the process by which material techniques are either consciously developed for specific functions, or, once developed, are adapted and made to serve specific social ends. In this he differs from Brecht, who keeps the concept of literary production free of the metaphoric identification of literary technique with technological advance, and understands it rather in terms of social function.

Let me conclude this section by mentioning briefly two concepts which seem to me to contribute to such an understanding. The first is Benjamin's view of commodity production as production of the *Immerwiedergleich*,[20] the eternal recurrence of sameness. The second is Kubler's concept of replications—that is, the "entire system of replicas, reproductions, copies, reductions, transfers, and derivations, floating in the wake of an important work of art." Kubler distinguishes between the nonidentity of new products (which he calls "prime objects") and the identity (a relative identity, imposed on the underlying nonidentity of the universe) of replicas. And this distinction implies a temporal dialectic of aesthetic evolution: "Without change there is no history; without regularity there is no time. Time and history are related as rule and variation: time is the regular setting for the vagaries of history. The replica and the invention are related in the same way . . . The replica relates to regularity and to time; the invention relates to variation and to history."[21] The replica belongs to the regularity of commodity production; the invention breaks or deflects the cycle of reproduction.

THE CATEGORY of marked change of *epochal* style raises in an acute form the question of the periodization of change. The two polar theoretical possibilities would be either to posit the organic self-sufficiency of stylistic change, so that each stylistic paradigm will obey necessary laws which dictate its rise and fall, or to reduce the stylistic break to an expression of a structural change in the socioeconomic base. A third, synthetic possibility would equate these two by conceiving of the organic unity of the spiritual and social manifestations of an epoch as the determinant of the coincidence of their limits; but to suppose the homogeneity of the historical epoch means surrendering the moment of discontinuity which is indispensable for a dialectical conception of historical movement.

One difficulty for Marxist theory in this respect has been Marx's bald statement in *The German Ideology* that superstructural forms "have no history, no development";[22] but to be properly understood, this statement must be read in the context of the anti-Hegelian thrust of the whole passage. Marx is arguing against the notion that history is moved by ideas, that its development is separate from that of socioeconomic processes, and thus he is denying not the history of superstructural forms as such but only their separateness from social practice. A more useful formulation is perhaps Engels's contention that the illusion of autonomy is constitutive of ideology.[23] In conservative theory the argument for autonomy always carries the implication of the necessary apoliticality of art and its freedom from market relations. The concept of an intertextual evolutionary dynamic seeks to circumvent this implication by positing both the relative autonomy of the literary series and a mediated intertextuality, in which the relation of text to text is primarily a relation of the text to the socially overdetermined state of previous texts.

This implies, further, the rejection of an organic conception of literary development, since "it is not so much the old that dies as the new that kills."[24] But what are the structural constraints placed upon development, if they are not those of an inner principle of formal growth? Jauss has proposed, in a discussion of the diachronic structure of genre, that for the metaphor of the organic cycle should be substituted "the nonteleological concept of the playing out of a limited number of possibilities."[25] If, shifting our perspective slightly, we think of a "work" as a productive transformation of raw material (that is, as a kind of *work*),[26] then the limits of its function and of its development are determined both by the nature of the material it elaborates (the particular mass of ideological values) and by the limited number of technical features which are more or less pregiven for the genre. This concept replaces that of an ontological determination of formal structure, and it describes the (historically modified) boundaries set on the representational and critical potential of a genre. The evolution of literary genres is therefore determined both negatively, through the break with the automatized norm, and positively, by the possibilities given in the formal genre features, the limited set of alternatives open at any point.

But the notion of a positive determination must be qualified in two ways. First, the formal and technical features of a genre are not *absolutely* pregiven, and the structural limits of development are therefore not marked out from the beginning; rather, these features are in most instances the result of previous development, a product of the exclusions and prohibitions created by the growth of the series, and of the possibilities of incorporating new material, of refunctionalizing formal elements, and of discovering new technical bases. Second, the formal-technical features of the literary genres—point of view; narrative structure; spatiotemporal categories; number of voices; author-text, speaker-text, and reader-text relations; and the number and kind of registers which can be absorbed— are capable of immensely rich development, and the time curve of most literary modes is almost indefinitely long.

Thus, although we can posit a double (positive and negative) determination of literary succession, we cannot speak, as Aristotle does of tragedy, of the "fullness of its perfect form"[27] or entelechy with respect to any genre, nor can we posit the predictability of new stages in the sequence. Furthermore, diachronic development is seen to be possible only through an intersection with the synchronic literary field: this is represented by the dominant norm, but necessarily involves the "extraliterary" factors of the discursive field, the relation to an audience, social function, and relations of dominance within the total social structure.

A more formalist model of aesthetic succession, and in many ways a rather precise description of the operation of formal prohibitions, is that of George Kubler. Using, like Thomas Kuhn, a notion of puzzle solving as the motive force of aesthetic change, Kubler elaborates the idea of an interconnected succession of solutions to formal problems, which he calls "linked solutions describing early and late stages of effort upon a problem." Because the sequence follows a definite path mapped out by the problem structure peculiar to it, it is possible for Kubler to argue that "every succession may be stated in the following propositions: (1) in the course of an irreversible finite series the use of any position reduces the number of remaining positions; (2) each position in a series affords only a limited number of possibilities of action; (3) the choice of an action commits the corresponding position; (4) taking a position both defines and reduces the range of possibilities in the succeeding position." Thus, "every new form limits the succeeding innovations in the same series."[28] Aesthetic succession is therefore primarily a process of constructive development and then progressive entropy, and the diachronic sequence follows a curve corresponding to the logic of its predetermined potentialities and limits. This logic is purely immanent: "The idea of seriation . . . presupposes a structural order in the sequence of inventions which exists independently of other conditions."[29] But Kubler also reinforces the notion of the finiteness of the series by adopting Göller's concept of *Formermüdung* to explain the exhaustion of the possible new solutions; this seems to suggest that the notion of an inherent structural order is inevitably bound up with metaphors of the organic. Finally, Kubler posits a dialectical interchange between new production and the past canon, which leads him to distinguish between the moments of production and of eventual assimilation (leading to further innovation). Innovation involves the obsolescence of prior positions in the sequence. "Yet prior positions are part of the invention, because to attain the new position the inventor must reassemble its components by an intuitive insight transcending the preceding positions in the sequence . . . The technique of invention thus has two distinct phases: the discovery of new positions followed by their amalgamation with the existing body of knowledge."[30]

I have quoted Kubler at some length because his theory seems to me to clarify some of the strengths and weaknesses of a purely formalist historiography. Its basic failure is already implicit in the initial thesis that "the forms of communication are easily separable from any meaningful transmission," and hence "the structural forms [of art] can be sensed independently of meaning."[31] The artificial separation of semantic and formal material distorts the functional integration of the two in the system of the text; in isolation from this system formal elements become abstract and undifferentiated. Further, Kubler's supposition that the "shaped time" of a sequence is determinate and unilinear ignores the complexity of the factors involved at each point. We should ask rather to what extent there is not *one* line of development but multiple possible "solutions" at each stage, one of which is chosen (or invented) not in accordance with an immanent logic but as a "blind" negation of occupied (and automatized) positions. We would thus think of the curve as being displaced, deflected, and modified by its reaction to the dominant norm, and through this by the specific historical conditions of artistic production and distribution (and by the corresponding institutions), by interrelations with other art forms, by *ad hoc* renovations (for example the introduction of new material), by technical innovation, and so on. The model of literary evolution as the working out of a calculus of possible forms presupposes a closed set of possibilities, and this can be only partly true (it is above all too technological a model). Diachronic development, which gives the appearance of being a purely internal process of change, should more accurately be described as the progressive sedimentation of a chain of synchronic interactions with other structures. More radically, we can argue that each period produces its own particular time, and that literary evolution is a bundle of such times rather than a sequence passing through a homogeneous frame.

VIKTOR ŽIRMUNSKIJ was one of the first to criticize the inadequacy of the Russian Formalists' view of literary change as a negative, reactional process, and to charge it with an inability to explain the direction of change.[32] But his own explanation of literary development in terms of correspondence to new world views reduces the text to a simply expressive function and minimizes the systematic constraints through which development occurs. A more serious formulation of this criticism is René Wellek's attack on the equation of aesthetic value with the evolutionary value of a text:

> It is another attempt to arrive at values in a value-proof way. The very act of choosing the significant objects, however, implies value-judgments in relation to the whole scale of values, not merely the criterion of newness. We recognize newness only by constructing a series of development which judges a certain trait as valuable. History has to construct series. But which series? The answer can only be that it must show the essential changes, i.e., the new thing should not only be different, but must be by its very novelty important for the tendencies or value-concepts dominating a history of art. Mere newness may not be in any sense valuable or essential.[33]

The demand that the constructed series show "the essential changes" restates Žirmunskij's demand for an explanation of the direction of change; and what this means, of course, is that the change must be shown to be motivated, to correspond to something beyond the literary series. We might have expected Wellek to require that the structure of the new text be shown to be positively correlated with social or class values; but he avoids this simple trap and walks into a more subtle one. The structure of the new product must have not only a negative but also a positive "importance," and this importance corresponds to the "tendencies or value-concepts dominating a history of art." But this is curiously circular, because it asks that the "tendencies or value-concepts" be used both to *construct* the series and to act as a *standard* for the series; such a history of art can only be an exercise in tautology.[34]

The real difficulty doubtless lies in the very restricted sense that Wellek allows to the concept of (mere) newness. It is a misreading of Russian Formalist theory to assume that this is equivalent to novelty or technical innovation. Rather, the breaking of the dominant literary norm system involves, as I have tried to demonstrate, a relation to the whole ideological

field and the production of a newness the force of which lies precisely in
its negativity. The Formalists' conception of the literary system, and their
rejection of historicism and any simple historical holism, excludes a view
of literary evolution as the working out of a preestablished pattern. Tynjanov and Jakobson make the point that, whereas an analysis of structural
laws will permit "the establishment of a limited series of actually existing
structural types (types of structural evolution)," it will not allow an explanation of "the tempo of evolution, or the chosen path of evolution
when several, theoretically possible, evolutionary paths are given. This is
owing to the fact that the immanent laws of literary (linguistic) evolution
form an indeterminate equation; although they admit only a limited number of possible solutions, they do not necessarily specify a unique solution."
The "direction" of change can be established only "by means of an analysis
of the correlation between the literary series and other historical series,"
and this means inserting the literary system into a structure of complex
determinations, not into an expressive totality.[35]

Formal and thematic innovation or refunctionalization can never, then,
be immediately expressive or imitative of changes in the structure of reality
(or of an institutionalized awareness of them). They have no necessity
which would correspond to a larger rationality of historical movement.
The negative progression of the literary series is a discontinuous dialectic
of formation and deformation; it is not even an "evolution" in the strict
sense of the word, because this sense is based on a conception of the
identity of the organism throughout its mutations, whereas social change
is endless, has no point of maturity, is not structured by a goal. The notion
of evolution can be useful only if we replace its connotation of biological
time, which "consists of uninterrupted durations of statistically predictable
lengths," with that of historical time, which is "intermittent and variable"
and which includes the uneven intervals between "events."[36]

We should perhaps ask how it is possible for the negative process of
deautomatization to produce a "positive" cognition. I would argue here
that the resemanticization of formal and thematic elements leads not to
the arbitrary production of *any* new meaning, but to one of three possibilities: (1) the only new meaning possible: but this is the historicist thesis,
relying on the postulation of a pregiven meaning in the course of history;
(2) the release of the multiplicity of meanings locked in the single authoritative meaning of the automatized word or structure: but this is
formalistic, since it stresses the act of release itself rather than its content;
or (3) a new meaning whose shape is determined by reaction to the

structure of the norm system; thus, a meaning which exists *as* a negation and in the determinacy of its negation, not in the determinacy of a new positivity. In this case the cognitive value of the new text is qualitatively determined by the limits of the system of canonized norms; it never establishes a wholly new configuration of meaning and can never do more than push beyond the norm or refunctionalize it. The break is never a *clean* break, and the text can never transcend ideology; it has a complex relationship to it, and its criticality can only ever be partial and itself historically conditioned. It is no objection to the cognitive value thus created to point out that the process remains within ideology: in a Marxist perspective, the categories of knowledge do not evolve toward a final "truth" but develop immanently in accordance with social and discursive determinations; their validity is that of a practice, not of an absolute and ahistorical adequacy to reality. The cognitive value of the break with the norm therefore lies in the suspension of meaning between a past and a future norm, in a state of determinate cancellation which has no transcendence. This does not imply negation for its own sake, since an avant-gardistic "originality" has no meaning once it is released from the state of tension linking the automatized structure to its breaking. But the ambivalence of this relation has no necessary influence on the content of the new text, as Julia Kristeva seems to propose when she writes of Lautréamont that "dialogue and ambivalence prove to be the only approach that permits the writer to enter history by espousing an ambivalent ethics: negation as affirmation."[37] Nor does it imply the indeterminate and purely formal openness which Eco, deliberately developing Crocean categories, has propounded as the essence of aesthetic creativity, and which he relates to a conception of the idiolectal status of the new text.[38] But one consequence which does seem to be indicated by the theory of the negative progression of the literary system is that the skeleton of the canon will always be present in the new product: as *mise-en-abyme* (the baroque topos of the *theatrum mundi;* emblems of writing in Bonnefoy or Robert Duncan); as a stylistic tension (Dickens's or Pound's pronounced shifts of register) or excess (Lezama Lima); or as the object of a philosophical thematization (Tolstoy, Proust, Musil). In all cases this skeleton will exist on various stylistic levels, and will be manifested both in its effects and in a tension which constantly strives to pull the text in contrary directions.

AT THIS POINT I need to introduce a substantial qualification of the model I have been using by trying to specify it historically. Turning the theory back on its own limits and conditions raises the question of whether, instead of a single and universal mode of literary evolution, there are not rather multiple epochally different modes, each influenced by and influencing a current theory of literary production. I have assumed, first, a sort of general aesthetic imperative which equates artistic value with opposition (usually on an implicit level) to the norms and values of a hegemonic class; and second, that all dominant classes depend upon the automatization of language in order to maintain their hegemony. That is, I have worked within a general modernist paradigm which derives its categories "from the dichotomy between conventional, clichéd language and experimental linguistic forms that dislodge those clichés" (Jochen Schulte-Sasse cites Adorno and Derrida as exemplary exponents of this view).[39] But I should immediately add that my argument is not dependent upon an espousal of avant-garde art or upon a dismissal of popular culture. The former is not necessarily estranging, the latter is not necessarily automatized. The model of change I have used makes no *a priori* judgment about where value is to be assigned and sets up no essential opposition, as do Adorno and Bourdieu in contrasting ways, between popular and bourgeois aesthetics (thus American jazz and blues—to take a musical example that Adorno conspicuously failed to comprehend—forced a rupture with the Western musical tradition in the early twentieth century more deep and pervasive than anything possible in the "classical" avant-garde). What matters for analysis is the social constitution of such oppositions, the specific interrelations thereby established, and the social function of these relations.

The connection between the theoretical model I have argued for and the modernist paradigm is a function of the specific historical break brought about by the avant-garde movements of the twentieth century. As Peter Bürger contends, this break "does not consist in the destruction of art as an institution but in the destruction of the possibility of positing aesthetic norms as valid ones. This has consequences for scholarly dealings with works of art: the normative examination is replaced by a functional analysis."[40] But this must not be taken to mean an objective or detached analysis: if the normative is taken as object of investigation, this is done from a position which is, by definition, within the play of values and so is itself subject to examination (and so on endlessly: the point where self-reflexivity stops is established practically and politically, not ontologically). In the same way, the destruction of the general validity of aesthetic norms establishes this principle as a new aesthetic norm: one more fragile, more relative, and therefore more difficult to transcend.

This norm is what I have called "modernism." The term is used with widely different meanings (in literary history it often describes a precisely delimited formation lasting from about 1910 to about 1930; in architecture it carries a sense—that of a full integration into capitalist rationality—almost precisely the reverse of the one that applies to other art forms); I use it to mean a general paradigm of literary production and reception which has lasted through most of the twentieth century. The modernist aesthetic is, in Schiller's sense, sentimental. It is characterized above all by (1) its attention to the status of the utterances it produces (although not, usually, by a political awareness of the social and institutional conditions of enunciation); (2) consequently an antimimetic impulse: the realities it constructs have a discursive rather than an ontological foundation; and (3) an antiorganicist impulse, working typically through the fragmentation of textual unity, through the play of contradictory genres of discourse, and through a splitting of the subjects of utterance. In all of this it is not so much opposed to a realist aesthetic as it is the culmination of the internal contradictions of realism.

This is clearly too simplistic and too unitary an account, but it will serve to delimit the frame within which I have been working. I have wanted to make clearly visible its difference from a naive aesthetic, which would be dependent upon a harmony between social and aesthetic "forms," a non-contestation of ideological values, and the ideal immediacy of form to content; but also to problematize the possibility of a postmodernist aesthetic which would fall into neither of these frameworks. The complexity of the organization of the modernist paradigm seems to me to anticipate those forms of radical difference proposed as postmodern. In most cases (apart from the various neo-avant-gardes) the models proposed—the films of Warhol or De Palma or Spielberg, video clips, advertising, new technologies *en bloc*, various forms of Third World art—offer no more than the possibility of a sentimental redemption of the naive: a typically modernist strategy, and one which is in many cases less radical than previous recuperations (automatic writing, the found object, and so on). This is to say that the claim for postmodernism tends to be either conservative (and this includes such conservative Marxist accounts as, for example, Peter Fuller's *Beyond the Crisis in Art*) or (in both senses of the word) naive.

A more sustained attempt to situate modernism historically, and so to project a politicized postmodernist aesthetic, has been made by Fredric Jameson, who argues that modernism has functioned as the ideology of consumer capitalism (that is, it has been in an expressive relation to this phase of capitalism, even, presumably, when anticipating it).[41] But this argument is curiously fused with another in favor of a realist aesthetic: classical realism (and its concern with "the referent") maintains a persistent validity insofar as "classical" capitalism continues to subsist as the foundation of consumer capitalism.[42] The periodization supplies the conclusion. The problem, though, with demanding a political rather than an aesthetic basis for new literary production is that there is no political art (indeed, to put it brutally, no politics) which cannot be read as style. This is a question of the institutional conditions of signification and available social functions, and questions of conditions and functions cannot be solved at a textual level. Within the framework of a sentimental aesthetic there can be no naive reading. Thus popular culture proposed as the form of the postmodern is always proposed in terms of a secondary, bracketed reading which does not escape the modernist paradigm. There is in fact a real glibness in many of the assumptions of an achieved postmodern condition; the glibness is that of "a state of post's and neo's in which novation is still considered to be valuable for its own sake even though it is a nostalgic ideal, and a cumulative notion of knowledge still prevails."[43] The modernist paradigm is both unworkable (as a dream of endless novation) and inescapable, and precisely *because* of its aporia (the "modern" as the perpetual present, the end of history which nevertheless remains subject to history). Until our historical space is totally altered, there can be no "beyond" of modernism which would not *thereby* be a moment of it.

The model of change I have used has, I think, general validity for the period of the capitalist mode (or modes) of production, which is still our horizon. It may also have a more generalized validity for other periods. In order to qualify the model, I first want to make an initial distinction between stable and dynamic economic formations, corresponding very roughly to the difference between oral and folk literatures and written literature. Second, I want to posit an important break in the system of literary production around 1800, when the autonomization of the arts (the result of a process set in motion by the introduction of printing— that is, by the increasing absorption of literary production into commodity production) is decisively accelerated; it is here that the oppositional and contradictory nature of literary evolution becomes fully apparent, when the tempo of change becomes more rapid, and artists are released from their immediate ties to the patron class. Jauss, who had originally worked with a similarly univocal model of aesthetic distance, has recently tried to construct a historical typology of the modes of literary activity. He distinguishes between a preformative and norm-giving stage, a motivating and norm-forming stage, and a transformative and norm-breaking stage.[44] His claim is that aesthetic theory has largely ignored the implications of the second stage, in which there is both a stylistic evolution and a freedom on the part of the artist to transform the aesthetic norm, and yet an absence of aesthetic distance between the new text and the canon of norms. It would be possible, however, to argue that this second stage constitutes a transitional phase between two polar modes of aesthetic production. Jurij Lotman's distinction between an "aesthetic of identity" and an "aesthetic of opposition" can perhaps serve to clarify this notion. The aesthetic of identity functions through a positive and constructive use of stereotypes, and through the confirmation of expectations; through a repetition of sameness on the basis of the difference of sameness; and through improvisation on the basis of strict rules. It covers folklore, medieval art, commedia dell'arte, classicism—and, we could perhaps add, popular fiction, television shows (quiz programs, serials), and spectacles (sports, religious rallies). The aesthetic of opposition is based on a concept of originality; on the breaking of expectations; and on deconstruction rather than construction—on complication rather than simplification. It is not, however, a creation without rules: it works through the destruction of a habitual system, but not through the destruction or absence of the systematic itself.[45]

Insofar as these can be seen as historical categories, we can posit that Jauss's second stage (covering, roughly, written literature of the prebourgeois period) will contain elements of both aesthetics: both a respect for the structure of the canon and a transformation of the canon which goes beyond a mere improvisation (the "battle of the books," the *querelle des anciens et des modernes,* marks, as Jauss has stressed, a decisive turning point in this phase of production). We could argue, for example, that in the medieval period it is the class-specific break between genres (for example between epic, romance, and novella) that carries the force of reaction to ideological conventions, whereas within the generic series development is likely to be constructive (the extension and elaboration of conventions). But obviously the precise historical process of transition needs to be examined in detail, and this is beyond the scope of my intentions here. I would contend, however, that although the model I have used can be applied rigorously only to the capitalist period, it is nevertheless relevant to the intermediate period as well.

It is, however, important that the limits of contestation be carefully defined. The concept of scandal which is inherent in Jauss's theory of aesthetic distance, for example, needs to be treated with a great deal more caution, insofar as it describes a phenomenon which is historically limited and which has in the meantime become institutionalized, and insofar as it ignores a whole series of important problems: that of the relative degree of legitimacy of an art form; that of the conjuncture at which a formal innovation may take on the force of scandal; that of the relation between literary innovation and literary fashion; that of the rapid obsolescence demanded by commodity production; and that of the institutional context within which innovation occurs. This last factor has been crucial to the thinking of both Brecht and Benjamin. Brecht thinks of the theater (the *Apparat*) as an economic institution which embodies the structural constraints of the social system insofar as there is a divorce between those who control the *Apparat* and those who produce for it.[46] Theatrical innovation is relatively meaningless (or at least ambivalent) as long as the institutional framework itself remains constant (of Brecht's plays only the *Lehrstücke* radically challenge, by their redefinition of the relation between spectators and actors and between theatrical and nontheatrical space, the *form* of the theatrical institution). And Benjamin applies the concept of the *Apparat* to institutionalized communication in general, arguing that within this framework, aesthetic distance is of secondary importance, and that

> to supply a production apparatus without trying, within the limits of the possible, to change it, is a highly disputable activity even when the material supplied appears to be of a revolutionary nature. For we are confronted with the fact . . . that the bourgeois apparatus of production and publication is capable of assimilating, indeed of propagating, an astonishing amount of revolutionary themes without ever seriously putting into question its own continued existence or that of the class which owns it.[47]

The degree of oppositionality—and the extent to which literary discourse can pass from a merely latent criticality to an open break with the hegemonic class—is dependent on the historically variable kind of sanction given to the reproduction of norms and the strength of the taboos on their violation. It is equally dependent on the directness of the relation between the dominant class and the literary producer, and thus, eventually, on the particular structure of relations of production and the organization

of the production process. Commodity production, which transforms relations of production into abstract and highly mediated relations, is the
necessary precondition for the emancipation of the arts (although this also
involves the *virtualization* of their authority and influence); it would be
senseless to look for an oppositional function before the historical preconditions for it existed. A theory of systems of literary production must
therefore depend on an analysis of the specific place and function of literary
discourse within a complex and determinate social formation, and on its
relations to other levels and to the particular play of social forces (including
its own tradition). Literary theory is not *Ideologiekritik* but a knowledge
of conditions and functions. It forms a unity with literary history, and its
descriptive categories are not separable from their content but must adapt
themselves to the structuredness of the material. "Every historical period
possesses its own laws";[48] the concept of art itself changes from period to
period, and theory must reflect and account for that change.

IN ONE SENSE what I have elaborated is the theoretical underpinning
for a descriptive literary history. Such a history would accept that, although
the process of canon formation is thoroughly political, and although the
canon is constantly being challenged, defended, and reconstituted, it is
nevertheless a historical given with determinate historical effects. The history of the formation of a literary canon is something like a crystallization
of the regimes of valuation which have governed this process.

But no description is neutral (although many pretend to be). Description and descriptive categories are always constituted as a moment of a
political interest. A "purely" descriptive literary history would tend both
to miss the possibility of thematizing its own interest and to gloss over
the possibilities of alternative histories, of hidden or repressed histories,
and of the redemptive reconstruction of the official histories. That means
that it would be likely to miss the complexity of the play of power and
exclusion through which canons are formed. Barbara Herrnstein Smith
gives a good recent account: she writes of a process in which deviant
judgments are made marginal or even pathological in relation to the nat-
uralized standards of those groups which validate "good taste." Because
aesthetic objects are always already culturally mediated, they come bearing
classificatory labels which "not only . . . foreground certain of their possible functions but also operate as signs—in effect, as culturally certified
endorsements—of their more or less effective performance of those functions." The evaluative regime produces texts for readers, but at the same

time it produces "generation after generation of subjects for whom the objects and texts thus labeled do indeed perform the functions thus privileged, thereby insuring the continuity of mutually defining canonical works, canonical functions, and canonical audiences."[49] Herein lies the danger of a descriptive history of canon formation: that it will become locked into this circle of mutually constituted categories and will have no access to excluded texts, functions, and readers, which lack historical effectivity.

A fully "objective" history is an activist, interventionist history. It understands that histories are fictions of power which can be rewritten, that the canon can be retrospectively changed or displaced (Donne, Louise Labé), or that the opposition of the canonical to the noncanonical, which is constructed and maintained by the force of cultural and educational institutions, can be radically transformed or can be taken itself as a text for analysis.

The categories I have used to try to rework the concepts of system and history—break, event, series, repetition, deviation, ideology—are necessarily internal to a specific regime of value and serve a particular political interest. This does not mean that they are simply and directly expressive of a coherent class position; but they are not neutral or universal categories. The identification of an event or a relation of power involves the mobilization of values in an act of construction, and it is important to be clear as to what the conditions of possibility of these values are. The limits of a Marxist intervention in the institution of literature are the limits of the petty-bourgeois intelligentsia. Given that class is complexly constructed across economic, political, and ideological positions, it is still broadly true that a critical literary theory will not directly address the working class, which is by definition excluded from the upper levels of the schooling system and from canonical literary culture. Reconstructing the curriculum so as to focus on popular culture is not in itself a solution to this exclusion; such a reconstruction seems often to rest upon a class essentialism which supposes a positive affiliation or "belongingness" between the working class and popular culture (thus blurring the heterogeneity of what the term covers) and between the bourgeoisie and canonical literary culture.[50] What I have suggested instead is the importance of the negative construction of value in the break with systemic norms; this process cuts across the division between the "legitimate" and the "popular," since the area from which a rupture with dominant norms will occur is never given in advance.

In another sense, of course, the reconstruction of the curriculum to include or concentrate on popular culture often has a definite strategic value. My argument is aimed only against the assumption that cultural norms, whether "high" or "low," have an intrinsic value which is distinct from any institutional and interpretive frame. This is part of a more general argument against the reduction of texts to a class consciousness or a particular set of determinants of textual production. Reductionism has been the weakness of most of the traditional sociologies of literature (those of Fügen or Escarpit, for example). There is a recent example in Peter Widdowson's influential anthology *Re-Reading English,* many of the contributions to which reject a textually oriented criticism in favor of an analysis of the social conditions of literary production: meaning is displaced outside the text, but displaced most significantly to another disciplinary discourse: that of history. The assumption that textual meaning can be read off from the conditions of its production is made possible by the elevation of an apparently nontextual mode of knowledge over one which is explicitly textual.

The assumption of discursive privilege on which this rests is made particularly clear in the work of Terry Lovell. The cognitive function of art is of secondary value, she argues, because the "truths" it produces would be assessable only "by reference to independently acquired knowledge of that to which they refer." Art may have the capacity to produce knowledge, "but the status of its truths *as* valid knowledge is determined elsewhere than in art, in the univocal language of science and history rather than the polysemic language of art." And in case we have missed the point, she spells it out for us: "If the goal of developing knowledge of the external world is what is at stake, then it could hardly be doubted that the methods and the conceptual language of science and history are better adapted to that goal."[51]

Lovell's argument depends in the first place upon an essentialization of discursive functions (based in a relation of appropriation of the nondiscursive real), and then upon an acceptance at face value of the socially validated authority of certain discourses over others. By contrast, the production of a less normative theory entails stressing the constitutive function of language, and the refusal of an inherent epistemological privilege to any one discursive formation. The essentialist question of how literature appropriates the real is replaced by the question of the knowledge effects historically generated by systems of literary discourse. These knowledge effects must be assumed to have no greater and no less "truth" than those produced in other discourses, but they have different kinds of historical effectivity, and a particular (although perhaps contested) ranking in a hierarchical economy of discursive formations. An epistemological relativism of this kind is the very opposite of that "scientific" detachment which results from the certainties of discursive mastery; on the contrary, it should make possible a process of political judgment of the knowlege effects produced, and therefore an avoidance of both a sterile historical cataloguing and an obliteration of the dynamics of textual activity in a sociologistic reduction. But these political judgments will be delayed: they will be not the reflex of a normative axiology but the outcome of an analysis of systems of production of value. What is crucial here is that the analyst is folded into these systems, is never at a vantage. The judgment that one text has been or can be used more productively than others, or that some readings are better than others (and calculations of this kind are not only inevitable but entirely appropriate for a politically committed criticism) will nevertheless be possible only within the limits of a definite and restricted frame of interest. Part of the power of a Marxist theory lies in its ability to make visible the frame from which its own categories and positions are derived.

6

Intertextuality

To this point, I have tried to argue for certain central pro-posals. First, I have tried to theorize the concept of represen-tation in semiotic terms; what is represented in the play of language is objects, conditions, and relations which are immanent in particular struc-tures of discourse and particular conditions of enunciation carrying the complex play of social power. Second, literary discourse is always consti-tuted as a historically specific system and is in a systematic relation to other discourses. And, third, this relation is one of interdiscursive repetition or transformation: the historical dynamic of the literary system is intertex-tually motivated, and intertextual relations establish the specific historicity of texts. Indeed, if "the text" is not a positive given but rather a differential structure, then "the very idea of textuality is inseparable from and founded upon intertextuality."[1] But such a statement poses a number of conceptual difficulties. How are we to consider the subordination and integration of one discursive structure to another? What is involved in the transformation of relations of discursive authority? And what are the analytical implica-tions of the concept of intertextuality (in particular, by what criteria of relevance do we identify intertextual structures and so construct a particular form of textuality in and for a reading)?

As an initial approach to these problems, let us look briefly at two possible models of interdiscursivity which illustrate some of the difficulties involved. The first is Jauss's situation of the text in relation to a unified horizon of expectations which is not purely literary but which forms a homogeneous structure determining the production and reception of new texts. The impact of the text within the diachronic process of production and repetition can be measured by integrating it into "the objectifiable system of expectations that arises for each work in the historical moment of its appearance, from a pre-understanding of the genre, from the form and themes of already familiar works, and from the opposition between poetic and practical language."[2] This concept has the advantage of relating literary evolution dialectically to a synchronic semiotic field which is defined both in terms of the literary norm and, through the "social index" of this norm, in terms of general ideological expectations: "An important work, one that indicates a new direction in the literary process, is surrounded by an unsurveyable production of works that correspond to the traditional expectations or images concerning reality, and that thus in their social index are to be no less valued than the solitary novelty of the great work that is often comprehended only later" (12).

The aesthetic distance between the given horizon and the norm-breaking new text is both a sociological fact and the basis for a judgment of aesthetic value. Jauss gives the example of two novels published in 1857: Feydeau's *Fanny* and Flaubert's *Madame Bovary*. Despite their superficial similarities as "realistic" treatments of petty-bourgeois adultery, Feydeau's novel, which was a contemporary best-seller, corresponded very closely to the fantasies of its public. *Madame Bovary*, by contrast, revolutionized the novel form through the *formal* innovation of "impersonal narration" and in particular through a use of free indirect discourse which caused its first readers moral uncertainty and brought upon the novel a judicial condemnation couched in a simultaneously aesthetic and ethical vocabulary ("a realism which would be the negation of the beautiful and the good and which . . . would commit continual outrages upon public morality and good manners," 27–28).

The problem with the concept of a horizon of expectations, however, is that it appeals to a phenomenology of consciousness rather than a theory of signifying systems and practices, and so remains vague about the structuring of *discursive* authority. In any case the "horizon" is described as an accumulation of quite heterogeneous values (generic conventions, experiential norms, language types), and Jauss offers no explanation of the mediations between them. In particular it is unclear in what relation the literary system stands to other discursive formations. Jauss's attempt to correlate literary and moral norms through the indirect mediation of the "opposition between poetic and practical language" (which is in any case a metadiscursive relation rather than an opposition) leaves unexamined the ways in which "poetic language" works other, literary and nonliterary, genres of discourse, and how this elaboration affects the relations of discursive authority involved. (I leave aside for the moment the problem of assessing the text only in relation to "the historical moment of its appearance.")

The second model is Kristeva's concept of the intertextual relation between literary discourse and its raw material. Drawing on Bakhtin, she argues that "each word (text) is an intersection of words (texts) where at least one other word (text) can be read," and thus "any text is constructed as a mosaic of quotations; any text is the absorption and transformation of another."[3] This depth beneath the textual surface suggests a dialectic of identity and difference between the text system and the systems it transforms. Kristeva defines intertextuality in terms of a concentration of alien discursive structures in the text:

> The poetic signified refers to other discursive signifieds in such a way that within the poetic utterance several other discourses are legible. There is thus created around the poetic signified a multiple textual space whose elements can be applied in the concrete poetic text. We shall call this space *intertextual*. Caught within intertextuality, the poetic utterance is a subordinated system of a larger whole which is the space of the texts applied in this whole.[4]

But if this intertextual space is larger than that of the text, it is also always contained, concentrated within the text. Literary discourse is both a part of the general discursive field and a particular mode of transformation of that field. Bakhtin was perhaps the first theorist to conceptualize literary representation as a representation of discourse, and so to "replace the static articulation of texts with a model where literary structure does not simply *exist* but is generated in relation to *another* structure. What allows a dynamic dimension to structuralism is his conception of the 'literary word' as an *intersection of textual surfaces* rather than a *point* (a fixed meaning), as a dialogue among several writings."[5] But although this conception of the activity of the text is indeed dynamic, it is not historical. It fails to allow for the diachronic interplay of norm and transformation, because the point of reference (the material which is to be transformed) lies outside the literary system. The "other" structure, the intertext, is not, as it is for Bakhtin, the dominant literary canon, but the world as text. The mediation of the literary system is simply disregarded.

Thus, instead of the social *determination* of the literary norm, we have the social text as *content* of the literary text. The structure of the French novel of the fifteenth century, for example, "can be considered the result of a transformation of several other codes: scholasticism, courtly poetry, the oral literature of the town, carnival. The transformational method therefore leads us to situate literary structure within the social whole considered as a textual whole."[6] The problem here is that the notion of a social text does not allow us to discriminate between the ways in which different kinds of code or discourse function in the literary text, and in particular to account for the specific function of the literary code. Two essential stages are omitted from the relation of the literary text to a cultural text: first, the texts to which the literary text most crucially reacts or refers are those which are ideologically dominant; second, within the structure of the literary text, literary discourse plays the role of dominant vis-à-vis nonliterary norms. Intertextuality is always in the first place a relation to the literary canon (to the "specifically literary" function and authority of an element) and only *through* this a relation to the general discursive field. This does not mean that literary texts are in some simple way "about themselves," but it does imply that reference to the authority of nonliterary modes of discourse is always structured by the force of reference to the literary norm.

To put this more precisely: the literary norm works, in the text, as a metonymic figure of general discursive norms. It works as a model of the authority of ideological categories, and it assigns to these categories the status (a status the text confirms or denies) of the natural, the *vraisemblable*. This metonymic reduction works in two ways. First, the social text is transformed into the terms and conventions of literary discourse. To ignore this mediation of the literary system, to relate a text to a horizon of expectations or a cultural text which is completely or predominantly non-literary, is to ignore the complexity of the enunciative shift involved in the elaboration of one generic structure by another (this enunciative shift in turn produces more complex forms of modality and more complex reality effects). Second, many texts (and not only the most self-conscious ones) tend to stress the centrality of the intertextual moment: to set up an overt metonymic equation between the contestation of literary norms and ideological norms, and to organize extraliterary reference (reference to the cultural text) around this equation. The literary canon acts as an exemplary mode of authority and comes to bear a heavy charge of value through which literature comes to "stand for" (although rarely *completely*) the whole realm of authoritative values.

The difference between these two processes is one of degree, not of kind; in both cases the analogy between literary and general discursive norms is not simply given but is produced by the text, and it rests on the constant presence of the canon as a threatening or reassuring intertext. The metonymic equivalence holds even for those texts which reproduce the norm: here the generic intertext "shows through," and with it the ideological values which have accumulated around it; and this may be reinforced by a validation of the ideologically "natural" in terms of "naturalness" generated by the canon ("*Nature* and *Homer*, were, he found, the same").

In disrupting and transforming the semiotic system governing social exchange, and displacing social instances into discursive instances, the text produces a "referential" function as a particular effect of language: social reference occurs on the level of the contradictory relationship between different structures of discourse. Thus, to take Kristeva's example of the fifteenth-century French novel, of the four dominant codes that she isolates ("scholasticism, courtly poetry, the oral literature of the town, carnival"), it seems likely that the first three would be associated with the literary canon, and the fourth would function as a part of the transformational and dis-ordering activity of the novel. Theodor W. Adorno and Max Horkheimer express this tension in more general terms as a result of the unity of (normative) "style" and power:

> The unity of style not only of the Christian Middle Ages but of the Renaissance expresses in each case the different structure of social power, and not the obscure experience of the oppressed in which the general was enclosed. The great artists were never those who embodied a wholly flawless and perfect style, but those who used style as a way of hardening themselves against the chaotic expression of suffering, as a negative truth . . . However, only in this confrontation with tradition of which style is the record can art express suffering.[7]

This is to say that literary texts thematize their relation to social power by thematizing their relation to the structure of discursive authority which organizes the linguistic form or the play of languages in their own textual structure (although to formulate the process like this is not to endorse Adorno's negative correlation of formal structure with the state of the historical dialectic; I have discussed this elsewhere).[8] Ross Chambers analyzes this process of self-reflexivity by adapting from Dällenbach's account of narrational *mise-en-abyme* (embedding) the categories of *mise-en-abyme* of the statement (*énoncé*), of utterance (*énonciation*), and of the code. The latter two categories are of particular relevance to Chambers's purpose of formulating a theory of explicit and implicit embeddings, realized either through intertextual reference or self-thematization. He distinguishes between "narrational" embedding—the representation of a communicational or narrative act or situation (*énonciation*)—and "figural" embedding—the representation of a figure (character or object) which in some way "stands for" art or narrativity. These modes appear in both "self-designating" and "duplicitous" narratives: "in self-designating narratives, the presence of 'narrational' embedding provides an immediate clue to the situational model the text is producing; in duplicitous narratives, in which 'narrational' embedding is either absent or very reduced in function, the reader's reliance on 'figural' embedding is proportionately greater."[9] To put it very crudely: reading is guided either by a reference to the code or by a metaphor of coding. Thus, to take Adorno and Horkheimer's example, an explicitly figural mode of embedding would occur when the ideological "harmony" of style is thematized through a stress on the concept of harmony itself— a concept which, in the medieval and Renaissance periods, because of its strategic place in a cosmology already performs the reduction of the political to the aesthetic.

Chambers argues that whereas narrational embedding has manifest analytic consequences, figural embedding has only latent consequences (I would prefer to say that the consequences have to be constructed in reading). In both cases, however, the function of embedding is to construct a model of an "appropriate" reading: that is, to make a paradoxical claim both to the unrestricted "meaningfulness" of the text as "literary" and to a restricted range of interpretive options.[10] In more general terms we could say that the process of embedding designates a particular literary system as its appropriate context. But we should be aware that such embedding is the way in which texts construct their relation to a context of overdetermined discursive authority. It is thus a productive activity, which thereby has the power to alter this context. At the same time, however, context is by definition beyond the control of the text, and moreover is not a singular structure but one which changes with the iteration of the text. The self-thematization of a text's intertextual context thus has a definite but limited value.

The following readings exemplify a range of possibilities of construction of intertextual reference: direct and explicit in the first case, mediated through the structure of genre in the second, and figural in the third.

This is the "Widow of Ephesus" tale from the *Satyricon* of Petronius:

Once upon a time there was a certain married woman in the city of Ephesus whose fidelity to her husband was so famous that the women from all the neighboring towns and villages used to troop into Ephesus merely to stare at this prodigy. It happened, however, that her husband one day died. Finding the normal custom of following the cortege with hair unbound and beating her breast in public quite inadequate to express her grief, the lady insisted on following the corpse right into the tomb, an underground vault of the Greek type, and there set herself to guard the body, weeping and wailing night and day. Although in her extremes of grief she was clearly courting death from starvation, her parents were utterly unable to persuade her to leave, and even the magistrates, after one last supreme attempt, were rebuffed and driven away. In short, all Ephesus had gone into mourning for this extraordinary woman, all the more since the lady was now passing her fifth consecutive day without once tasting food. Beside the failing woman sat her devoted maid, sharing her mistress' grief and relighting the lamp whenever it flickered out. The whole city could speak, in fact, of nothing else: here at last, all classes alike agreed, was the one true example of conjugal fidelity and love.

In the meantime, however, the governor of the province gave orders that several thieves should be crucified in a spot close by the vault where the lady was mourning her dead husband's corpse. So, on the following night, the soldier who had been assigned to keep watch on the crosses so that nobody could remove the thieves' bodies for burial suddenly noticed a light blazing among the tombs and heard the sounds of groaning. And prompted by a natural human curiosity to know who or what was making those sounds, he descended into the vault.

But at the sight of a strikingly beautiful woman, he stopped short in terror, thinking he must be seeing some ghostly apparition out of hell. Then, observing the corpse and seeing the tears on the lady's face and the scratches her fingernails had gashed in her cheeks, he realized what it was: a widow, in inconsolable grief. Promptly fetching his little supper back down to the tomb, he implored the lady not to persist in her sorrow or break her heart with useless mourning. All men alike, he reminded her, have the same end; the same resting place awaits us all. He used, in short, all those platitudes we use to comfort the suffering and bring them back to life. His consolations, being unwelcome, only exasperated the widow more; more violently than ever she beat her breast, and tearing out her hair by the roots, scattered it over the dead man's body. Undismayed, the soldier repeated his arguments and pressed her to take some food, until the little maid, quite overcome by the smell of the wine, succumbed and stretched out her hand to her tempter. Then, restored by the food and wine, she began herself to assail her mistress' obstinate refusal.

"How will it help you," she asked the lady, "if you faint from hunger? Why should you bury yourself alive, and go down to death before the Fates have called you? What does Virgil say?

> Do you suppose the shades and ashes of the dead
> are by such sorrow touched?

No, begin your life afresh. Shake off these woman's scruples; enjoy the light while you can. Look at that corpse of your poor husband: doesn't it tell you more eloquently than any words that you should live?"

None of us, of course, really dislikes being told that we must eat, that life is to be lived. And the lady was no exception. Weakened by her long days of fasting, her resistance crumbled at last, and she ate the food the soldier offered her as hungrily as the little maid had eaten earlier.

Well, you know what temptations are normally aroused in a man on a full stomach. So the soldier, mustering all those blandishments by means of which he had persuaded the lady to live, now laid determined siege to her virtue. And chaste though she was, the lady found him singularly attractive and his arguments persuasive. As for the maid, she did all she could to help the soldier's cause, repeating like a refrain the appropriate line of Virgil:

> If love is pleasing, lady, yield yourself to love.

To make the matter short, the lady's body soon gave up the struggle; she yielded and our happy warrior enjoyed a total triumph on both counts. That very night their marriage was consummated, and they slept together the second and the third night too, carefully shutting the door of the tomb so that any passing friend or stranger would have thought the lady of famous chastity had at last expired over her dead husband's body.

As you can perhaps imagine, our soldier was a very happy man, utterly delighted with his lady's ample beauty and that special charm that a secret love confers. Every night, as soon as the sun had set, he bought what few provisions his slender pay permitted and smuggled them down to the tomb. One night, however, the parents of one of the crucified thieves, noticing that the watch was being badly kept, took advantage of our hero's absence to remove their son's body and bury it. The next morning, of course, the soldier was horror-struck to discover one of the bodies missing from its cross, and ran to tell his mistress of the horrible punishment which awaited him for neglecting his duty. In the circumstances, he told her, he would not be tried and sentenced, but would punish himself then and there with his own sword. All he asked of her was that she make room for another corpse and allow the same gloomy tomb to enclose husband and lover together.

Our lady's heart, however, was no less tender than pure. "God forbid," she cried, "that I should have to see at one and the same time the dead bodies of the only two men I have ever loved. No, better far, I say, to hang the dead than kill the living." With these words, she gave orders that her husband's body should be taken from its bier and strung up on the empty cross. The soldier followed this good advice, and the next morning the whole city wondered by what miracle the dead man had climbed up on the cross.[11]

Narrative theorists have long had a predilection for the short tale: its peculiar effect of self-containment makes it possible and plausible to seek an equally self-contained point or a finite set of deep-structure categories. Yuri Scheglov, for example, has produced a generative account of this story which describes its surface textual features as expressive expansions of a thematic kernel, which he formulates as "the infidelity and depravity of women."[12] Clearly, the explanatory force of such a description is not going to be found in its interpretive insight, its grasp of enunciative modality, or its feminist acumen. But it is also, I think, flawed as a technical methodology: first because it is a necessarily self-validating account which can do no more than confirm what it already knows (it could never discover that it was initially wrong); and second because it conceives of theme or meaning as a static origin rather than a process. In the same way, a structuralist description (or its Greimassian complication) of the binary oppositions organizing the tale (life/death, sacred/profane, up/down, bodily functions/spirituality, poetry/prose, and so on) would have no nontautologous criteria to justify its choice of categories or to prevent their multiplication to infinity, although its concern with relations rather than origins might make it better equipped to explain the structure of paradox which produces the narrative twist.

In his brief analysis of the story, Bakhtin remarks on the repetition of a certain kind of movement between categories:

At its simplest, the narrative is an uninterrupted series of victories of life over death. Life triumphs over death four times: the joys of life (food, drink, youth, love) triumph over the widow's gloomy despair and longing for death; food and drink as the renewal of life near the corpse of a dead man; the conceiving of new life near the tomb (copulation); and saving the legionnaire from death by crucifying a corpse. Introduced into this series is the additional, and classical, motif of theft; the disappearance of the corpse (the absence of a corpse being equal to an absence of death, in a this-worldly suggestion of resurrection). The motif of resurrection is present in its most straightforward expression, that is, the resurrection of the widow from her helpless grief and from the grave-like gloom of death into new life and love; in the comic aspect of laughter, there is as well a sham resurrection of a dead man.[13]

Bakhtin then goes on to comment on the story's economical and realistic reworking of a folkloric complex with cultic origins. I shall return to these comments later, but for the moment I want to take up Bakhtin's idea of a *layering* of narrative transformations, and to suggest a slightly more complicated model in which the movement of the text is not simply from death to life but from one form of life through death to a qualitatively different form of life, and in this process a movement from the realm of social sanctions and decencies to the realm of profane values associated with bodily functions. Like Bakhtin, I order these transformations along four levels:

Level 1: a movement from life to death, governed by the social norm of marriage; then a movement from death back to life, initiated by the juxtaposition of the dead husband and the lover and ending in a choice of the latter's living body over a dead body recognized as interchangeable with other dead bodies.

Level 2: a movement from an excess of chastity (*tam notae . . . pudicitiae*), repeated in the invocation of Dido, to a transgression of the rules of fidelity and chastity (breaking the fast, succumbing to the soldier), culminating in a second, ironic state of excess, the inexplicable "resurrection" of the husband on the cross.

Level 3: a movement from descent into the tomb, associated with a negative parody of sexuality (the widow moans and lacerates herself), to ascent from the tomb and onto the cross. The spatial dimensions (tomb and cross) simultaneously suggest a gendered partition of space between womb and phallus.

Level 4: a movement from the first disposal of the husband (which is sacred and involves laying him down) to the second disposal (which is profane and involves raising him up). This movement is mediated by two approximations to death: the apparent death of the woman in the tomb and the soldier's threat to kill himself with his sword.

A number of mediators assist in each of these movements: the maid, food, the lines of poetry, the dead thief.

In schematic form, this analysis yields a particular ordering of paradigmatic repetitions, represented in the table below. It must be stressed that this analysis is not meant to represent an inherent categorical structure. It is a grid constructed in order to give an account of the paradox or ambiguity around which the tale is organized, and it is therefore no less self-validating than Scheglov's model. It makes a difference, however, that my model is self-consciously so and makes no claim to be a representation. I read the four vertical columns as follows:

Column 1: the realm of social regulation—specifically, moral and religious standards governing sexual behavior and the ritual disposal of the dead. This realm is split between those characters (parents, magistrates,

Socially Sanctioned (spirit)		*Profane (body)*	
1. Life (social norm)	Death (tomb)	Death + life (juxtaposition of dead husband and lover)	Life (lover; breaking of norm of chastity)
2. "Prodigy" (excess chastity)	Dido (fidelity and self-destruction) poetry	Eating of food (infidelity) prose	"Miracle" (profane resurrection)
3.	Descent tomb negative sexuality (moaning, laceration) womb	Ascent cross positive sexuality phallus	
4. First disposal of husband: sacred laying down	Pseudodeath of lady in tomb	Threatened death of soldier by sword	Second disposal of husband: profane raising up
LIFE		DEATH	LIFE

governor) who enforce social norms and the woman, who respects them to excess. This excess motivates the plot, setting up the need for one state to be transformed into another.

Column 2: the realm of death, dominated by the tomb and by the continuation of social, religious, and sexual norms in death. This realm is the negation of life: sexuality takes on the perverted form of self-laceration and a suicidal drive, and the figure of Dido acts as a complex model of the relations between sexual fidelity, sexual infidelity, and death.

Column 3: the realm of death, not as the negation of life but as a passage to rebirth. Here we pass from social regulation to the bizarre juxtaposition of the corpse of the husband with the lover. The cross, the instrument of death, is also the phallus and the sword: this is a realm of paradox, where everything also means its opposite. And it is the realm of the body, not dissociated from death but in proximity and tension with it: eating and making love still take place within the tomb.

Column 4: the realm of a qualitatively transformed life, transcending social regulation (or rather subverting it); physical love inspires a new moral code ("better to hang the dead than kill the living") and generates a "miracle" which inspires laughter rather than religious awe.

Jurij Lotman, in *The Structure of the Artistic Text*, distinguishes between plotless texts and narratives: plotless texts construct static taxonomies (telephone directories, maps, descriptions), whereas plot is always a movement across taxonomic boundaries.[14] In the case of this tale we can take the central vertical line, dividing the "sacred" or "spiritual" realm from the "profane" realm of bodily functions, as the main axis around which this story turns. But the force of the story seems to me to reside in the fact that this is not a simple passage from one half of a dichotomy to the other; far more important is the asymmetry between the categories of body/spirit and of life/death. It is this asymmetry that gives the story its paradoxical force. What it suggests is that the passage from spirit (or moral norms) to body cannot simply be equated with the passage from death to life, or vice versa; rather, the sexuality which constitutes the central rite of passage is seen to have two contradictory aspects, both of which are intimately associated with death.

To come to some such conclusion about the story's thematic structure is to remain within the game of interpretation—a limited game insofar as it tends to offer an explanatory grid derived from a larger framework as an immanent textual structure; and a problematic game in its construction of an impossible textual closure. One way out of this game would involve setting the tale in relation to its immediate narrative frame. The story is introduced like this:

> Meanwhile Eumolpus, our spokesman in the hour of danger and the author of our present reconciliation, anxious that our gaiety should not be broken, began, in a sudden moment of silence, to gibe at the fickleness of women, the wonderful ease with which they become infatuated, their readiness to abandon their children for their lovers, and so forth. In fact, he declared, no woman was so chaste or faithful that she couldn't be seduced; sooner or later she would fall head over heels in love with some passing stranger. Nor, he added, was he thinking so much of the old tragedies and the classics of love betrayed as of something that had happened in our own time; in fact, if we were willing to hear, he would be delighted to tell the story. All eyes and ears were promptly turned to our narrator, and he began.   (*Satyricon*, 121–122)

And it concludes with the words, "The sailors greeted this story with great guffaws, while Tryphaena blushed to her ears and tried to hide her head in embarrassment against Giton's shoulder" (125). The telling of the story is thus precisely equivalent to the speech-act structure Freud described as characteristic of the dirty joke—a structure in which,

> in addition to the one who makes the joke, there must be a second who is taken as the object of the hostile or sexual aggressiveness, and a third in whom the joke's aim of producing pleasure is ful-filled . . . When the first person finds his libidinal impulse inhibited by the woman, he develops a hostile trend against that second person and calls on the originally interfering third person as his ally. Through the first person's smutty speech the woman is exposed before the third, who, as listener, has now been bribed by the effortless satis-faction of his own libido.[15]

But, if the "exposing" of the widow and the female listener is clearly part of the point, the story cannot nevertheless simply be reduced to the func-tion prescribed by this frame, since the *reader* is situated at another level of framing. Rather, the misogynistic message corresponds to one dimen-sion of the text—that of a conventional morality which is perhaps objec-tified in all those impersonal observers who accompany the progress of the story ("the women from all the neighbouring towns and villages," "all Ephesus," "all classes alike agreed," "any passing friend or stranger would have thought," "next morning the whole city wondered"), and in the narrator's sententious clichés ("None of us, of course, really dislikes being told that we must eat, that life is to be lived"; "Well, you know what temptations are normally aroused in a man on a full stomach"; "As you can perhaps imagine, our soldier was a very happy man"). This rhetoric of inclusion is relativized by the internal structure of the story to the public realm of social norms—the first of my four vertical columns.

At least as interesting a feature of the introductory passage is Eumolpus' claim to be thinking not "so much of the old tragedies and the classics of love betrayed as of something that had happened in our own time" (*nec se tragoedias veteres curare aut nomina saeculis nota, sed rem sua memoria factam*: not to be thinking of old tragedies or famous names but of a thing which had happened within his own memory). Fiction and legend are here opposed, in the constitutive gesture of realist fiction, to personal witness. It is an entirely conventional gesture designed to reinforce the reality effects of the text, and Bakhtin is wrong to lay so much emphasis on the "credibility" of a "completely real-life narrative" (222–223). The basic categorical structure of the story derives from the transposition of the categories of another story (an "old tragedy" with "famous names"): the fourth book of the *Aeneid*. Two direct quotations stress the connection: both are from the passage (Book 4, lines 31–53) in which Dido's sister and confidante, Anna, urges her to forget her dead husband and give herself to Aeneas. In both stories ties of piety which seem to be binding even beyond death are broken in a transgressive union with a stranger, a soldier. Petronius' tale is thus explicitly a repetition of the first half of Book 4. But Book 4 as a whole is a tragedy (it draws in its turn on Euripides' account of the desertion of Medea by Jason), and thus quite contrary to the spirit of the Milesian tale. It is an ideologically ambivalent narrative, managing both to celebrate the superiority of Aeneas' masculine values over Dido's weakness and to expose the brutality of these values. But in both aspects the moral point is clear: inchastity is condemned either because it puts an obstacle in the way of historical destiny or because it entails the suffering and death of the woman.

In light of this, "The Widow of Ephesus" can be read as a direct reversal of the heroic ideology of the epic poem. Structurally, this reversal is achieved through a parodistic selection which omits the tragic outcome but repeats a number of its motifs: the opposition between Dido's enclosed bedchamber and the high funeral pyre becomes the opposition between the underground vault and the cross; the sword with which Dido stabs herself becomes the sword with which the soldier—not the widow—*nearly* stabs himself. This reversal is repeated at a stylistic level in the relation, internalized within the tale, between verse (and a "high" literary decorum) and prose (and the demotic Latin of the *Satyricon*). The stylistic reversal generates a moral universe which not only differs from that of the heroic poem (and the ideology of empire it celebrates) but actively undermines it. In one sense, of course, this is a relation to the epic genre and its associated values and authority rather than a relation only to this particular intertext; and the pattern is repeated elsewhere in the *Satyricon* through the mock-heroic poems, *Halosis Troiae* and *De bello civili*, with their direct parodies of Virgil and Lucan, as well as through the parodic relation to the degraded epic form of the Greek romance.

Bakhtin claims another intertextual source for the story, a folkloric complex closely associated with the Hellenistic-Oriental mysteries; he mentions in particular the Christian cult and its thematics of burial, sacramental eating, and resurrection, but the Orphic cults and their rituals of descent into the underworld would also be relevant. The status of this material must remain conjectural, but if Bakhtin's guess is correct it means that the categories of my analysis can now be retrospectively justified (although not validated) in terms of this double intertextuality: on the one hand the inversion of the body/spirit opposition would derive from the parodic relation to Book 4 of the *Aeneid*, and on the other hand the constructive use of folkloric material would give the thematics of a passage through death. It is the relation between these two discursive complexes that would generate the ambiguity around which the story is productively organized. This is not offered as a solution to the methodological problem of establishing and accounting for the categories of analysis; but it does suggest that a minimal opening out of the text to its constitutive intertextual relations is the precondition for specifying a methodologically adequate object of analysis.

My second reading is of the relation between a novel that works within and upon the generic framework of the thriller, Don DeLillo's *Running Dog* (1978), and four novels by Robert Ludlum to which it seems particularly close: *The Scarlatti Inheritance* (1971), *The Rhinemann Exchange* (1974), *The Gemini Contenders* (1976), and *The Holcroft Covenant* (1978). The Ludlum novels vary considerably, but their underlying structure is something like this: a present order is disrupted by the intrusion of a hidden or secret story associated with the fascist past (the intrusion takes the form of an inheritance or an assignment). The hero is then involved in a quest for or a struggle over a lost object. He is opposed by an antagonist who is identified with the resurgence or repetition or reincarnation of the fascist past, and their struggle, their duel, is organized along contractual lines. The lexical emphasis of the titles themselves (inheritance, exchange, contenders, covenant) suggests this quasilegal regulation of the contest. Thus in *The Rhinemann Exchange* it is the balance of perfectly equal forces which makes possible the exchange (of industrial diamonds for the design of a high-altitude gyroscope); it could not take place if advantage were given or taken, since any weakness would destroy the exactness of the symmetry; but this balance is maintained only through a protracted process of bluffing, feinting, and dealing in which each side defensively tests out the other. Hero and antagonist increasingly come to resemble each other (or this mirroring is displaced onto the two sides in the contest). Scarlett/Kroeger, the American who has defected to the Nazis in *The Scarlatti Inheritance*, is shadowed by the obscure government accountant, Canfield, in a relation which is as much one of sexual rivalry as it is political. The gemini of *The Gemini Contenders* are twin brothers divided by character and politics; one of them, the increasingly obsessive killer Andrew, is in turn hunted by the brother of a man he has murdered. The antagonist in *The Holcroft Covenant*, Tennyson, is the "real" assassin known as the Tinamou, but he is doubled by a simulacrum whom he has trained and will now sacrifice; at the end of the novel the defeated hero, Holcroft, becomes a counter-Tinamou and assassinates Tennyson. But if in all cases this mirror structure is or becomes clear, the same is not true of the totality of forces involved in the plot. Rather, the progression of the quest for the lost object involves a sorting out of participants whose identity is initially unclear and who irrupt into the plot through apparently random acts of violence; there is a gradual revelation of the forces by which the hero is being manipulated, and with this knowledge the hero moves from passivity (or blind activity) to control of his own destiny. In some cases this means a movement from identification with one side to alienation from both: the hero becomes an outlaw.

Of the four Ludlum novels the most interesting is perhaps *The Gemini Contenders*, because of its extension of the plot over two generations of a family; because the plot constructs a directly political emblem of the social divisions caused by the Vietnam war; and because the lost object around which the plot revolves turns out to be deeply ambiguous in its import. This object, an Aramaic parchment apparently written from a Roman prison by Simon of Bethsaida, claims that a substitute was crucified in place of Christ, and that Christ took his own life in despair three days later: the truth of the Christian myth is its profane, bungled parody, a switching of positions that changes nothing and everything. But although this degree of ambiguity is of unusual intensity, it is nevertheless important to add that in Ludlum's novels ambiguity is always recuperated at another level as a device for forwarding plot. It is structured by an epistemological framework that permits final resolutions and clear courses of action. The ideological burden of the novels is carried most forcefully at this level of formal structure rather than at the level of an overtly thematized political ideology (Kennedy liberalism) or the level of a cliché-ridden verbal texture. It is an ideology of individual action and control, of the rediscovery of individual identity at the end of a process of alienation, and of the ultimate, regulated meaningfulness of history as the vehicle of American destiny. It is this level of formal structure that is internally eroded by *Running Dog*.

Running Dog's plot centers on a quest for a film purportedly shot in Hitler's bunkers in 1945, and reputedly pornographic. To the extent that the intensity of the struggle over it is far in excess of its intrinsic worth, this lost object works in the novel as a kind of fetish. One man, a systems engineer named Ludecke, has already been killed for it. Its brokerage is handled by Lightborne, a small-time dealer in phony antique erotica, who eventually negotiates a sale to a "twenty-two-year-old master of distribution and marketing," Richie Armbrister.[16] The film is also being sought by a crime boss, Vincent Talerico, and by Senator Lloyd Percival. Obscurely involved in this quest is a maverick intelligence organization, Radial Matrix, a secret arm of a bureaucratic entity called PAC/ORD which is currently under investigation by Percival's Senate committee. According to Percival, Radial Matrix

> was in fact a centralized funding mechanism for covert operations directed against foreign governments, against elements within foreign governments, and against political parties trying to gain power contrary to the interests of U.S. corporations abroad. It was responsible for channeling and laundering funds for unlisted station personnel, indigenous agents, terrorist operations, defector recruitment, political contributions, penetration of foreign communications networks and postal agencies. (74)

A Radial Matrix agent, Glen Selvy, who acts as a buyer of erotica for Percival, is in a position to exercise political blackmail. Moll Robbins, a reporter for *Running Dog*, "one-time organ of discontent" (21), is drawn into the double secret of the film and of Radial Matrix through her relationship with Selvy, but the two are then carried apart by divergent plot strands: Moll's employer is blackmailed by PAC/ORD, and Moll is unable to print an inside story on the committee investigations; she is denied access to the world of semiofficial terror but remains connected to the quest for the film. Selvy is marked for assassination by Radial Matrix and becomes a fugitive; pursued by two ex-ARVN rangers, he travels to his former training ground near the Mexican border to meet his death. Intercut with his flight is an account of the eventual screening of the movie.

The role of Radial Matrix, Senator Percival explains at one point to Moll, is to "satisfy the historical counterfunction" to the history of reform, "to invent new secrets, new bureaucracies of terror" (74). But the paranoia induced by secrecy and conspiracy is part of a more general technical possibility of total surveillance. Earl Mudger, the ex-CIA operative who runs Radial Matrix, explains that "it's the presence alone, the very fact, the superabundance of technology, that makes us feel we're committing crimes. Just the fact that these things exist at this widespread level. The processing machines, the scanners, the sorters. That's enough to make us feel like criminals. What enormous weight. What complex programs. And there's no one to explain it to us" (93). Coming from Mudger this is glib and deeply suspect. Equally dubious (at once trite and cynical) is Lightborne's complaint:

> "Go into a bank, you're filmed," he said. "Go into a department store, you're filmed. Increasingly we see this. Try on a dress in the changing room, someone's watching through a one-way glass. Not only customers, mind you. Employees are watched too, spied on with hidden cameras. Drive your car anywhere. Radar, computer traffic scans. They're looking into the uterus, taking pictures. Everywhere. What circles the earth constantly? Spy satellites, weather balloons, U-2 aircraft. What are they doing? Taking pictures. Putting the whole world on film."
> "The camera's everywhere."
> "It's true."
> "Even in the bunker," she said.
> "Very definitely."
> "Everybody's on camera."
> "I believe that, Miss Robbins."
> "Even the people in the bunker under the Reich Chancellery in April 1945."

"Very definitely the people in the bunker."
"You believe that, Mr. Lightborne."
"I have the movie," he said. (149–150)

Film and information technologies (the complete commodification of information) alter the directness of the world: it becomes more intensely mediated, the product only of its mappings. Tourists photograph each other in front of a smashed-up car in Times Square or a Wild West town in Texas, endowing the real with an authenticity which is the pure effect of its photographic reproduction. A gunman wearing shooting glasses and ear protectors shoots up a bar where Selvy and Moll are drinking, and the kids in the street decide that "it was Stevie Wonder. You see his head set? He was shooting to the music" (67). At a more sinister level, Mudger warns Moll that he has the technical capacity to mix her and the senator's voice prints to produce a tape of "last night's amorous activities" (92), and he explains—perhaps not truthfully, but plausibly—that "the Senator and PAC/ORD aren't nearly the antagonists the public believes them to be. They talk all the time. They make deals, they buy people, they sell favors. I doubt if Lomax knows whether he works for PAC/ORD or Lloyd Percival, ultimately" (89–90). History is doubled back on itself, visible only in its reflections, repetitions, ambiguities. Richie Armbrister is obsessed "not only by his impending assassination but by the conflicting reports that would ensue," and especially by the police cover-up (189). Percival's wife has been reading the twenty-six volumes of the Warren Report for the last nine years.

One way of explaining why this world has become deceptive would be to say that it is written filmically, as an array of surfaces. A window in a car next to Moll's taxi is rolled down and "reflections gradually vanished, replaced by Earl Mudger's smiling face" (164)—itself a *further* image of deception. A cop complains to a plainclothes detective that it has become impossible to tell who are the police—"It used to be you could go by the clothes. But you can't go by the clothes anymore" (8). Senator Percival is first seen "still wearing orange makeup from an earlier TV appearance" (20). But this is not just a matter of disguise or of appearances: if there is no substantial reality behind surfaces, then mediated constructions of the world themselves become substantial. The state of Moll's hair "was extreme enough to be taken as a style" (29). This slight recomposition has the effect of an aesthetic ordering. The view from a window is of "a vacant lot that might have been a Zen garden of rubbish" (35): might have been, but isn't, except in the perception that transforms it. The aesthetic is poised precariously between Being and virtuality. The same kind of detachment, but turned ironically back upon itself, informs the description of Harlem: "People who don't make the trip every day have a tendency to grow silent as the train passes through Harlem. It isn't shock or gloom so much as sheer fascination that brings on the hush. The pleasure of ruins. The eye's delight in finding instructive vistas. It's so interesting to look at, so numbly colorful, especially from this distance, and while moving through" (42). As the black slums are transformed into landscape, action and violence are transformed into gesture. At the same time Selvy is discussing with Lomax Percival's connection to the murdered Ludecke, "in a park a group of young Orientals practised the stylized movements of *t'ai chi*, a set of exercises that seemed to some degree martial in nature" (27). Such stylizations operate a displacement between action and effect, so that the world is experienced *après-coup*, as "aftereffect" (35) or "preview" (234) or *déjà-vu* (31); it has the structure of the cop's dream, in which "I was there but I wasn't there" (5). When stylization is taken more seriously, less ironically, however, it becomes the metaphysical support of violence. Mudger's cult of weaponry is a mystique of pure amoral technique, but at the same time a cult of its specialized jargons. A knife handle he is making "would be burl maple. The names of things. Subtly gripping odors. Glues and resins. The names. Honing oils. Template. Brazing rod. The names of things in these two rooms constituted a near-secret knowledge . . . You couldn't use tools and materials well, he believed, unless you knew their proper names" (119). It is this cult, he says, that sustained the American soldier in Vietnam:

> Technical idiom was often the only element of precision, the only true beauty, he could take with him into realms of ambiguity.
> Caliber readings, bullet grains, the names of special accessories . . . Spoken aloud by sweaty men in camouflage grease, these number-words and coinages had the inviolate grace of a strict meter of chant.
> Weapons were named, surnamed, slang-named, christened, titled and dubbed. Protective devices. Bearings of perfect performances. Reciting these names was the soldier's poetry, his counterjargon to death. (208–209)

And the operations of Radial Matrix continue to be couched in a dense medium of corporate jargon (the order to assassinate Selvy is a "phasing into adjustment" in relation to "the subject," 138).

It should be clear by now that *Running Dog* is a novel "about" representation, and more particularly about the politics of representation. Its preferred metaphor for this (as in DeLillo's first novel, *Americana*) is film, and what seems to be special about film is its capacity for faithful capture of the past, for the transmission of authenticity. Film seems to guarantee the solidity of history, to ensure a special access to historical truth. But the other claim made for film is that it heightens eroticism. Lightborne complains that his collection of erotic objects is "innocent" because "it doesn't move . . . Movement, action, frames per second. This is the era we're in, for better or worse . . . A thing isn't fully erotic unless it has the capacity to move" (15). The lost movie is sought with such intensity not because of its documentary value but because of its erotic value—a value which is merely enhanced by its historical authenticity, or rather by its association with a powerful historical myth. (The connection is specified in *The Gemini Contenders*, where reference is made to a Nazi commandant in Warsaw who "has been compromised. On film . . . his proclivity for children has been duly recorded," and to another who has "seen too many motion pictures in which he was a prominent player. Sheer pornography."[17]) Lightborne's version is this:

> So you have this pornographic interest. You have the fact that movies were screened for [Hitler] all the time in Berlin and Obersalzburg, sometimes two a day. Those Nazis had a thing for movies. They put everything on film. Executions, even, at his personal request. Film was essential to the Nazi era. Myth, dreams, memory. He liked lewd movies too, according to some. Even Hollywood stuff, girls with legs . . . You see he's endlessly fascinating. The whole Nazi era. People can't get enough. If it's Nazis, it's automatically erotic. The violence, the rituals, the leather, the jackboots. The whole thing for uniforms and paraphernalia. He whipped his niece, did you know that? (52)

And what he expects from the movie is a piece of theater about the last days of the Reich—"people in overcoats listening to Bruckner. Hitler handing out vials of poison . . . the operatic quality, the great flames" (95).

What he eventually sees is rather different—not history but history repeating itself as farce. There are in fact two movies in the novel; the other one is Chaplin's *The Great Dictator*, a parody of Hitler by Chaplin but also, within the text of the movie, a parody of Chaplin-as-Hitler by Chaplin-as-tramp, "a burlesque, an impersonation" (61). The lost film, Eva Braun's home movie, gives its audience not the grand opera of "the century's ultimate piece of decadence" (20), not "the madness at the end. The perversions, the sex" (257), but the sad comedy of Hitler miming Chaplin, complete with the "sweet, epicene, guilty little smile. Charlie's smile. An accurate reproduction" (236), and a Chaplinesque walk exaggerated by a muscular disorder (235), and a moving of the lips which imitates (alludes to) the speechlessness of the silent movies (237). The ultimately real imitates its imitation (which in turn is imitated within *The Great Dictator*). "Look," says the disgusted Lightborne, "he's twirling the cane. A disaster" (237). Not that the film is a lie, a failure of truth, but rather that "it was all so real. It had such weight. Objects were what they seemed to be. History was true" (188). True, yet yielding no final or secure truths whatsoever: whose *is* "the world's most famous moustache" (60)?

Running Dog works at a number of different levels of intertextuality. At the most general level it refers to a world structured by its representations; more specifically it explores the epistemological ambiguity of film; and it refers constantly and in quite particular ways to the genre of the thriller (including its filmic versions). I have suggested that it is especially close to the novels of Ludlum, but closeness of reference to specific texts is not the most important criterion: it is generic structures, the forms of knowledge they make available, and the authority they carry which are the crucial consideration.

One of the advantages offered by the popular thriller is a workable *formal* solution to the question of how to write a novel: it delivers certain resources of story and plot construction, a repertoire of *topoi*, a ready-made thematics of conspiracy and paranoia, and so on. *Running Dog* uses this framework (as DeLillo's *Ratner's Star* uses science fiction) as a machine for generating words and representations, but it then reworks the genre in such a way as to refuse and expose its ideological implications. In the place of Ludlum's "good" plotting we are given a "bad" plot that tails off in defeat and bathos (and in the black joke of the last paragraph); instead of character differentiation we are given stretches of terse, solipsistic dialogue which blur the differences between speakers; instead of a passage from illusion to truth we encounter only a world of surfaces and reflections. What is performed is not an ideologically "correct" contestation of the certainties of the Ludlum novels: there is no sign of class analysis and no discussion of political alternatives in *Running Dog*. Its subversion of the genre is immanent, tied to what it undermines, and productive only in its inventive negativity. But this work of negation, it should then be said, is already potentially present in the sophisticated form of the genre that Ludlum develops. The labyrinthine plotting, the complex primary and secondary doublings, the persistent tension between ambiguity and revelation—all of these offer a material which can be worked against the grain of the genre. It is the material itself which in part determines the possibility and the limits of its textual working.

My third text for analysis is Hölderlin's *Natur und Kunst, oder Saturn und Jupiter*.[18]

> Du waltest hoch am Tag und es blühet dein
> Gesetz, du hältst die Waage, Saturnus Sohn!
> Und teilst die Los' und ruhest froh im
> Ruhm der unsterblichen Herrscherkünste.

> Doch in den Abgrund, sagen die Sänger sich,
> Habst du den heilgen Vater, den eignen, einst
> Verwiesen und es jammre drunten,
> Da, wo die Wilden vor dir mit Recht sind,

> Schuldlos der Gott der goldenen Zeit schon längst:
> Einst mühelos, und grösser, wie du, wenn schon
> Er kein Gebot aussprach und ihn der
> Sterblichen keiner mit Namen nannte.

> Herab denn! oder schäme des Danks dich nicht!
> Und willst du bleiben, diene dem Älteren,
> Und gönn es ihm, dass ihn vor allen,
> Göttern and Menschen, der Sänger nenne!

> Denn, wie aus dem Gewölke dein Blitz, so kömmt
> Von ihm, was dein ist, siehe! so zeugt von ihm,
> Was du gebeutst, und aus Saturnus
> Frieden ist jegliche Macht erwachsen.

> Und hab ich erst am Herzen lebendiges
> Gefühlt und dämmert, was du gestaltetest,
> Und war in ihrer Wiege mir in
> Wonne die wechselnde Zeit entschlummert:

> Dann kenn ich dich, Kronion! dann hör ich dich,
> Den weisen Meister, welcher, wie wir, ein Sohn
> Der Zeit, Gesetze gibt und, was die
> Heilige Dämmerung birgt, verkündet.

You rule high in the day and your law flourishes, you hold the scales, Son of Saturn, and apportion destinies and rest happy in the fame of the immortal arts of ruling.

Yet into the abyss, the singers tell themselves, you banished once the holy father, your own, and there has long been lamentation below, there where the wild ones are rightly before you,

by the god of the golden age, who is innocent: once effortless, and greater than you, although he uttered no command and none of the mortal called him by name.

Then down with you! or else don't be ashamed to give thanks. And if you wish to remain, then serve the more ancient one, and grant him that the singer name him before all others, gods and men.

For, as your bolt of lightning from the clouds, so from him comes what is yours, and see! what you have plundered testifies to him, and every power has grown out of Saturn's peace.

And once I have felt in my heart what is living, and what you have shaped grows dark, and had changing time joyfully fallen asleep for me in its cradle:

Then I will know you, Kronion! then will I hear you, the wise master, who, like us, a son of time, dispenses laws and reveals what the holy twilight conceals.

As I suggested earlier, certain ideologically overdetermined categories (harmony, order, concord and discord, coherence, energy, paternity, art, nature, and so on) offer at different times the possibility of a semantic fusion through which a text can thematize its own ambivalent relation to the structure of social power. In this poem the structural symmetry of the four terms nature:art/Saturn:Jupiter (a symmetry between the philosophical and the mythopoetic) opens the way both to a "structuralist" reading and to its impossibility: the impossibility of building the repressed realm of nature, of nonlanguage, of absence, into a positive formal calculus. This impossibility is worked out in the tension between the classical and classicizing strophic form and the strained contortion of the syntax (but these are already generic characteristics of the Horatian ode), and in the complex play and patterning of enunciative positions.

Structurally the poem moves through a series of pronominal transformations: a stanza addressed to Jupiter; two stanzas spoken indirectly by *die Sänger* (the singers) about Saturn, who is absent as a speaker and has to be represented by the poets or the poem's "I"; two stanzas which move from address to Jupiter to statement about Saturn; one stanza in which

Intertextuality 149

the poet (the poem's speaker) speaks in the first person; and a final stanza in which the poet, speaking in the first person, addresses Jupiter. If we can locate three main subjects of enunciation in the poem (Jupiter, Saturn, and a composite subject made up of "the singers" and "I"), then we can see it being divided roughly equally between these subjects. The movement from Jupiter to Saturn to Jupiter and Saturn to *Ich* to the final fusion of Jupiter and *Ich* is also a movement from speech in the second person (stanza 1) to speech in the third person (stanzas 2 and 3) to a mixture of second and third person (stanzas 4 and 5) to a mixture of first and second person (stanzas 6 and 7). In these terms the poem can be seen as attempting, in stanzas 4 and 5, a synthetic resolution (of Jupiter and Saturn, of second- and third-person speech), which fails because of the purely antithetical nature of the categories involved. Stanza 6 then replaces the substitutional speech of "the singers" with the first-person speech of the "singer" of this poem and creates the possibility of an alternative resolution through the fusion, in the last stanza, of *Ich* and *du*, "I" and "thou." This fusion—which is also based on a fusion of three different time scales, which I shall discuss shortly—indicates in the first place the potential union of Jupiter and Saturn, of art and nature; but at a second level it indicates the replacement of Saturn (who is speechless) by the poet, and the unity of poetry and the logos, revelation and law.

The poem's argument is initially set up in the indicative mood, which points to an actual state of affairs. In stanza 4 the imperative mood of the verb begins the process of attempted overcoming of this state; *ist erwachsen*, "has grown," in stanza 5 indicates the extension of the past into the present, which is the basis for the ambiguous future perfect of stanza 6 and the present-of-potentiality, a disguised conditional, of the last stanza. This movement is developed from the association established between art and domination: *Herrscherkünste* ("arts of ruling") expresses with wonderful clarity the alliance between art and a civilization based on repression,[19] and the ambiguity is reinforced by the contrast between the legal register of *walten, Gesetz, Waage* ("rule," "law," "scales") on the one hand and, on the other, the vocabulary of hymnic praise (*ruhest froh im / Ruhm der unsterblichen*, "rest happy in / the fame of the immortal"). It is similarly underlined by the union of the organic and the cultural in *es blühet dein / Gesetz* ("your law / flourishes"), and by the ambivalent value of *Tag* ("day"). At a second level this set of paradigmatic oppositions is worked out as an opposition between language and silence. Saturn is characterized by the fact that *Er kein Gebot aussprach und ihn der / Sterblichen keiner mit Namen nannte* ("he uttered no command and none of the / mortal called him by name"), or at best that *es jammre . . . der Gott* ("there has been lamentation . . . by the god"). His realm is prelinguistic, whereas Jupiter incarnates the legality of language, language as law: he is named, defined, and distinguished, whereas Saturn must be lent a language by the poets. Here the central ambiguity of the poem serves to create a paradoxical asymmetry: language is polarized into logos and language as silence, and poetry withdraws from the realm of art to seek speech in the inarticulate realm of nature. The singers speak, but can speak their secret (the name of the once nameless god) only to themselves (*sagen die Sänger sich*, "the singers tell themselves"). This displacement of poetry, of language as song, from art to nature entails a further polarization: poetry is divided between the harmonious unity of nature, an undifferentiated and prelinguistic state, *for* which the poet can speak (*dass ihn . . . der Sänger nenne*, "that the singer name him") but which cannot speak *through* him; and nature as anarchy, *die Wilden vor dir* ("the wild ones before you"), the Titans who stand for revolt and subversion, and who are intimately associated with the present outcast condition of Saturn (note that mention of the Titans occurs between *es jammre* and *der Gott*, between the present state and the indication both of its subject and of a contrasting previous state; in this interrupted transition the verb is transformed by the delayed adverb from a straightforward present tense to a quasiperfect tense).

The resolution of these antinomies is carried out through a transition to first-person utterance and to a complicated sequence of tenses: a perfect and a pluperfect (*Und hab ich erst . . . gefühlt / Und war . . . mir . . . entschlummert*), which are doubtless to be read as future perfects, followed by a present (*Dann kenn ich dich*) which must be read as a future or a conditional tense. The future perfect points to the utopian nature of this resolution, but it is paralleled at the same time by a thematic resolution of temporal categories: from the opposition of the timelessness of Saturn (he exists *before* time, since as Kronos/Chronos he is not subject to time, and he is the seed from which everything in time grows)[20] and the false immortality of Jupiter (who is associated with the word *unsterblich*, "immortal") comes the recognition of Jupiter as Kronion, a son of time *wie wir* ("like us"). This insertion of Jupiter into a finite time framework (which gives a new significance to *hoch am Tag*, "high in the day," and the *unsterbliche Herrscherkünste*, "immortal arts of ruling") modifies the purely utopian aspect of the last stanza. The projected unity of repressed nature and repressive Logos, of the naive and the sentimental, of Greece and Germany, and of Greek strophes with the German language, is set in a future which is a historical future; and this points both to a reunification of language and logos in *Kunst* and to the annihilation of the *Herrscher-künste*. The poem thematizes social power (the power of the usurping father/son, the ruler) through a turning back on itself as language, a subversion of its own legality by a repressed and primordial silence.

THE CONCEPT of intertextuality makes possible precisely a *formal* analysis of texts: not in the sense that meaning would be taken to be inherent in formal properties, but in the quite opposite sense that it is only within a system of intertextual relations that the function of formal elements can be assessed. (Lotman gives the example of the different significance attaching to an absence of rhyme in the ancient epic, in contemporary verse, and in verse written in a period in which rhyme is the poetic norm.)[21] To describe (construct) the network of relations in which a text is constituted is to account for the conditions of its textuality, its historical modality, but equally to account for the way the text constructs itself in and as a specific *relation* to these conditions. But if the concept of intertextuality is not to remain gestural, a number of methodological questions need to be faced: how explicit should the identification of intertextual structures be? How does such an identification differ from the traditional practices of source criticism? What can function as an intertext, and what is its analytical status? And to what uses can the construction or reconstruction of intertextual relations be put? One—entirely apolitical, entirely "formalist"—set of answers to these questions is offered by the poetics developed by Michael Riffaterre. Since his work has at least the virtue of being detailed and explicit, it may serve as a point of theoretical entry.

In order to be read properly (whatever this may mean), the poetic text demands a double reading: in the first place a heuristic construction of the referential coherence of the text (the *mimesis*)[22] and at the same time a registration of the anomalies and incompatibilities which cause problems for such a construction; then subsequently a retroactive attempt to translate the contradictions of the first level into a coherent order of significance (*semiosis*). In this process "the reader's acceptance of the mimesis sets up the grammar as the background from which the ungrammaticalities will thrust themselves forward as stumbling blocks, to be understood eventually on a second level" (6). The construction of textual unity at this second level involves a transformation of semantic material, and we could say that transformations are of one of two kinds: *intratextual* (the elaboration of a text from a semantic core) and *intertextual* (the elaboration of a text in relation to other texts). Although Riffaterre blurs this distinction, we could say that the former involves a relation to a matrix, and the latter involves a relation to a hypogram.

A *matrix* is a simple kernel of which the poem can be seen to be the expansion; the poem results "from the transformation of the *matrix* . . . into a longer, complex, and nonliteral periphrasis" (19). The matrix is a purely hypothetical structure (it is not the real origin of the text but rather the reader's reduction of the text to a simple kernel); and it is an invariant which is realized in successive variants. The full text of a poem is generated by either the expansion or the conversion of a matrix sentence into more complex forms.

The process of expansion is clearly intratextual; but conversion is in fact a transformation of *inter*textual material: for example, the transformation of the value given to a cultural cliché, a quotation, or a "descriptive system" (a restricted semantic field, 63). Because he needs the concept of matrix as a guarantee of textual unity Riffaterre tends, I think, to confuse the intratextual matrix with the intertextual *hypogram* (meaning a semantic structure—thematic field, cliché, norm, or actual text—which is referred to and transformed by a particular poem). Witness his analysis of Eluard's "Toilette":

> Elle entra dans sa chambrette pour se changer, tandis que sa bouilloire chantait. Le courant d'air venant de la fenêtre claqua la porte derrière elle. Un court instant, elle polit sa nudité étrange, blanche et droite. Puis elle se glissa dans une robe de veuve.

> She went into her little room to change. The kettle was singing. The draft from the window slammed the door behind her. For a brief moment she stood polishing her nakedness, strange, white, erect. Then she slipped into a widow's dress.   (*Semiotics of Poetry*, 117)

Riffaterre argues convincingly that the poem's title indicates "not an orderless fragment of realism" but a particular genre of painting (the sensuous depiction of a woman's toilette). In relation to this stylized genre the poem can therefore be seen as "a well-ordered morphological system comprising a limited number of stereotypes. The form of this system is dictated by its first word, and its realism flows from the intertextual conflict between the explicit derivation," that is, the text as "orderless fragment of realism," "and its implicit traditional derivation, normally a symbol of fantasies of luxury and pleasure" (119). There is thus a "double derivation" from the title, which is both internal matrix and intersemiotic reference. But I think one could as simply say that the intertextual reference to the genre of painting is internalized and becomes the core from which the text is generated. *Conversion*, in other words, is the process by which the intertextual functions as a generative force within the text, and it is different in kind from the simpler process of expansion. (But note that the fantasy of unity fails to account for everything in the text: Riffaterre's derivation does not account, for example, for the images of closure, or the metaphor of polishing, or the black/white opposition, or the possibility of reading the poem as a sexual allegory: there is no given unity of the text.)

A long statement at the end of the book illustrates the way Riffaterre moves from the concept of matrix to an implicit recognition of the intertextual (hypogrammatic) basis of the text: In the process of reading,

> the poem's content, that is, what the detour [the switching of levels] turns about, is perceived or rather rationalized as an equivalent form at its before-detour, pre-transformation stage [that is, as a matrix]. The reader more or less explicitly subsumes this content as a colloquial or ordinary-language version of what he is reading. The paradox is that while the poetic text is interpreted as a departure from a norm, that imaginary nonliterary norm is in effect deduced, or even retroactively fantasized from the text perceived as departure. But no matter what the reader may think, there is no norm that is language as grammars and dictionaries may represent it: the poem is made up of texts, of fragments of texts, integrated with or without conversion into a new system. This material (rather than norm) is not the raw stuff of language: it is already a stylistic structure, hot with intensified connotations, overloaded discourse.   (164)

In other words, the "matrix" is a convenient fiction and is in any case a structure of cultural norms to which the poem refers intertextually. The material of the poem is a material of normative structures of meaning, "texts," not a simple lexical matrix.

The hypogram, then, is a conventional structure of meanings and of relations between meanings. This structure may be diffuse (sets of connotations, meanings that "go together" or that can be substituted for one another); it may have the more precise and specific form of a formula (clichés, sayings, cultural norms, conventional epithets); or it may be an actual text, usually well known and stereotyped, so that it has the status of an established and normative meaning. The hypogram is whatever can be taken for granted as a familiar point of departure, an authoritative cultural meaning. Its crucial importance for poetry derives from the fact that poems are made out of pre-existent meanings; they *transform* meaning rather than creating it out of nothing. Texts are made out of the styles and ways of speaking embedded in language; out of cultural norms; out of the conventions of genre; and out of other texts. This is true, as Riffaterre demonstrates, even of the least controlled, least consciously "literary" form of literature, the automatic writing of the surrealists, which like all other poetic texts is obtained by a systematic process of conversion.

"Conversion" and "transformation" are used more or less interchangeably by Riffaterre to describe the construction of poetic significance out of the "ungrammaticalities" of the surface text. Here it may seem that what is transformed is the hypogram *rather than* the mimesis; but if we recognize that the verisimilitude of the mimetic text is a conventional mode of authority, then we can perhaps recognize that this mimesis is in fact equivalent to the normative structures of meaning that Riffaterre labels "hypograms." The representation of the "real," in other words, is an intertextual reference to cultural modes of authority; what we take for granted as reality are the codes of cultural and literary convention. Riffaterre never quite makes this recognition, but it is surely implicit in his definition of the poetic text as deviation from a norm which at times he refers to as mimesis and at times as hypogram.

The criticisms to be made of Riffaterre's theoretical presuppositions are reasonably obvious and need be only briefly rehearsed. They concern above all the problematic of error within which he works. A practice which declares itself to be descriptive of the process of reading quickly turns out to be normative and elitist. Rather than being in a mutually conditioning relation to the text (such that both "text" and "reader" would be categories constituted within a particular regime of reading), the reader "is taken as the standard of normal usage and the poem as that which violates it. The reader's very normality represents mistakenness according to the logic of the poem, just as the deviance of the poem represents ungrammaticality in the normal semantics of everyday language. The thrust of the theory is . . . to correct the reader."[23] The corollary of this is the possibility of a "correct" interpretation, which depends above all on the identification of the *only possible* intertext; this in turn can be identified as such by the fact that text and intertext are in a strictly homologous relation, "variants of the same structure."[24] Reading, in other words, is restricted by the limited number of "solutions" available to the "puzzle" of the text, and in particular by the finite number of hypograms to which the text refers; the reader "is under strict guidance and control as he fills the gaps and solves the puzzle" (*Semiotics of Poetry*, 165). Even in those cases where the intertext cannot be identified, the text still "holds clues (such as formal and semantic gaps) to a complementary intertext lying in wait somewhere."[25] In the usual circular manner the possession of truth is guaranteed by an objectively given structure which is truly known only by the theorist. This structure is ultimately independent of any reader and any interpretive grid. The anomalies or ungrammaticalities on which reading is built are objectively present in the text; every literary text "contains certain subliminal components that guide the reader towards a single stable interpretation of that text."[26] Guiding and controlling, the singleness and stability of truth: it requires little imagination to construct the political homologues of these metaphors.

And yet Riffaterre's work has a certain value, in part for his stress on the range of levels at which an intertext may be actualized, in part for his practice of interpretation, which is frequently illuminating as *a* reading of a text. But the important point to make is that any particular construction of a set of intertextual relations is limited and relative—not to a reading subject but to the interpretive grid (the regime of reading) through which both the subject position and the textual relations are constituted. Certainly some constructions of intertextual reference work better than others; but any construction derives from an interpretive interest, and this means that the relevant prehistory of texts will change as their present historical space changes. In Jonathan Culler's words, "there are no moments of authority and points of origin except those which are retrospectively designated as origins and which, therefore, can be shown to derive from the series for which they are constituted as origin."[27]

It is Culler who has most forcefully problematized the analytic applicability of the concept of intertextuality. In its initial elaboration by Kristeva and Barthes the term was not necessarily restricted to particular textual manifestations of signifying systems; rather, it designated the general conformation of a culture as a complex network of codes with heterogeneous and dispersed forms of textual realization. The force of the concept was precisely that it formulated the codedness (hence the textuality) of what had previously been thought in nonsemiotic terms (consciousness, experience, wisdom, story, culture). With the later work of Kristeva, however, there arises the problem of a distinction between precise and diffuse forms of intertextuality. In a criticism that applies equally to Kristeva's identification of specific intertexts for Lautréamont's *Chants de Maldoror* and *Poésies* (an identification which goes so far as to name the particular edition of the intertext used) and to Riffaterre's and Harold Bloom's identification of a single relevant intertextual origin, Culler argues that intertextuality "is a difficult concept to use because of the vast and undefined discursive space it designates, but when one narrows it so as to make it more usable one either falls into source study of a traditional and positivistic kind (which is what the concept was designed to transcend) or else ends by naming particular texts as the pre-texts on grounds of interpretive convenience" (109). The concept should not be narrowed to designate "a single anterior action which serves as origin and moment of plenitude" but should cover rather "an open series of acts, both identifiable and lost, which work together to constitute something like a language: discursive possibilities, systems of convention, clichés and descriptive systems" (110). But this methodological imperative then conflicts with the practical requirements of exegesis. The concept of intertextuality can be made workable only if it is focused and given precision of reference; but such a narrowing of its range then weakens its power to describe the full network of textual determinations and relations (111).

Laurent Jenny formulates this paradox in terms of a distinction between "weak" and "strong" forms of intertextuality (for example, the distinction between thematic allusion on the one hand and an explicit, extended, verbally and structurally close reference on the other).[28] The point of this is to differentiate between such different forms of intertextuality as "a citation, a plagiarism, and a simple reminiscence" (40): that is, between modes of reference which will be functionally quite dissimilar. A more difficult (but also a more crucial) question is whether one can speak of an intertextual relation to a genre: that is, a relation which, in simple or complex form, is absolutely determinant for every text and yet which is not, strictly speaking, a relation to an intertext. The problem this poses is that it would "mingle awkwardly structures which belong to the code and structures which belong to its realization." But in fact, Jenny concedes, any rigid distinction between the levels of code and text is not tenable: "Genre archetypes, however abstract, still constitute textual structures" (42). This seems to me an important insight (akin to Riffaterre's point that literary signification takes place in relation to "an intertext either potential in language or already actualized in literature"),[29] and it is extended in the argument that the material of intertextual discourse is "not just words, but bits of the already said, the already organized, textual fragments" (45): that is, organizations of discourse anywhere along the scale between text and register. We could add that reference to a text implicitly evokes reference to the full set of potential meanings stored in the codes of a genre.

In this sense the precise identification of a specific intertext may turn out to be a relatively trivial operation. What is crucial to interpretation is rather the possibility of constructing what must have been the canonic structures against which the text is shaped. Particular intertextual references (Emma Bovary "soiling her hands" on lending-library novels and, later, on the historical romances of Scott, for example)[30] may be important clues in this process of construction but can never be an end in themselves. The textual prehistory constituted by the literary system, the canon, and particular intertexts are not pregiven facts to be established but structures to be elaborated on the basis of their textual definition. Literary competence or "expertise" may be useful in this activity but cannot be decisive.

Similarly, the determination of the *level* at which the authority of a literary system and a canonic norm is confirmed or challenged is never given in advance but is always the product of an interpretive interest. This authority may be referred to at the level of verbal detail, of formal or thematic microstructure, at the level of enunciative positioning or narrative macro-structure, at the level of generic structure or of a contradiction between generic structures, and so on; and the "messages" constructed at these different levels may be mutually contradictory. Referral may involve direct invocation of an intertext, as in parody or pastiche, or a purely implicit relation to an intertextual system; and it may involve greater or lesser degrees of interdiscursive and intersemiotic reference. But the starting point of analysis (which both determines and is determined by the *ends* of analysis) is not an objective historical system or an objective textual ordering; it can only be an assessment of the strategic value (the fruitfulness, the pleasure, the didactic or political interest) of a particular construction of relevant relations.

The analysis of intertextual relations is to be distinguished from source criticism not only by its stress on the process of reading rather than on the establishment of "external" facts as the beginning and the end of its activity, but also by its emphasis on the functional integration of intertextual material. This is to say that such material is rarely simply embedded in a text but is rather transformed in accordance with an internal textual logic, a logic of "conversion," to use Riffaterre's term. Paul De Man once wrote that "a literary text simultaneously asserts and denies the authority of its own rhetorical mode."[31] If we set to one side De Man's monumentalization of the "literary," this seems to me an adequate description of how the internalization of canonic and generic authority tends to produce a peculiar tension which is then projected onto the syntagmatic axis of the text. There can be no total break with literary norms, since deautomatization can occur only as a relation and an ongoing textual process. It is the reproduction or citation of normative literary structures (a metrical schema, a code of sexual representation, a level of decorum) which makes possible the play of expectations, blockages, deviations, reversals, and complications which typically constitute this textual process. And one of the most important ways in which the patterning of relations of textual authority and disruption is built up is through the play of canonic and noncanonic discourses.

WHAT A TEXT "distinctively and characteristically represents is not images, ideas, feelings, characters, scenes, or worlds, but discourse";[32] not a pretextual world, but a "world" which is discursively constructed. It refers to realities embedded in the knowledge conditions (particular semantic categories, appropriate subject positions and rhetorical modes, rules of use and availability) of particular genres of discourse; or more precisely, as David Silverman and Brian Torode argue, to realities which are constructed in the relations between genres, since "it is the play of reference from one language to another language that suggests the reference of language to a reality other than language."[33] The most developed account of this play is in Bakhtin's poetics of the novel. Let me quote a central passage:

> The novel can be defined as a diversity of social speech types (sometimes even diversity of languages) and a diversity of individual voices, artistically organized. The internal stratification of any single national language into social dialects, characteristic group behaviour, professional jargons, generic languages, languages of generations and age groups, tendentious languages, languages of the authorities, of various circles and of passing fashions, languages that serve the specific sociopolitical purposes of the day, even of the hour (each day has its own slogan, its own vocabulary, its own emphases)—this internal stratification present in every language at any given moment of its historical existence is the indispensable prerequisite for the novel as a genre. The novel orchestrates all its themes, the totality of the world of objects and ideas depicted and expressed in it, by means of the

social diversity of speech types and by the differing individual voices that flourish under such conditions. Authorial speech, the speeches of narrators, inserted genres, the speech of characters are merely those fundamental compositional unities with whose help heteroglossia can enter the novel; each of them permits a multiplicity of social voices and a wide variety of their links and interrelationships (always more or less dialogized). These distinctive links and interrelationships between utterances and languages, this movement of the theme through different languages and speech types, its dispersion into the rivulets and droplets of social heteroglossia, its dialogization—this is the basic distinguishing feature of the stylistics of the novel.[34]

I have previously registered my objection to Bakhtin's essentializing of the genre of the novel in relation, particularly, to poetic discourse. But the great power of his conceptualization of the transformational activity of novelistic discourse is that it allows the high-order textual constructs of plot, character, narrator, space, time, and so on, to be thought of as complex discursive effects, reality effects produced in the intertextual operation of one discourse upon another.

By using the concept of discourse genre, it becomes possible to analyze a text as a play of voices—that is, of utterances made from shifting positions specified by the registers the text invokes. These positions are not necessarily actualized as those of a personified speaker: they are positions appropriate to a *kind* of speaker. Taken in this discursive, nonontological sense, the concept of voice has the advantage over traditional concepts such as point of view that it is not in the first instance subordinate to concretizations drawn from a represented world[35]—that is, to the "consciousness" or "vision" of characters or the narrator. There is, therefore, no sharp division between discourse which is assigned, directly or indirectly, to a character, and discourse which has its source in other texts. The narrative process can be theorized as a structure which knits together heterogeneous discourses; everything in the text is language.

Free indirect discourse, which became a major narrative device only in the nineteenth century, is of particular interest for the linguistic analysis of narrative in that it foregrounds the number of different contexts of enunciation from which the discourse of the text originates. It can most economically be described as a "dual voice" situated between narrative and represented voice and combining aspects of the homogeneous modality of indirect speech (the conformation of the tense sequence and personal pronouns in the embedded clause to those of the main clause) with aspects of the split modality of the quoting of direct speech (deictics referring to the context of the quoted speech; the use of exclamations, incomplete sentences, oral intonation patterns, and so on).[36] It is this ambivalence both of grammatical structure and perspective which emphasizes the shifting directionality of narrative. Barthes has in fact argued that this sense of direction is characteristic only of the classical novel, although I think that the indeterminacy of the modern text could be seen as a special case of the plural voice. According to Barthes,

> in the classic text the majority of the utterances are assigned an origin, we can identify their parentage, who is speaking: either a conscious- ness (of a character, of the author) or a culture (the anonymous is still an origin, a voice) . . . The best way to conceive the classic plural is then to listen to the text as an iridescent exchange carried on by multiple voices, on different wavelengths and subject from time to time to a sudden *dissolve*, leaving a gap which enables the utterance to shift from one point of view to another, without warning.[37]

An analysis of the following extended passage from *Little Dorrit* will demonstrate the way in which these tonal shifts correspond to a play of quotations from or allusions to a number of different registers.

> Arthur Clennam went on to the present purport of his visit; namely, to make Plornish the instrument of effecting Tip's release, with as little detriment as possible to the self-reliance and self-helpfulness of the young man, supposing him to possess any remnant of those qualities: without doubt a very wide stretch of supposition.[38]

The last phrase initiates the first major shift of voice in this passage. Subjective adverbs or adverbial phrases of assertion such as "without doubt" tend to function as indices of free indirect discourse.[39] The "supposition" which in this phrase ironically negates that of the preceding phrase may be either Clennam's or that of a moral spokesman whose voice is suddenly foregrounded. More probably it is a fusion of the two, in which Clennam's opinion is supplemented by a voice more open and sarcastic than his own.

> Plornish, having been made acquainted with the cause of action from the Defendant's own mouth, gave Arthur to understand that the Plaintiff was a "Chaunter"—meaning, not a singer of anthems, but a seller of horses—and that he (Plornish) considered that ten shillings in the pound "would settle handsome," and that more would be a waste of money.

The capitalization of "the Defendant" and "the Plaintiff" perhaps indicates that the intonational stress is a quotation from Plornish, who is in awe of the legal register he is adopting. If that is so, then this sentence contains three different modes of rendition of Plornish's speech—direct speech, indirect speech, and free indirect discourse—in addition to the parenthetical voice of the authoritative narrator.

> The Principal and instrument soon drove off together to a stable yard in High Holborn . . . [The reference to Clennam's desire to "make Plornish the instrument of effecting Tip's release" is an internal quotation; in this elaborated form as a ponderous circumlocution it works at the same time as a quotation from legal jargon.] where a remarkably fine grey gelding, worth, at the lowest figure, seventy-five guineas (not taking into account the value of the shot he had been made to swallow for the improvement of his form), was to be parted with for a twenty-pound note, in consequence of his having run away last week with Mrs Captain Barbary of Cheltenham, who wasn't up to a horse of his courage, and who, in mere spite, insisted on selling him for that ridiculous sum: or, in other words, on giving him away.

This sentence of free indirect discourse fuses the narrator's discourse with the hyperbolic discourse of horse trading. The parenthetical phrase, "not taking into account the value of the shot he had been made to swallow for the improvement of his form," is of a higher degree of complexity. In its continuity with the free indirect discourse, it seems to be from the same source, but the contradictory content indicates that the voice is that of the narrator miming the alien register.

Although I have identified voice as having its source in secondary concretizations (Plornish, the narrator), this in no way contradicts the principle of the priority of discourse over the quasi-real entities which are its effects, since in the novel the assignment of a source to discourse functions precisely as a means of constructing these totalities; they are confirmed by being produced. That the assignment of discourse to a character is a secondary operation subsequent to its identification as a register is indicated by the fact that the source of the free indirect discourse here is not immediately located. The passage continues:

> Plornish, going up this yard alone and leaving his Principal outside, found a gentleman with tight drab legs, a rather old hat, a little hooked stick, and a blue neckerchief (Captain Maroon of Gloucestershire, a private friend of Captain Barbary); who happened to

be there, in a friendly way, to mention these little circumstances concerning the remarkably fine grey gelding to any real judge of a horse and quick snapper-up of a good thing, who might look in at that address as per advertisement.

To be a character is to be both a source of discourse and an object of discourse; but there is no necessity for the jargon of horse trading to have been located in a particular speaker. The source could equally well have been left indefinite—that is, assigned to a *type* of speaker. Every register specifies a limited number of positions of utterance appropriate to it, and these positions may vary or may not be further specified as an object of the discourse of the text. The continuation of the free indirect discourse after the description of Captain Maroon of Gloucestershire has the effect of simultaneously *identifying* him retrospectively as the source of the passage about the "remarkably fine gelding" and *defining* him as the kind of speaker who would likely to fill the position of utterance appropriate to that register.

Analytic priority is therefore given not to character but to those normative genres of discourse which may or may not be assigned to a specific person. In this passage I would identify four main registers: that of nineteenth-century realist narrative, that of commercial transactions, legal jargon, and Cockney dialect. The narrative norm governs three distinct voices: that of a neutral narrator, that of the moralizing narrator who condemns Tip, and that of the narrator who parodies Captain Maroon. If the phrase "without doubt a very wide stretch of supposition" can be read as a fusion of the narrator's voice with Clennam's, however, then we could argue that there is also a direct correspondence between Clennam's perspective and the narrative norm. Legal jargon is assigned in one case, indirectly, to Plornish, and in the other case—the phrase about "the Principal and instrument"—to a narrative voice quoting and perhaps parodying itself. The commercial jargon is assigned indirectly to Captain Maroon; and Cockney dialect, which is technically not a register but which seems in this case to be functioning in the same way, is assigned directly to Plornish.

The interest of this typology is, I think, that it allows us to analyze the novel in terms of relations between different kinds of discursive authority, each producing specific reality effects, and in particular between literary and nonliterary structures of discourse. The force of the norms of nineteenth-century narrative lies in their monologic authority. Through their projection of a world which is objective and external to the formal structures through which it is enunciated, they sustain an authoritative definition of the real as a moral universe. The other genres invoked in this passage are still subsumed beneath this authority; but at the same time they work to break the monopoly of verisimilitude held by the omniscient narrator. Bakhtin's concept of dialogic discourse—discourse which is oriented toward and in some way influenced by an alien discourse—is relevant here.[40] Parody, stylization, the projected narrator, free indirect discourse, any discourse which stresses the act of speaking and its relation to other acts of speaking would function as a kind of double voice. Clearly the distinction between monologic and dialogic discourse is one of degree, since I have argued earlier that all literary discourse is a relation to previous discursive structures. But one could define monologic modes of discourse in terms of the suppression of alternative ways of speaking and the *reproduction* of official norms, and dialogic modes in terms of the pluralization of the text and the *transformation* of official norms. Further, it is those registers specified as appropriate by the genre—in this case particularly the morally superior discourse of the omniscient narrator—which tend to embody official values, whereas those registers drawn from other realms, and particularly those which transgress stylistic decorum, tend to subvert the authority of the dominant discourse.

I want now to try to define this dominant discourse more precisely in terms of the options made possible by the genre. The form of the novel that Dickens developed was a complex hybrid, and despite the huge quantity of commentary on his work, there is hardly any substantial analysis of the different subgenres which were fused in the making of this form. Bakhtin, in a number of useful passages in *The Dialogic Imagination*, speaks of the English comic novel's "comic-parodic re-processing of almost all the levels of literary language, both conversational and written, that were current at the time": those of the parliament, the court, of journalism, business, scholarship, epic and biblical styles, and the sermon (301). The linguistic norm, however, is an automatized "common language" from which the authorial voice distances itself. This authorial voice takes the form of "pathos-filled, moral-didactic, sentimental-elegiac or idyllic" discourse, and "in the comic novel the direct authorial word is thus realized in direct, unqualified stylizations of poetic genres (idyllic, elegiac, etc.) or stylizations of rhetorical genres (the pathetic, the moral-didactic)" (302). But this analysis seems to me to miss the major organizing subgenres from which the Dickensian novel is built. Very schematically one could say that these are a multistranded form of the picaresque derived basically from Smollett; and a form of Gothic which perhaps owes more to Victorian melodrama than to the Gothic novel proper. The characteristic structure of the Gothic form is the double time scale which links a surface plot to a second plot buried in the past (it is from this oedipal plot structure that the modern detective story developed). The structure of the multistranded picaresque, however, is essentially synchronic, a juxtaposition of simultaneous narratives. What happens in the fusion of these two forms is that the principle of resolution of diachronically separate strands is extended to the synchronically separate strands. The discourse of the novel knots together plot structures which are both temporally and spatially dispersed. Miss Wade formulates this double teleology early in *Little Dorrit*: "In our course through life we shall meet the people who are coming to meet *us*, from many strange places and by many strange roads . . . and what it is set to us to do to them, and what it is set to them to do to us, will all be done" (63).

Among the plurality of narrative modes in *Little Dorrit* it is the Gothic register which carries the burden of official moral authority. It serves as the vehicle for a moral melodrama centered on the figure of Little Dorrit and expounding the themes of filial love, forbearance, and Duty. The fatality of its unfolding turns the narrative itself into a representative and instrument of the ineluctable laws of moral retribution. The rhetoric of the Gothic register is a rhetoric of doom and judgment, which is relativized only by its discordant juxtaposition with other registers.

At the same time, however, the Gothic mode permits the thematization of material which effectively subverts the surface moral code. This material relates to a past which is suppressed and which thereby contaminates the present, producing the disorder which motivates the contingencies of the plot. It is thematized through a number of different strands of imagery. At the very center of the book is the image of the dead travelers in the mortuary at the Great Saint Bernard monastery, frozen in an eternal gesture. Similarly, the imagery of imprisonment refers not only to physical confinement but to the retardation of time. The light of Chapter 1 is not only imprisoned but is "the light of yesterday week, the light of six months ago, the light of six years ago. So slack and dead!" (46); and the mirror in Miss Wade's apartment is "so clouded that it seemed to hold in magic preservation all the fogs and bad weather it had ever reflected" (376). Flora lives in a "sober, silent, air-tight house" pervaded by the smell of old rose-leaves and lavender (186); and she herself is described, in a bold simile, as behaving "with a caricature of her girlish manner, such as a mummer might have presented at her own funeral, if she had lived and died in classical antiquity" (192). Mrs. Clennam, finally, is the focus of a whole series of images of the obscure preservation of secrets: the watch with its admonitory inscription striving to force the past into the present; the cellars of the house and the strong room, "stored with old ledgers, which had as musty and corrupt a smell as if they were regularly balanced, in the dead small hours, by a nightly resurrection of old book-keepers" (95); and more generally the neighborhood of the house, the streets of which "seemed all depositories of oppressive secrets" (596).

The secret which haunts the novel is of course brought to light in the dénouement, which unfolds the suppressed narrative within the present in order to restore and complete the order of narrative. But this story of wills and codicils, with all its improbable complexities, can surely not be anything other than a rationalization, screening a repressed oedipal configuration—a structure of the positions of symbolic Father, symbolic Mother, and symbolic Child and the relations of attraction and identification between them—which is the unconscious of the text. Part of the force of the Gothic mode, indeed, lies in this potential to bring repressed material so close to the textual surface without ever breaking through it.

The most interesting identification in the suppressed story is that which the codicil makes between Little Dorrit and Arthur Clennam's real mother (848). But the identification is in fact much more complex. Clennam's relationship to Little Dorrit is never that of a peer; nor, as the difference in their ages might suggest, is it merely a paternal relationship. Rather it is a component of a structure in which the relations of father/son and mother/child are fully reversible. When Clennam lies ill in prison, Little Dorrit announces herself to him as "your own poor child"; and yet she at once adopts a maternal role, nursing him "as lovingly, and GOD knows as innocently, as she had nursed her father in that room when she had been but a baby, needing all the care from others that she took of them" (825). The reference to the nursing of her father is to a previous passage which invokes the myth of Euphrasia suckling her father, King Evander, during his imprisonment: "There was a classical daughter once—perhaps—who ministered to her father in his prison as her mother had ministered to her" (273–274). Both of these passages state the strong paradox that the female child is the mother of its own father. They identify Clennam, the lover, with Mr. Dorrit; and in both cases the emphasis on the innocence of the act of nursing suggests the probable incestuousness of one or both of these relationships.[41]

At the same time, this transformation of irreversible parent-child relations into reversible and incestuous relations, both for Clennam and for Little Dorrit, works as a negation of sexuality insofar as it sublimates Little Dorrit as a de-eroticized mother figure. In this sense it completes the lack left by Mrs. Clennam's vacating of the position of mother, and it reinforces that predominant Dickensian myth of the foundling who has lost its real parents. But if the sublimation accords closely with the official moral ethos of the novel, it nevertheless fails to displace Mrs. Clennam from her generically and symbolically central role as a type of that other, randomly evoked figure of the suckling mother: the Capitoline she-wolf (668). Equally threatening is the motherless lesbian, Miss Wade, whose "History of a Self-Tormentor" directly contradicts the moral authority of the narrative discourse by developing a set of incompatible counterreadings. Only since Dostoevsky, however, has it been possible for the seriousness of the moral melodrama built around Miss Wade and Tattycoram to be appreciated.

The other way in which the Gothic register allows for internal contra-diction is a function of its position outside the representational mainstream of the nineteenth-century realist novel. Henry James expressed this neatly when he wrote of *Our Mutual Friend* that it is "so intensely *written*, so little seen, known, or felt," and contrasted the "habitual probable of nature" to the "habitual impossible of Mr. Dickens."[42] Consider the following passage:

> As he went along, upon a dreary night, the dim streets by which he went, seemed all depositories of oppressive secrets. The deserted counting-houses, with their secrets of books and papers locked up in chests and safes; the banking-houses, with their secrets of strong rooms and wells, the keys of which were in a very few secret pockets and a very few secret breasts; the secrets of all the dispersed grinders in the vast mill, among whom there were doubtless plunderers, forg-ers, and trust-betrayers of many sorts, whom the light of any day that dawned might reveal; he could have fancied that these things, in hiding, imparted a heaviness to the air. The shadow thickening and thickening as he approached its source, he thought of the secrets of the lonely church-vaults, where the people who had hoarded and secreted in iron coffers were in their turn similarly hoarded, not yet at rest from doing harm; and then of the secrets of the river, as it rolled its turbid tide between two frowning wildernesses of secrets, extending, thick and dense, for many miles, and warding off the free air and the free country swept by winds and wings of birds. (596–597)

The reality effects of this text—the structure of images imbued with a particular moral ethos—are effects specific to the Gothic genre. That genre constructs an order which emphasizes the subjective apprehension of a threatening environment, and the main verb of each of these three sentences is a verb of subjective perception: the streets "seemed" to Clennam; he "could have fancied"; "he thought of." By means of these verbs the text moves outward from the indicative mood to the subjunctive mood, and this movement toward the realm of the possible is constructed on a framework of Gothic *topoi*: crime, shadow, church vaults, graves, the river. In this process language takes on a large degree of autonomy, building up alternative worlds on the basis of collocations which are conventional for the genre. It is the stylized discursive patterns of the genre, in other words, which enable the solidification of a reality which is clearly based in the rhetorical play of language: in the repetition of the word *secret*; in the assonance of "winds and wings of birds"; in the concealed iambic pentameters of the second half of the third sentence. In this mode the claim to linguistic transparency is considerably weaker than in what we have come to think of as the classic nineteenth-century realist text—which may mean that we have misjudged the extent to which not only the novels of Dickens but other "realist" texts as well foreground the discursive status of their reality effects.

This autonomization of language is of course not restricted to the Gothic genre, although it is arguable that the peculiar ontology of the Gothic mode provided much of the antirepresentational impetus of Dickens's writing. Much of the comic force of his novels depends on a similar process of literalization of the hypothetical or the figurative. For example, young John Chivery is described by his mother as sitting among the clotheslines in his back yard because "he feels as if it was groves" (303). The phrase is later quoted literally by the narrator: "Here the good woman pointed to the little window, whence her son might be seen sitting disconsolate in the tuneless groves" (304). A more extended example of this playing of literal against figurative meanings is the description of Mr. F.'s Aunt,

> an amazing little old woman, with a face like a staring wooden doll too cheap for expression, and a stiff yellow wig perched unevenly on the top of her head, as if the child who owned the doll had driven a tack through it anywhere, so that it only got fastened on. Another remarkable thing in this little old woman was, that the same child seemed to have damaged her face in two or three places with some blunt instrument in the nature of a spoon; her countenance, and

particularly the tip of her nose, presenting the phenomena of several
dints, generally answering to the bowl of that article.   (198)

Here the initial analogy with a doll generates a supposititious owner of the
doll who is then linked with a series of predicates; and this chain moves
so far away from the original figurative status of the association that Mr.
F.'s Aunt does indeed assume the qualities of the doll, and becomes the
inhabitant of an uncertain realm somewhere between the animate and the
inanimate. A similar process turns Mrs. Merdle synecdochically into a
"Bosom" and by a further metonymic extension into a display case for
jewelry (293).[43]

Through these devices the novel is able to a certain extent to subvert
that monolithic moral reality carried predominantly (but contradictorily)
by the Gothic mode. This subversion is in fact thematized in *Little Dorrit*
through the opposition of official to nonofficial linguistic forms. Official
language is conceived in terms of the avoidance of the taboo: Dorrit erects
a wall of "genteel fictions," "elaborate forms," and "ceremony and pre-
tence" against his knowledge that his daughters work (114); and after the
family's rise to wealth, Fanny, speaking in accordance with Mrs. General's
regime of linguistic censorship, refers to Clennam as "that very objec-
tionable and unpleasant person, who, with a total absence of all delicacy,
which our experience might have led us to expect from him, insulted us
and outraged our feelings in so public and wilful a manner on an occasion
to which it is understood among us that we will not more pointedly allude"
(506). Circumlocution of this order becomes a generalized social theme
in the description of the Circumlocution Office: the self-perpetuation of
the governing class depends upon the self-perpetuating proliferation of
bureaucratic language.

These forms of the official are adequately treated at an overt thematic
level. A more important subversion of the ideological authority of monologic forms of language occurs through the value given to the opposition
between written and spoken forms, and in particular the stress on idio-
syncratic styles of speech, either directly represented or incorporated into
the narrative discourse. The speech of many of the lower-class characters—
for example the Plornishes—is a deformation of standard forms and so
works both as parody and as a simple comic incongruity. The really complex idiolects are those of Flora and Mr. F.'s Aunt. Flora's rambling strings
of free association are almost impenetrable because she in fact speaks both
parts of a dialogue. This means that she can assume total comprehension

of her presuppositions because there is no need of a response from the actual interlocutor, whom she uses as a prop. In the case of Mr. F.'s Aunt this tendency to hermeticism becomes complete. This lady had "a propensity to offer remarks in a deep warning voice, which, being totally uncalled for by anything said by anybody, and traceable to no association of ideas, confounded and terrified the mind. Mr. F.'s Aunt may have thrown in these observations on some system of her own, and it may have been ingenious, or even subtle: but the key to it was wanted" (199). The failure of signification undermines the rationality of the novel's moral universe as a kind of threatening madness. And it is in this very opacity of the signifier that much of the violence and the neurotic energy that underlie the text are able to rise to the surface.

It is in the articulation of different modes of language, different registers, that the reality effects and the fiction effects of the literary text are generated. This articulation involves relations of dominance and subordination between registers, and this clash of languages is a clash of realities—that is, of moral universes. The text can be defined as the process of these relations of discursive contradiction; and it is here that ideological value is confirmed or challenged, and textual historicity generated.

7

Text and System

Borges's "Pierre Menard, Author of *Don Quixote*" is a perfectly serious joke that we are still learning how to take seriously.[1] This story of an obscure provincial "novelist" who by an immense labor (the traces of which are lost) managed to produce a fragmentary text coinciding completely, at the verbal level, with several chapters of *Don Quixote* has usually been read as a meditation on the nature of reading and the nature of authorship. Macherey and Mike Gane both stress that Menard's enterprise "poses the question of reading in the most active possible manner: writing."[2] Alicia Borinsky notes that it "puts into play the question of authorship as the production of voice and, in doing so . . . questions the kind of continuity that exists between that hypothetical voice and its discourse" (although she herself then restores the ontological link between author and text by reconstructing the voice of "Borges" as that of "the aristocracy of intelligence in Argentine political history").[3] But in another sense the question of authorship is quite secondary. It is true that the narrator locates the difference between the two texts within a biographical framework; but his explanation of why it is that "the text of Cervantes and that of Menard are verbally identical, but the second is almost infinitely richer" (Borges, 49) is made in terms of the different systems of intertextuality within which the second is inscribed. Thus its disdainful avoidance of the Hispanicizing exoticism popularized by Mérimée "indicates a new approach to the historical novel. This disdain condemns *Salammbô,* without appeal" (48). The apparent anachronism of the discourse on arms and letters is explained by reference to "the influence of Nietzsche" (48). And the address to "truth, whose mother is history," which in the seventeenth-century text is "a mere rhetorical eulogy of history," becomes in the twentieth-century text, written by "a contemporary of William James," a radical epistemological proposition (49).

The point is surely that, once we have disposed of the red herring of authorship, what is at stake is the historicity of a single, verbally self-identical text; what the parable suggests is that "textual 'identity' under changing conditions becomes 'difference.' "[4] The question I deliberately begged in the last chapter, which dealt with "internally" constructed intertextual structures, was that of those intertextual relations not constructed or controlled by the text. This is the question of the instability of the "internal," the fact that intrinsic structures are not given but are variably constructed in accordance with changing intertextual relations. Let me propose, schematically, that every text is marked by a multiple temporality: the time of its production (the "internal" time of its rewriting or repetition of prevailing literary and ideological norms), and the times of its reception (in which this textual process is transformed by its entry into new intertextual relationships). The serial or lateral movement of a text between systems produces new texts, and new kinds of text. Such a formulation should in principle preclude an ontological definition of literary function, and Bennett in fact argues that it opens the way to a properly Marxist theorization of the extended production of literary discourse. The value and function of texts should "be viewed differently according to the different places they occupied within the received cultures of different societies and different historical periods," and "literariness" would depend primarily "not on the formal properties of a text in themselves but on the position which those properties establish for the text within the matrices of the prevailing ideological field. Literariness resides, not in the text, but in the relations of inter-textuality inscribed within and between texts."[5]

The force of this is to build into Marxist theory a fuller conception of the historicity of the text, accounting not merely for its pastness but also for its productive interaction with historically distinct systems. It is not a question of denying the specific difference of literary texts from other language types but rather of constructing this difference as an object of historical understanding and of accounting for its effect in each case on the selection and semantic transformation of the literary corpus. And it is because the literariness of a text, its very existence *as* a "literary" text, is not an innate property that methodological priority must be given to the literary system or systems in which it is assigned its function. The mode of operation of a text cannot be pregiven by the structure of the genre since relations of signification, and hence the status of genre conventions themselves, are prescribed within a specific social articulation of discursive functions.

Thus the following texts[6] are all realizations of the "same" genre conventions and even of the "same" initial production:

> . . . so full of bloud, of dust, of darts, lay smit
> Divine Sarpedon that a man must have an excellent wit
> That could but know him; and might fail—so from his
>   utmost head
> Even to the low plants of his feet his forme was altered.
> All thrusting neare it every way, as thick as flies in spring   5
> That in a sheepe-cote (when new milke assembles them)
>   make wing
> And buzze about the top-full pailes. Nor ever was the eye
> Of Jove averted from the fight; he viewd, thought ceaselessly
> And diversly upon the death of great Achilles' friend—
> If Hector there (to wreake his sonne) should with his javelin
>   end   10
> His life and force away his armes, or still augment the field.
> He then concluded that the flight of much more soule
>   should yeeld
> Achilles' good friend more renowne, and that even to their
>   gates
> He should drive Hector and his host; and so disanimates
> The mind of Hector that he mounts his chariot and takes
>   Flight   15
> Up with him.
>
> (Chapman, *Homer's Iliad,* Book 16)

> Now great *Sarpedon,* on the sandy Shore,
> His heav'nly Form defac'd with Dust and Gore,
> And stuck with Darts by warring Heroes shed;
> Lies undistinguish'd from the vulgar dead.
> His long-disputed Corpse the Chiefs inclose.   5
> On ev'ry side the busy Combate grows;
> Thick, as beneath some Shepherd's thatch'd Abode,
> The Pails high-foaming with a milky Flood,
> The buzzing Flies, a persevering Train,
> Incessant swarm, and chas'd, return again.   10
>   *Jove* view'd the Combate with a stern Survey,
> And Eyes that flash'd intolerable Day;
> Fix'd on the Field his Sight, his Breast debates
> The Vengeance due, and meditates the Fates;
> Whether to urge their prompt Effect, and call   15

The Force of *Hector* to *Patroclus'* Fall,
This Instant see his short-liv'd Trophies won,
And stretch him breathless on his slaughter'd Son;
Or yet, with many a Soul's untimely flight,
Augment the Fame and Horror of the Fight?   20
To crown *Achilles'* valiant Friend with Praise
At length he dooms; and that his last of Days
Shall set in Glory; bids him drive the Foe;
Nor unattended, see the Shades below.
Then *Hector's* Mind he fills with dire dismay;   25
He mounts his Car, and calls his Hosts away.

(Pope, *The Iliad of Homer,* Book 16)

And now not even a clear-sighted man could any longer have known
noble Sarpedon, for with darts and blood and dust was he covered
wholly from head to foot. And ever men thronged about the dead,
as in a steading flies buzz around the full milk-pails, in the season of
spring when the milk drenches the bowls, even so thronged they
about the dead. Nor ever did Zeus turn from the strong fight his
shining eyes, but ever looked down on them, and much in his heart
he debated of the slaying of Patroklos, whether there and then above
divine Sarpedon glorious Hector should slay him likewise in strong
battle with the sword, and strip his harness from his shoulders, or
whether to more men yet he should deal sheer labour of war. And
thus to him as he pondered it seemed the better way, that the gallant
squire of Achilles, Peleus' son, should straightway drive the Trojans
and Hector of the helm of bronze towards the city and should rob
many of their life. And in Hector first he put a weakling heart, and
leaping into his car Hector turned in flight.

(Lang, Leaf, and Myers, *Iliad,* Book 16)

        No longer
could a man, even a knowing one, have made out the godlike
Sarpedon, since he was piled from head to ends of feet under
a mass of weapons, the blood and the dust, while others
    about him
kept forever swarming over his dead body, as flies   5
through a sheepfold thunder about the pails overspilling
milk, in the season of spring when the milk splashes in the
    buckets.
So they swarmed over the dead man, nor did Zeus ever
turn the glaring of his eyes from the strong encounter,

but kept gazing forever upon them, in spirit reflective,   10
and pondered hard over many ways for the death of
    Patroklos;
whether this was now the time, in this strong encounter
when there over godlike Sarpedon glorious Hektor
should kill him with the bronze, and strip the armour away
    from his shoulders,
or whether to increase the steep work of fighting for more
    men.   15
In the division of his heart this way seemed best to him,
for the strong henchman of Achilleus, the son of Peleus,
once again to push the Trojans and bronze-helmed Hektor
back on their city, and tear the life from many. In Hektor
first of all he put a temper that was without strength.   20
He climbed to his chariot and turned to flight, and called to
    the other
Trojans to run.

                    (Lattimore, *The Iliad of Homer*, Book 16)

And nobody, including those who saw him lie,
A waxen god asleep on his outstretched hand,
Could know him now.

> *But if you can imagine how*
> *Each evening when the dairy pails come in*   5
> *Innumerable flies throng around*
> *The white ruff of the milk,*
> *You will have some idea of how the Greeks and Trojans*
> *Clouded about Sarpedon's body.*

And all this time God watched his favourite enemies: 10
Considering. Minute Patroclus, a fleck
Of spinning radium on his right hand—
Should he die now? Or push the Trojans back still more?
And on his left, Prince Hector, like a golden mote—
Should he become a coward for an hour   15
And run for Troy while Patroclus steals Sarpedon's gear
That glistens like the sea at early morning?

    The left goes down.
In the half-light Hector's blood turned milky
    And he ran for Troy.   20

                    (Logue, *Patrocleia of Homer*)

To these I might have added Maginn's 1850 translation of passages of the *Odyssey* into an archaicizing ballad form; Worsley's translation of the *Odyssey* into Spenserian stanzas (1861); Mackail's Pre-Raphaelite version of the *Odyssey* (1903); and Rouse's (1938) and Rieu's (1950) renditions of the Homeric epics as novels of action. But these few examples will suffice to demonstrate the ways in which the "same" text is a radically different piece of poetry in the context of different systems. The question of the relationship of these texts to an "original" text is not irrelevant, but this original is not the notional Homer of the eighth or ninth century B.C., not an author or a text situated at a fixed (and unreconstructable) point of origin; it is a sixteenth- or an eighteenth- or a twentieth-century "Homer," a particular mode of authority of the classical.

The texts demonstrate too the extent to which this mode of authority is fused with the major ideological categories of particular social formations; as this authority decays, the fusion becomes less intrinsic, and translation becomes an active recuperation of social content, until in the final text the diminished authority of the classical allows it to be used in direct contradiction to other modes of social authority, including its own vestigial academic prestige.

Chapman's text is imbued with a metaphysical conception of human agency: this concern is realized through the use of key ambiguities ("plants," a lexeme which is now obsolete but which must, even in the early seventeenth century, have functioned as a latent organic pun; "forme," which is ambivalently a material and a spiritual concept; and "disanimates / The mind of Hector," in which the strong presence of the Latin root tends to override the literal sense and foreground the tension between human agency and divine intervention); through a syntax which depends heavily on the use of nontransactive verbs ("lay smit," "was altered"), which replaces the main verb of the second sentence with a present participle, and which elides the warriors in the indeterminate "all"; and through the allegorization of "Flight."

Pope's text works through a categorical framework which opposes and relates glory to death and then overlays this opposition with the dichotomized categories of social class: Sarpedon's "heav'nly Form" loses all rank and distinction to become one with the "vulgar dead." Patroclus, by contrast, balances the categories: "Trophies," "Fame," "Praise," and "Glory" are played against "short-liv'd," "Horror," and "his last of Days / Shall set"; this balancing means both the triumph of social hierarchy over death ("Nor unattended, see the Shades below") and yet also, in the dialectical perspective of a second reading, the opposite of this: death destroys social status, *and* social status survives death. This effect, or this *expectation,* of detached equivocality is achieved in part through the exploitation of syntactic ambiguity, especially in the use of participles ("high-foaming," "Fix'd") and causal sequencing ("To crown . . . he dooms," "and that . . . bids him"). "Thick" in line 7 refers both backward to "Combate" and forward to "Flies," and in this transition the individual warriors are subsumed within the two moments of the metaphor: the hypostatized action, which "grows" and is "busy," and the train of flies, a thoroughly Popean image of the disaffected mob. The vantage point here is that of Jove, an absolute monarch who is nevertheless subject to the ultimate constitutional check of the Fates.

The Lang, Leaf, and Myers translation is much less confident about its own social relevance; it is an ornamental text insofar as it uses Anglo-Saxon heroic models which certainly "translate" Homer but do so into categories which are dead. Zeus dealing "sheer labour of war," for example, is dubious because it is imitating an archaic concept of fate. Archaism both of vocabulary ("darts," "steading," "helm") and syntax ("was he covered," "even so thronged they") is the predominant stylistic feature, and its effect is to increase radically the redundancy of the text. In the extended simile there is a double stylistic tautology: "ever men thronged about the dead" / "even so thronged they about the dead"; "the full milk-pails, in the season of spring" / "when the milk drenches the bowls." The chiasmic geometry of the simile is autonomized and frozen by its lack of any function except self-reference. Surface elegance screens an underlying incoherence. Where the previous texts had drawn up a balance sheet of honor and death, here it simply "seemed" to Zeus "the better way." Similarly the nominalized form "the slaying of Patroklos" blurs considerations of tense and causality.

Lattimore's text relies much less on surface archaism, but it is equally academic and in fact it follows closely the syntax of Lang, Leaf, and Myers. In the extended simile, "steading" is replaced by "sheepfold," which is modern English; "bowls" by "buckets," which is comprehensible; and "buzz" by "thunder," which is stronger but less appropriate. But the structure of chiasmic repetition remains unchanged. Lattimore's hexameter attempts a partial recuperation of an oral mode—through the use of feminine endings, spondaic feet ("more men," "steep work"), repetition ("forever . . . ever . . . forever," "strong encounter"), and formulaic epithet ("the strong henchman of Achilleus, the son of Peleus"); but these devices serve only to underline the distance between the two texts and the subordination of the later piece of writing to an alien text.

Logue's *Patrocleia,* by contrast, actively insists on its difference from this alien text, and uses anachronism as a way of identifying the authority of the classical with the ideologies of militarism and patriarchy. The text is a countertext, a deconstruction (but also an explication) of the social force of a literary norm. The fragmentation of epic homogeneity is achieved through a juxtaposition of lyrical discourse with politicized techniques of disruption. On the one hand lyrical cohesion is established through the binding together of chains of imagery which integrate the extended simile into its context: "clouded" not only refers to the mass of flies/warriors (this perspective is extended and defined in the wanton God's consideration of the "fleck" and "mote") but also picks up the opacity of "milk," which then goes forward to "Hector's blood turned milky," and perhaps also to the "half-light." Yet the simile is detached from its context, not only graphically but also by the stress on its rhetorical function ("if you can imagine how"). The play of perspectives, corresponding partly to the paragraphing, is of a novelistic complexity: line 1 particularizes point of view to participants in the action, and so subjectivizes the metaphor of the (syntactically ambiguous) second line. Line 4 reasserts narratorial objectivity. The third paragraph switches to the vantage point of a detached God, but also sets up a tension with the irony of "favourite enemies" and the intrusively figurative language of "spinning radium," "like a golden mote," and "that glistens like the sea at early morning." The lineation of the last paragraph then switches the perspective to that of a detached commentator undermining heroic rhetoric.

Five different Homers, then: five modes of collusion and conflict between social categories and an economy of literary conventions which works these categories and which also, especially in the later texts, works their refraction and their consolidation in previous literary economies. Translation makes the point neatly; but the same is true of a single linguistically constant text in its passage through time. *Don Quixote* is a component of every subsequent Spanish literary system, and to a lesser degree of most subsequent European systems, but it is a slightly different text in each case. This productive power of the literary system (the system is of course also partly produced by the tradition it incorporates) means that it cannot simply be defined empirically as a collection of texts. The system is rather a normative regime, a semantic code which governs the nature and the limits of literariness and the relations of signification which are socially possible and legitimate for the genres it recognizes. It produces new texts, and new texts from old texts, and new ways of reading and writing and framing texts; but since the invention of Literature some time in the eighteenth century, it has also produced the appearance of the universality and autonomy of the literary text.

LET ME RECALL the three levels at which Tynjanov defines the concept of system. It refers in the first instance to the literary text as a hierarchically ordered structure of elements. But the text is constituted as such only in its intertextual relation to the codes of the literary system, and in particular in its integration to the subsystem of the codes of genre. At a third level the text and the literary system are defined, given a determinate shape and function, through their relation to the "system of systems"—let us say their interdiscursive relation to other signifying formations and to the institutions and practices in which these are articulated. At each of these levels the concept of system works dynamically: time is a structural component of the system in the form of a play of actual or potential discontinuity between the levels of code and message.

I have suggested that the concept of literary system is equivalent to that of a discursive formation. But it should be clear that the mode of existence of the formation is not "merely" discursive, or rather that discourse is defined in such a way as to include its particular conditions of possibility: it constitutes a complex unity of semantic material, rhetorical modes, forms of subjectivity and agency, rules of availability, specific discursive practices, and specific institutional sites. All of these may overlap with the constituents of other discursive formations, and any formation will tend to be internally contradictory: the space of a discursive system is not unitary or homogeneous. What binds it together, more or less, is the normative authority it wields as an institution, an authority which is more or less strictly exercised and which is always the attempted imposition of a centralizing unity rather than the achieved fact of such a unity. Institutional authority, which by definition is asymmetrically distributed between "central" and "marginal" members of the institution, is deployed in particular to maintain the purity and the solidity of boundaries, and this involves both defining appropriate and inappropriate practices of language and restricting access to these practices to certified or qualified agents. The converse of this is the establishment of the "internal" categories of the institution as a particular range of possible functions. In the case of the literary system this means defining the functions of author, reader, and text and the possible relations between them; and delimiting the specificity of literary discourse, as though it were ontologically grounded. In terms of this normative regulation (and despite the diversity of the literary genres) the "literary" is reified as a distinct and unitary language game, and the logics of its forms (its genres, its rhetorical strategies and densities, its degrees of "keying")[7] are coded as being appropriate to the institution.

Peter Bürger has described in similar terms the conditions of constitution of the aesthetic:

> Works of art are not received as single entities, but within institutional frameworks and conditions that largely determine the function of the works. When one refers to the function of an individual work, one generally speaks figuratively; for the consequences that one may observe and infer are not primarily a function of its special qualities but rather of the manner which regulates the commerce with works of this kind in a given society or in certain strata or classes of a society. I have chosen the term "institution of art" to characterize such framing conditions.[8]

But rather than describing the full set of social practices and conditions which govern the commerce with and constitution of the work of art, Bürger tends to equate the institution with a particular set of discourses about art (manifestos, for example) which, as aesthetic ideologies, are only a part of the total aesthetic apparatus. As a counterexample it might be worthwhile to consider briefly the systemic conditions of constitution of the Homeric texts.

Marthe Robert gives an incisive account, in *The Old and the New,* of their contradictory activations in antiquity. The primary function of the epics is pedagogic: they are thought to incorporate a code of morality, a summary of wisdom, a compendium of the most varied forms of knowledge, and information about the smallest details of life. Even Plato, in the *Protagoras,* recommends that the teacher have his students learn by heart the "works of good poets" in which "they meet with many admonitions, many descriptions and praises and eulogies of good men in times past, that the boy in envy may imitate them and yearn to become even as they."[9] In daily life the Homeric texts have almost the force of law. At the same time, however, this pedagogic authority is contested by the existence in antiquity of a tradition of logical and moral criticism of the texts. It is in order to close off this contradiction that the texts are reconstituted within a new institution of reading: that of allegorical exegesis. Here "Homer" is construed as the author of scientific, philosophical, mystical, or political treatises *disguised* as works of fiction. The distinction between the letter (the textual surface) and the inner meaning, corresponding to a further distinction between the ordinary (naive) and the initiated reader, makes possible a sacralization of the texts which endows them with the highest conceivable spiritual authority (they are constituted as Scriptures) (83). This exegetical activity is the basis for a succession of later exegetical practices: the great Alexandrine commentaries, for example; the syntheses of neo-Platonism and Christianity in the allegorizing recuperations of Homer for the Renaissance; or the contemporary research of philologists, archaeologists, and anthropologists. One of the most important changes of direction was that brought about by the radical historicism of nineteenth-century philology. This new paradigm of reading constructed the Homeric epics as the manifestation of the spirit of a folk, which entailed redefining the author function in such a way that it could be filled by a group ("the people") rather than an individual. In addition, the Romantic revolution stressed the Aryan origins of the epic (which it read through the model of folklore) and established strict concordances between all the European epic cycles (86): hence the Victorian translators' use of Anglo-Saxon heroic models, and the dispute between Newman and Arnold as to whether the ballad form is the appropriate vehicle for capturing the primitive purity of the Greek epics.[10] The dominant metaphor here is that of the "childhood of humanity," the organic historicism of which has plagued Marxist literary theory ever since Marx used the phrase (it is drawn directly from Hegel's *Ästhetik*) in a famous passage of the *Grundrisse*.[11]

Moral and exegetical pedagogy have been the most important supports of the different regimes of reading through which the Homeric texts have been variously constituted; but other institutional bases have at different times provided their conditions of possibility. One of the most recently excavated is that of the tradition of bardic recitation. As a result of the work of Milman Parry and Albert Lord (originally on twentieth-century Yugoslavian epic recitation), we now have a very different understanding both of the mode of composition (cumulative, formulaic, dependent on particular mnemonic trainings, and fusing the functions of author and performer) and of the conditions of enunciation of the Greek epic cycles (ritual recitations in an oral, preliterate culture, with a mix of functions including the repetition/commemoration of a stable world order, the filiation of the present with this past order, together with various profane informative functions).[12] A complementary account (for example Charles Autran, *Homère et les origines sacerdotales de l'épopée,* summarized in Robert, 89–91) stresses the cultic function of the epics and their close link with the caste of priests. The poems are written (composed) in a language which was *always* archaic and archaicizing, an artificial composite of different dialects drawn from the ritual language of the cults. In this perspective, the epics combine the functions of religious propaganda and legitimation of the nobility; they appear as "a collection of pious legends, designed to perpetuate the continuity of the great heroic families, which take pains to establish their divine ancestry" (91). Hence the structural importance of genealogies and nomenclatures, "which prove by continuity of lineage the theocratic origins of the aristocracy and royalty." In short: "Composed on command and according to absolutely fixed rules, the epic contains only the truth of the priestly caste on which it depended. This caste exploited the prestige and the influence of poetry, and expressed in turn its solidarity with a political and social system—the aristocracy—identified with the order of the world" (91).

But it must be stressed that this function of class legitimation is a recurrent function of the Homeric epics, not necessarily in terms of any inherent formal or thematic properties but purely and simply through their fetishized value as the Classic. Pope's translation appropriates their prestige for the culture of a restored aristocracy. At the height of the British Empire the classics continue to form the basis of the civil service entry examinations,[13] and in both England and France constitute the major point of distinction between the "elaborated" and "restricted" training offered by the secondary and primary schooling systems.[14] Rather than having a continuous value (or manifesting a "transcendence of historical conditions"), the Homeric epics are one of the means by which claims to cultural and hence political continuity are validated. Two contradictory moments of this process of constant retotalization and reintegration of the past into a qualitatively different present are, on the one hand, the cultural renaissances in which new class ideologies seek a legitimation and an expressive "mask" in material from a different period, and on the other hand, the ideological mechanisms of eternalization—the museum, the school text, the reference book, the television adaptation—which strip the "masterpieces" of their specific historical differences. It is the clarification of these mechanisms that becomes relevant, since, in Macherey's words: "Homer's *Iliad,* the 'work' of an 'author' exists only for us, and in relation to new material conditions into which it has been reinscribed and reinvested with a new significance: however odd it may seem, it did not exist for the Greeks and the problem of its conservation is thus not a relevant one. To go further: it is as if we ourselves had written it (or at least composed it anew)."[15]

The forms of rewriting of the Homeric texts differ radically with the historically different forms of literary system in which they occur, but in all cases the rewriting is the result of a complex articulation of the literary system with other institutions (the school, religion), institutionalized practices (moral or religious training, commemoration, or else a relatively autonomous aesthetic function), and other discursive formations (religious, scientific, ethical). The ties between the literary system and its institutional bases may be close or they may be relatively loose, and the functions of the system are not necessarily homogeneous. But the system is always a network of norms and of processes and sites for the implementation (or contestation) of these norms.

What the literary system crucially governs are ways of reading, the interpretive grids through which texts are constituted. The concept of reading and of the reading subject has been the focus of intensive theorization in recent years, but it is also the site of an extraordinary lack of clarity. The status of "the reader" has been especially murky. The commonsense assumption that the reader is an empirical individual quickly leads both to an atomistic relativism and to an inability to theorize the modes of textual inscription of reading. Conversely, a concentration on this inscription can hypostatize it as an immanent textual structure and so lead both to a disregard of the differences between the uses made of texts and to a disqualification of "deviant" readings. Empirical readers, inscribed readers, and ideal or informed or normal readers all have an uncanny ability to duplicate the readings preferred by the critic.

Similarly intensive theorization of reading has taken place in communication studies, where it assumes the more general (and perhaps more urgent) form of a debate about conflicting models of the communication process. David Morley gives a useful summary of two opposed traditions. On the one hand there is that of the Frankfurt School's account of the effects of "mass culture," in which manipulative signifying practices are seen as having a relatively ineluctable and unmediated impact; and with it that of the journal *Screen* (the unification is unfair but convenient), which describes the positioning of viewers such that they are shaped as unitary subjects in the apprehension of the imaginary unity of a discourse. On the other hand there is a tradition of research into the behavioral effects of the media or into the selective use of cultural messages ("uses and gratifications" analysis); in this tradition the emphasis is on the diversity of appropriations of texts. Morley himself attempts to reconstruct a heterogeneous range of readings of a single text across a number of social groups (ambivalently classified in terms of "subculture" or of "class") and so to explore the effects of the television text at the level of "the structuring of discourses and the provision of frameworks of interpretation and meaning."[16] Part of the power of his analysis lies simply in the radical incompatibility of the twenty-eight reconstructed readings of the television program *Nationwide*. But the analysis is also theoretically provocative in its elaboration of Paul Willemen's argument for a lack of smooth fit between the subject position constructed for a viewer/reader in a particular text and the range of subject positions constructed in other discourses and practices.[17] If analysis is expanded from the "abstract signifying mechanisms" of a text toward "the field of interdiscourse in which it is situated,"[18] then it becomes clear that the text produces no *necessary* effects, since the historical "subject" exceeds the subject positions of a text:

> The "subject" exists only as the articulation of the multiplicity of particular subjectivities borne by an individual (as legal subject, familial subject, etc.), and it is the nature of this differential and contradictory positioning within the field of ideological discourse which provides the theoretical basis for the differential reading of texts and the existence of differential positions in respect to the position preferred by the text.[19]

Or more concisely, in Claire Johnston's words, "Real readers are subjects in history rather than mere subjects of a single text."[20] The problem with any such formulation, however, is that it tends easily to slip back into talk of a *non*contradictory subject, a subject unified as "real," "historical," or (for Morley) "empirical."[21] Any such realism of the subject then restores precisely that opposition of subject and object, reader and text, which, in its assumption of entities fully constituted prior to the textual process, is the major weakness of traditional theories of reading.

One of the most cogent cases against this polarity is that argued by Stanley Fish in the process of redefining his early commitment to a reader-centered aesthetic. This aesthetic had relied upon a strong demarcation between text and reader, conceived as independently constituted entities; even the relatively greater emphasis he laid upon "the structure of the reader's experience" still left intact the text/reader dichotomy. (In any case this reader was only ever *derived* from the text: at times from some "objective" structure such as an interpretive crux, at times from the absence of such a structure, as when Fish postulates "a reading that is fleetingly available, although no one has acknowledged it because it is a function not of the words on the page but of the experience of the reader.")[22] But, as Fish comes to argue, the problem with any such opposition of subject to object is that it takes for granted "the distinction between interpreters and the objects they interpret. That distinction in turn assumes that interpreters and their objects are two different kinds of *a*contextual entities, and within these twin assumptions the issue can only be one of control: will texts be allowed to constrain their own interpretation or will irresponsible interpreters be allowed to obscure and overwhelm texts?" (336). The way out of this bind is to recognize that text and reader are categories given by particular interpretive strategies, and that the criteria of interpretation are therefore internal to discourse rather than given by the reality of texts or readers (238).

Once the interpretive process is understood in this conventionalist manner, a number of interesting consequences ensue. One is that it becomes necessary to dispense with an ontologically grounded differentiation between language varieties:

> When we communicate, it is because we are parties to a set of discourse agreements which are in effect decisions as to what can be stipulated as a fact. It is these decisions and the agreement to abide by them, rather than the availability of substance, that makes it possible to refer, whether we are novelists or reporters for the *New York Times*. One might object that this has the consequence of making all discourse fictional; but it would be just as accurate to say that it makes all discourse serious, and it would be better still to say that it puts all discourse on a par.   (242)

A second consequence is that language is seen always to be determinate in relation to a particular context; it is not limitlessly plural, but it is also not *inherently* determinate. And this means that there may be a plurality of determinate and stable meanings for a plurality of contexts. Underpinning this understanding of the constitutive status of discourse is the premise that linguistic and interpretive norms "are not embedded in the language (where they may be read out by anyone with sufficiently clear, that is, unbiased, eyes) but inhere in an institutional structure within which one hears utterances as already organized with reference to certain assumed purposes and goals" (306). Reading is thus relativized to the semiotic and situational constraints of a discursive formation, the institutional dimension of which Fish calls the "interpretive community." It is this dimension which makes possible agreement and disagreement—not as relations of truth and error but as a coincidence or conflict of interpretive frames.

Fish's attempt to theorize the institutional determinants of reading through the concept of the interpretive community is seriously flawed, however, by its inability to account in any sort of political terms for contradiction within or between communities and by its disregard of the relations of power which sustain communities. A complementary theorization of reading as a semiotic institution is that of Mircea Marghescou. Noting the plurality of possible valid readings of a text, Marghescou concludes that none of them therefore has a formal necessity. What they all have in common, however, is that they insert the signifier into a new semantic field in which it tends to the realization of all its semantic possibilities. This functional constant is not an effect of the particular speech situation or of the formal structure of the message; nor is it the product of a subjective intention, because it is a shared semantic code which gives information about the operability of a text. Marghescou designates as the *regime* of a text this supralinguistic semantic code which assigns the message to its type and labels it with directions for use without specifying a particular content. In itself, he argues, the text is a purely virtual entity, and "only a regime designating the textual function through opposition to its linguistic function and above all to other possible semantic functions could give form to this virtuality, transform the linguistic form into information."[23] Unlike the phenomenological concept of an "aesthetic attitude," the regime is conceived not as a fact of consciousness, nor even as an intersubjective consensus, but as a semiotic constraint.

These formulations make it possible to consider the interpretive process in systemic terms. The regime, the semiotic institution, determines the historically specific mode of existence of texts, as well as the point at which the line between the literary and the nonliterary is drawn. Further, the categories of text, author, and reader have the status not of entities but of variable *functions;* they are products of determinate practices of reading, produced by, not given for, interpretation. These functions in turn mediate the textual transactions of real readers and writers, circumscribing both the actual operations each can perform and their representation of each other as textual functions.[24] Writer and reader are not the fixed and isolated origin and conclusion of the textual process, nor is their relationship that of a constant factor to an uncontrolled variable (as is the case with Wolfgang Iser's oscillation between and, in practice, ultimate conflation of an "implied reader," understood as an *overt*—"intended"—textual function, and a real reader external to the textual process).[25] Both "writer" and "reader" are the categories of a particular literary system and of particular regimes within it, and only as such are they amenable to theorization. But these categories are therefore unstable, and they shift in value as texts are translated from one literary system to another. Finally, interpretation, and a limited and definite range of contradictory interpretive strategies, are themselves constituted as determinate social practices within a specific historical regime. In short, the regime of reading is what allows readers to do work upon texts, to accept or transform readings offered as normative, to mesh reading with other social practices and other semiotic domains, and indeed to formulate and reformulate the categories of the regime itself.

From this theoretical basis it becomes possible to move to a meta-interpretive level where our concern is not with the rightness or wrongness of a particular reading but with the formal and social conditions and preconditions of interpretation: that is, with an analysis of the politics of reading and the historicity of readings—the synchronic and diachronic heterogeneity of interpretation. This shift of level has been characteristic, I think, of much recent literary theory, under the double influence of structuralism's construction of its theoretical goal as a poetics rather than a practice of reading, and the demand made by reception theory that our own reading be relativized to the chain of prior interpretations. The move seems to me a positive one for two reasons: first, because of its generosity toward disparate readings, its insistence not on disqualifying invalid readings but on recognizing the politically and historically relative validity of different interpretations;[26] and second, because it opens the way to an inscription of our own situation (political, methodological, historical) in the object of analysis as a component of that object.

For Marxist criticism such a shift of level entails paying particular attention to the institutions within which literary criticism adopts the form of a practice: that is, above all, to the educational apparatuses, which promote specific forms of circulation of writing and specific valorizations of certain kinds of writing,[27] and which seek to impose a hegemonic "consensus" while making available certain possibilities of resistance. What is crucial here is that the literary system not be thought of as a monolithic unity. It is systematic only in the sense of providing a space of dispersion, but not in terms of any underlying epistemic coherence; certainly there is no necessary structural or functional homology between discursive formations.

Tony Bennett has used the concept of a reading formation to theorize the construction of text-reader relations within contradictory interpretive frames (and in particular to theorize "the necessary disparity which exists between the discourses of criticism and the reading formations, circulating outside the academy, through which popular reading is organized").[28] His argument is directed against that sleight of hand by which particular class-specific discourses of value elevate their criteria of judgment into universally normative principles which can be appealed to against the criteria of other, contradictory discourses of value. Bennett's interest is in the rim of social and institutional conditions governing interpretation, and in the political possibility of choice between one socioepistemological frame and another. But a possible consequence of this stress is that the details of any particular interpretation will be seen as relatively unimportant to the extent that they will be derivable from the hermeneutic protocols given as the preconditions of reading. The question of what happens within an interpretive frame once it is chosen or imposed is left open: it is a technical question, a question of application or realization.

Against any such objectification of the conditions of reading and valuation one must stress that aesthetic judgment is always a judgment about the determinate ideological force to be attached to an utterance in a particular historical conjuncture. Value and meaning can be read off neither from the "text itself" nor from the rules of a reading formation, because the act of judgment involved is situational, political, and itself helps to construct "the text," the interpretive frame, and an overlapping but contradictory relation to competing interpretive positions. Clearly this varies historically: some frames are more rigid than others, and different kinds of text tend to demand more or less work of the reader. But in all cases the interpretive frame is not simply *prior* to particular readings, inexorably governing them, but is inferred, guessed at, constituted by a reading. Interpretive frames are fuzzy and continuously negotiable; and any account of the literary system needs to be accompanied by a continuous deconstruction of the concept of system.

THIS EMPHASIS on the textuality of knowledge involves at the same time an expansion of the concept of text. Rather than being thought as a fixed entity with a definite structure, the text is conceived of as shifting and unstable, a system of relations continuously and variably interrelated with other systems of different orders. Textuality thus becomes a function of an intertextual network and of the institutions (the literary system, the regime of reading, the codes of genre) through which this network is constructed and either maintained or shifted.

The focus of analysis is then turned to the multiplicity of constructions of textuality, both diachronically, as the serial reinscriptions of the text, and synchronically, as the contradictory modes of its social constitution.

"The text" is not separate from these variant constitutions and their determinants, and its "meaning" becomes a function not of its origin but of its multiple historicities.

In the last section of this chapter I want to examine the process of intertextual inscription through which the novels of the Australian writer Frank Hardy, and especially his first novel, *Power Without Glory,* have been constituted as social texts. *Power Without Glory* is a social-realist novel based in part on the life of John Wren, a politically powerful boss of organized illegal gambling in Australia. It was published in 1950, at the height of the Cold War, and the communist Hardy was prosecuted for libel in a trial whose political resonances were heightened by impending legislation to outlaw the Australian Communist Party.

Hardy's novels have proved notoriously difficult for orthodox literary history to handle. Adrian Mitchell, writing the fiction section of the *Oxford History of Australian Literature,* uses the reductive categories of school, movement, and tradition as tools with which to denounce "the propagandist intentions of socialist realism." Hardy "is altogether too programmatic, and shows little sensitivity to writing. In some respects he is hardly a novelist at all. *Power Without Glory* (1950) is a long-winded, ambitious documentary study of corruption and extortion, clumsy in structure and style, and only partly salvaged by Hardy's moral fervour. His true ear is for the anecdote, the pub yarn." In the later novel *But the Dead Are Many* "the supervising pattern is so tight that the novel appears to exist for the fugue form, rather than to derive advantage from it. The contrapuntal action and the characters' self-preoccupation fail to interest because in the first place the characters are themselves uninteresting. Only towards the end does the pressure of real feeling begin to emerge." And the achievement of works in this tradition is put "in its proper literary perspective," finally, by reference to the novels and short stories of Christina Stead, Martin Boyd, Hal Porter, and Patrick White.[29]

The perspective and the sociocritical assumptions at work here are in no way different from those employed twenty years earlier by H. M. Green in his *History of Australian Literature*. Green wrote of *Power Without Glory* that

> it is written to a formula, and its men and women are little more than factors in an equation, so that, though extremely vigorous and by no means without bloodshed, it is a bloodless story; a number of leading politicians and other public men are introduced with little

disguise, but none of them is really alive. Crammed with action and incident, the book is almost structureless and quite without perspective and the style is crude and commonplace, so that it is monotonous and dull; nevertheless, it has sincerity and force, and there is no doubt about its author's talent, if he cared to devote it to literature instead of social propaganda.[30]

Finally, to stress that, while judgments of value may vary slightly, the theoretical framework underlying these literary histories remains constant, here is Harry Heseltine writing in Geoffrey Dutton's *Literature of Australia:*

> After the lapse of a decade, the impact of *Power Without Glory* has considerably diminished. Yet it still impresses as an honest, if clumsy, piece of work, unquestionably inspired by sincere indignation and a desire for reform. Hardy's chief literary strategy is thoroughly familiar in Australian writing—documentation, depending on an overwhelming accumulation of detail. Fiction, under the weight of such a technique, can easily collapse into a mass of undiscriminated data, unless it is buttressed by the author's immediate and passionate interest in his material. Hardy has enough of that kind of interest to retain for *Power Without Glory* some lasting merit as a work of art; its importance as a document in social history may in the long run be even greater.[31]

These judgments, made within the terms of a shared liberal-humanist ideology, hold in common these presuppositions: that there is a clear distinction between an aesthetic and a documentary function of texts; that ethical values are a proper component of the aesthetic function, but political values are not; that aesthetic worth is in part determined by the ethical commitment (the "sincerity") of the author; and that narrated subjects must be so constructed as to attract empathetic identification. More fundamental than all of these, however, is the assumption that the proper task of the literary historian is not the examination of the function of cultural capital within a social formation but its evaluation; and what is evaluated is a firmly constituted entity, "the text," whose meaning and value are objectively ascertainable and independent of what Benjamin calls the text's "afterlife" (*Nachgeschichte*).[32]

It is this problem of what constitutes "the text," and of the place it can be assigned in a historical series, that I want to examine with reference to *Power Without Glory*. A passage in Hardy's account of the prosecution of the novel for criminal libel makes it clear that the question of the relevance of context to the determination of meaning is a serious one which can be enforced by judicial as well as by academic authority:

> Judge Martin argued, "Unless reading the Author's Note is to show the intention was not to portray an actually living man; that his intention was to portray what Mr Campbell calls a composite fictional figure, that is the only reason for reading the Author's Note."
>
> "With respect," [the defense attorney] Starke said, "I cannot concede Your Honour's proposition is correct."
>
> "What do you suggest is the reason for reading the note?"
>
> "Because it has to be read—it is part of the context."
>
> "It is not part of the context at all, Mr Starke. It is not part of the book."
>
> "Your Honour, I speak of context as the whole publication—everything between the covers—and I do submit this Author's Note . . . I say with a great deal of confidence, sir, that the Author's Note should be taken or may be taken to be part of the context of the publication by the jury."
>
> But the Judge was insistent.[33]

The judge's literal insistence is one we should be wary of, because it gives legal sanction to precisely that fetishization of the text which makes possible the constitution of the "literary" as an autonomous realm with intrinsic characteristics. If we disregard his ruling, however, we might notice that many of Hardy's books (*Power Without Glory, The Hard Way, The Outcasts of Foolgarah*) contain both a fictional text and a metatext which doubles the text on a different ontological level. Correspondingly, in all the books subsequent to *Power Without Glory* there is an internal doubling of the act of writing: Paul Whittaker writes about the process of writing about his alter ego Jim Roberts in *The Four-Legged Lottery; The Hard Way* splits the author into two characters, Frank Hardy and Ross Franklyn, in an alternating narrative structure; the author F. J. Borky is seen at work in *The Outcasts of Foolgarah* on a novel which is obviously *The Outcasts of Foolgarah;* Jack self-consciously reconstructs the life of his double, John Morel, in *But the Dead Are Many;* and in *Who Shot George Kirkland?* Ross Franklyn writes about the writing of a novel called *Power Corrupts,* and after his death is doubled by a biographer who gradually comes to identify with him. Increasingly the effect of this is to produce a baroque structure of *mise-en-abyme,* a self-reflexive structure of obsessive repetition.

I use the word *repetition* here in a Freudian but not in a psychological sense, since what concerns us is a textual pattern rather than an individual act of consciousness.[34] Although the metatextual and internal doublings are synchronic in form, their persistence through a series of texts indicates that they are motivated by a diachronic relation to the traumatic moment of the publication and prosecution of *Power Without Glory*. Specifically, the later texts repeat the primal scene of that novel's exclusion from the Australian literary market in the Cold War period, and the primal ambivalence, established in the scene of the court, of the relation between the real and the fictional. In this process the "mirror" of the traditional representational novel (the one that gives a "reflection of life") is transformed into the mirror image of Frank Hardy/Ross Franklyn in *The Hard Way* and then into the multiplication of endlessly receding mirror images in *But the Dead Are Many* and *Who Shot George Kirkland?* The effect of this is to destroy the epistemological privilege of representational discourse. The text which seemed to derive its veracity from its relation to the real must now be seen as being constituted in an ambivalent relation to other levels of textuality. *Power Without Glory,* for example, is a productive transformation of "extracts from *Hansard,* from old newspapers and magazines, from Royal Commission Reports, from documents in Melbourne and Sydney libraries" (*The Hard Way,* 44) and of secondhand accounts of Wren and his period; but it mixes a novelistic discourse with a historical and a sociological discourse in such a way that language working referentially ("In 1889, the overseas price of wool fell, goods had accumulated far in excess of the market, land and property prices began to collapse") serves to validate the language of fiction ("John West was sacked, together with most of the other boot workers").[35] The appeal to a transcendental reality is a way of obliterating the novel's own status as text, and in this it merely reproduces the generic norms of the realist novel. *The Hard Way,* with its mixture of autobiography and third-person autobiographical fiction, begins a process of playing with and undermining this mode of validation which is carried through more fully in the later texts.

The crucial question here is that of the referentiality of fictional signifiers; and at the heart of this question is that of the semiotic status of proper names. The issue is not merely an academic one: it has consequences in law. Two opposing views on the nature of fictional signification were presented at the trial. The defense argued that "by a work of fiction is meant something which is the product of the author's imagination but which does not represent an actual situation, fact or character" (*The Hard Way,* 190). A witness for the prosecution, John Wren, Jr., argued, however, that a work of fiction "is a work which can deal with real people about whom lies are written" (190). The difference is that between conceptions of discourse as primarily an act of *signification* or an act of *reference*.

The paradox is that Hardy is committed to both views. The author's note to the first edition of *Power Without Glory* outlines a Lukácsian aesthetic of representation of the "typical," the *essentially* real: "Characters—that is, people—cannot be invented, they must be based on persons drawn from real life . . . But no single person, as he exists, is concentrated or typical enough for literature; something must be added, something taken away. In every person there are characteristics typical of many people . . . Sometimes actual historical events and people will be portrayed, often composite incidents and characters" (*The Hard Way*, 196). And his career as a writer began when he was told that "literature is life" (35). In order to defend the novel, however, he was obliged to stress its difference from life, its fictionality. Yet the prosecution was in the equally difficult position of having to defend a proposition that was simultaneously true and false. In order to identify the character "John West" as a representation of John Wren, they went so far as to introduce as exhibits the "real" chair and the "real" print of Beethoven described in the novel (184). At the same time they needed to deny that Wren had committed any of the crimes attributed to West—and this involved a substantial portion of the book.

Niall Brennan summarizes the complexity of the legal issue involved by pointing out that "as it stood in the public eye, Mrs. Wren had been accused by Hardy of adultery. She could be exonerated of this charge only if it could be proved that the likeness of John West to John Wren was sufficient to implicate her; namely, if Hardy's picture of West was an accurate picture of Wren, then Mrs. Wren could say she was innocent of adultery and had therefore been libelled." The defense, however, was able to point to a number of obviously fictional incidents in the book, many of them involving crimes, and to argue that these fictional incidents "weakened the identification, rather than besmirched the character."[36]

The theoretical problem at issue here is that of the ontological realm occupied by proper names. John Searle argues in *Speech Acts* that, although proper names seem to be purely referential, to be sui generis, unique particulars, they nevertheless entail descriptive predicates; they have a function of signification as well as a referential function, and the latter depends on the former, on our ability to distinguish essential and contingent identifying descriptions. In other words, if both the speaker and the hearer associate some identifying description with the name, then the utterance of the name is sufficient to satisfy the principle of identification, for both the speaker and the hearer are able to substitute an identifying description. The utterance of the name communicates a proposition to the hearer. It is not necessary that both should supply the same identifying description, provided only that their descriptions are in fact true of the same object.

The crucial point for our purposes is that "the uniqueness and immense pragmatic convenience of proper names in our language lies precisely in the fact that they enable us to refer publicly to objects without being forced to raise issues and come to an agreement as to which descriptive characteristics exactly constitute the identity of the object. They function not as descriptions, but as pegs on which to hang descriptions."[37] It is this inherent ambiguity of the function of proper names—an ambiguity that is in sharp conflict with the precision required of legal definition—that allowed Hardy to claim in *The Hard Way* that the degree of referentiality of the character "John West" depended as much on the code of the hearer as on the code of the speaker ("I have never claimed that the characters in the book are real people but apparently some people see themselves in it. If so, certain men in high places are guilty of bribery and murder," 26).

But the ambiguity of proper names used in the everyday world is further complicated when we consider the twofold question of the status of *fictional* proper names and the status of public persons like the "legendary" John Wren—that is, a John Wren who is already partly fictional, who is known by "hearsay" and is therefore as much a cultural unit as a private person. Hardy attempts to broach the theoretical problem involved here by distinguishing between four modes of signification in the novel. We could schematize this distinction as follows:

Signifier	*Signified*
1. Real	Real
2. Fictive	Fictive
3. Fictive	Real
4. Real	Fictive

The first class would cover the use of the real name of a real person: Billy Hughes, for example. The second class covers most of the minor characters in the book: invented characters with invented names. The third class is that of the "composite fictional character": an invented name—West, Malone, Thurgood—grouping selected semes or characteristics of real people—Wren, Mannix, Theodore (an interesting case in a later novel is the fictive character "Buratakov," who is the author of a real book, *The A.B.C. of Communism*). For the fourth case Hardy gives the example of the character "Eddie Corrigan," an actual person whom Hardy inserted into a different, fictional story (*The Hard Way*, 116).

The crucial factor here, however, is that all these signifier/signified relations are bracketed within a fictional frame. The novelistic signifier is an "imitation" of another signifier, whether this be real or fictive (thus the novel's signifier "Billy Hughes" is a fictional representation of the real signifier "Billy Hughes," which in turn refers to an actual person). Brennan makes this point in relation to the third class in order to prove the referential function of these proper names:

> The names were imitated as to their initials, their vowels and their metrical structure. Closer imitation of names was hardly possible. John West seemed to be the man we all knew about. His tote was in Jackson Street, Carringbush, rather than in Johnson Street, Collingwood. The childish way in which Hardy fabricated these names— substituting even affixes like "-bush" for "-wood"—indicated either a deliberate attempt to portray a character, or else a paucity of ability to dream up his own names.[38]

But the essential point here seems to me to be the slight divergence of the fictive signifiers from the real signifiers, the difference which is constitutive of signification (as opposed to the principle of identity which is the basis of reference).

I shall draw this part of my argument to a close by suggesting that there are two overlapping ontological realms in *Power Without Glory*: the Fictive, and the Fictive Real (in which "John West" has a status similar to that of the fictional character "Richard Nixon" in Robert Coover's *Public Burning*). These realms have as their counterparts outside the novel the realm of the Real (which is always a hypothetical realm) and that of the Real Fictive: a realm in which John West replaces John Wren in the public mind; in which people report having witnessed events invented by the novelist (*The Hard Way*, 119–120); and in which a library in the Collingwood area is named the Carringbush Public Library. These categories are in fact quite different from the ontological categories informing a Lukácsian aesthetics of representation, and potentially open the way to a quite different politics of writing.

The problem of the status of fictive signification is not adequately confronted by the academic distinction between the aesthetic and the documentary, a distinction which presupposes the possibility of an unmediated representation of factuality. Nor is it adequately confronted by the court's solution of a complex ontological problem by legal fiat (a solution which led to the farce of the Australian Broadcasting Commission's filming the television series *Power Without Glory* on the basis of advice from the Attorney General that the novel had been found by a court of law to be fiction).[39] The arbitrariness of the separation of discourse into two inherently distinct realms can be easily demonstrated by reference to a book which claims to give a purely factual, documentary account of John Wren: Hugh Buggy's *The Real John Wren*.[40]

In the preface and the foreword to this book five guarantees are given for the epistemological privilege of the narrative. The first concerns Buggy's authority as an author: unlike Hardy, who relied on "gossip," he was an intimate friend of Wren's. The second is that "the author Hugh Buggy was, during his career, regarded as the doyen of journalists. He was a writer intensely interested in the first fifty years of the twentieth century and the canvas he painted was immense. He had the ability of being able to translate into his writing a vivid portrayal of the events of that period." *Ut pictura poesis:* Buggy is a better novelist than Hardy. The third credential is a social guarantee of truth: "How corrupt can a man be when he could count amongst his close associates the following friends . . ." (there follows a list including the president of the Returned Servicemen's League, the Catholic archbishop and the governor of Queensland, two Australian prime ministers—Scullin and Lyons—E. G. Theodore, Archbishop Mannix, Dr. Evatt, and Arthur Calwell). And the author of the preface, John Wren, Jr., goes on to ask: "How can Hardy substantiate his allegations when you evaluate the calibre of the people I have mentioned?" The fourth guarantee is that of education and religion. Hardy's charge of adultery against Mrs. Wren is untrue because she "is a highly educated and God-fearing lady. She has led a spotless and saintly life, and I am certain that she would gladly face death rather than commit adultery." Finally, the foreword by Arthur Calwell—signed "Deputy Leader of the Federal Parliamentary Labour Party"—tells us that "this book is not a biography of

John Wren . . . rather it is a presentation of the facts—which means the truth—in answer to the scurrilous and vicious attacks to which he was subjected from time to time over the years."

The book is therefore authorized by the highest levels of Australian society as the discourse of truth. In fact there seems almost to be an excess of guarantees; and a reading of the book quickly makes it apparent why this should be so. The first reason is that Buggy's facts have their source largely in John Wren himself: "It was in his rare reminiscent moods that he told me many things which threw a different light on some of the fantastic stories that have been told about him" (2). The second reason is that this discourse of factuality is even more novelistic than *Power Without Glory*. Buggy specializes in the evocative cliché, the mixed metaphor, essentialistic characterization, scenic condensation, and narrative teleology. A small sample:

> It was Melbourne Cup Day, 1890, and the stage was set for the triumph of the great Carbine. Colonial aristocracy in full flower—top-hatted, arrogant and ostentatious—moved on Flemington with all the pomp of a regal progress. Democracy in its blue serge suit, its wing collar, and its hard bowler hat gazed with respectful awe on the debonair gallants and the chaperoned lovelies . . .
>
> Nobody, least of all the gentry, gave the sandy-haired youth a second glance as he dodged the spanking turnouts. They were not, of course, clairvoyants. They did not know that they had just passed the opening chapter in one of the greatest success stories Australia has known.   (7–9)

The discourse of the real, in other words, is a *discourse*. It follows certain conventions, and its criteria of validity are internal to it, not located in a domain which would transcend discourse. In this case they overlap with novelistic criteria—to such an extent that one is led to wonder whether Hardy might not himself have written the book, in a characteristically tortuous act of parodic self-punishment. This use of narrative models derived from fiction is true even of more respectable historical accounts of Wren. Niall Brennan, for example, writes as follows of the methodology used in writing *John Wren, Gambler: His Life and Times:* "What I have done is to try to get an impression from a survey of all available material and when it has begun to assume a consistent pattern, then I have tried to tell the story in a broad outline; not in microscopic detail which is always tedious, but with some attention to the aim of a narrative."[41] Brennan's version of the founding of Wren's fortune through his win on

Carbine is in fact taken almost word for word from Buggy; but the worst of the purple prose is edited out, leaving an apparently dispassionate and objective account. In other words, the verisimilitude established in this text involves a second mediation of a story deriving ultimately from Wren. Brennan constructs a highly mediated narrative in accordance with narrative conventions and ideological codes, and in this process becomes a mirror image of the novelist Frank Hardy. To Brennan's accusations of ideological bias, of having distorted the truth about Wren, Hardy replied in a review article that Brennan's book was "a distorted image in the mirror of Brennan's own pre-assumptions," and that Brennan had naively accepted Wren's own "image projections."[42]

In this play of mirrors the real is endlessly deferred through its reiterated variant intertextual production. No discourse has an ultimate epistemological privilege (including this one), and it is Hardy's recognition of this that is partly responsible for the structure of repetitions characteristic of the later texts—a structure that works to fill that space in *Power Without Glory* which was supposed to be filled by the real, and that succeeds only in doubling and displacing it into further acts of writing.

It is clear that *The Hard Way,* which recounts the myth of the publication and prosecution of *Power Without Glory* and which was written explicitly as an act of exorcism, is both a compulsive repetition of that novel and a key mediation between it and the later texts. The first of these (although its date of publication precedes that of *The Hard Way*) is *The Four-Legged Lottery.* Through the use of a dual time scale which opposes the narrated time, the story of the gambler Jim Roberts, to the hesitant, arresting movement of the narrative time of Paul Whittaker producing the manuscript in prison, the novel foregrounds writing as its theme. In a number of ways, too, it implies an equivalence between the manuscript and *Power Without Glory.* The narrator occupies the place Frank Hardy would have occupied had he been convicted of libel in 1951: his writing material is supplied by the same character (the Bush Lawyer) who, in the prison scene in *The Hard Way,* promised to supply the material to Hardy if he were sent to Pentridge prison. When the manuscript is smuggled out of the jail, Whittaker writes: "The book is an established identity. Unknown people are taking risks for it; treating it with respect. This has given me a strange sense of recognition, and I write with more confidence."[43] This repeats the account of the printing and distribution of *Power Without Glory* by strangers who ran a constant risk of violence from the Wren machine. And Whittaker's crime is embezzlement, which is equivalent to the crime attributed to Hardy by a drunken prisoner. Told that Hardy was in jail for writing a book, the drunk replied: "Uttered a crook cheque, did yer. Hope yer beat the rap" (*The Hard Way,* 16).

The crime for which Jim Roberts is hanged is the murder of a corrupt bookmaker, who is of course equivalent to the corrupt tote operator John Wren—with one slight difference. At the moment of the murder, "something clicked in Jim's mind and Pittson became a symbol of all the frustrations and disappointments of his life. Instead of an adversary weak and full of fear, he imagined himself confronted with a powerful, evil enemy. He must destroy that enemy or be destroyed" (*The Four-Legged Lottery,* 218–219). The significant difference here is that the power of the enemy is now "imagined," recognized as a fantasy. In other ways, however, the novel is deeply dependent on fantasy structures. In *The Hard Way* these lines from Henry Lawson had been used as a straightforward denunciation of incarceration: "If the people knew what the warders know . . . and felt as the prisoners feel—if the people knew, they would storm their jails, as they stormed the old Bastille" (76). In *The Four-Legged Lottery* this becomes: "If decent citizens knew the revolting sexual abnormality practised in the jail they would tear down the jails and reform the prison system" (117). In an anticipation of the rape of Commissar McKakie by the warders in *The Outcasts of Foolgarah,* the jail becomes Sodom, a mythical site of homosexual rape. Its function is to displace the erotic intensity of the homosexual attachment ("mateship") between the two protagonists, each of whom is a projection of Hardy, and one of whom—like Morel in *But the Dead Are Many* and Ross Franklyn in *Who Shot George Kirkland?*—is both punished by death and redeemed by an act of writing.

The Outcasts of Foolgarah is perhaps the most successful of Hardy's novels, and it is the one least under the shadow of *Power Without Glory.* Only in the author's note, which recounts the fifteen-year saga of threatened censorship and nonpublication, does it allude to the earlier text.[44] It is structured on a Marcusean model of repressive tolerance and the revolutionary potential of social outcasts (the source of Jack Beasley's description of Hardy as "the laureate of the lumpen proletarians" and of the novel as a parody of *Power Without Glory,* "its miasmic by-product").[45] Its rhetoric is indeed populist rather than Marxist, but it largely avoids the folkloristic sentimentality of Hardy's short stories. In its use of scatological language and imagery, its scurrilous characterization ("Sir William Big-ears"), and its foregrounding of the signifier through the phonetic reproduction of Australian speech patterns and the use of rhyming slang, it approximates closely the genre of Menippean satire. The opposition of the "affluent society" to the "effluent society" picks up precisely the categorical structure that Bakhtin isolates as defining the carnivalesque;[46] but unlike the inversions of medieval carnival, and unlike the other dual structures in Hardy's texts, this opposition is not so much a mirroring as the structure-in-contradiction of class conflict.

But the Dead Are Many is equally close to a Bakhtinian model, in this case that of the polyphonic novel.[47] This is so in a quite literal sense: the book is built on the model of a fugue, weaving voices (or "subjects") in relations of contrapuntal complementarity or conflict so as to create a sustained ambiguity as to the source of utterance. Analytically one can reconstruct three more or less distinct levels. The first is the narrative of Morel's journey into suicide. Initially, at least, it is unclear whether this is a text written by Morel (it switches between first- and third-person reference) or whether it is a "fictional" trace written by Morel's alter ego, Jack. This level is interwoven with a set of third-person texts which are in fact transcriptions from fragmentary autobiographical documents, but which are inserted in such a way that they could be "unwritten" remembrances subordinated to the predominantly first-person structure of the first level. These two levels occasionally blur together in Morel's consciousness ("Am I catching a train or in the garden of the psychiatric hospital balancing a notebook on the knee of a faded check dressing gown, writing without conviction"),[48] and they merge with the third level, the bracketed editorial interventions by Jack, relating to the time of writing, and the increasingly obtruded unbracketed narrative of Jack's pursuit of the dead Morel.

It seems likely that it is Hardy's status as a social realist that has made it difficult for critics to appreciate the implications of this deliberately ambiguous polyphonic structure. John Docker, for example, writes in an otherwise perceptive paper that Hardy "is being naively pretentious and has created a great deal of unnecessary and slightly ridiculous machinery for himself." He makes the obvious but irrelevant point that the technique of novelistic counterpointing is at least as old as the epistolary novel, then continues: "More importantly, the use of different voices allows Hardy to break with the social realist tradition of the omniscient narrator."[49] He nevertheless concludes by insisting on the different novel Hardy should have written. Cecil Hadgraft similarly denounces the failure of *But the*

Dead Are Many to be either an account of political infighting or, curiously, a conventional spy thriller. And he too is uneasy with the shifts in the source of utterance:

> These do not make for easy reading: narrative and statement and comment change places abruptly and even confusingly. An additional complication is that third-person narrative is intermingled with these two others. Then it almost becomes a guess who is writing—the author, or the character standing outside himself, or another character. The overall effect of the obliquity is a mild sort of obfuscation, a slight blurring, as of our difficulty in understanding one another.[50]

The authority and the location of the speaking voice are of course a cornerstone of the realist tradition. In breaking with this convention, *But the Dead Are Many* can be seen as a kind of unwriting of *Power Without Glory*. "Morel" (which "imitates" the name of Paul Mortier) is of course the most novelistic of all proper names (Frédéric Moreau, Proust's Morel, Paul Morel in *Sons and Lovers*); and the doubling of Morel by Jack, and of Buratakov/Bukharin by Morel, represents a formal subversion of the unity of novelistic character. Thematically too there is an unwriting of the myth of the publication of *Power Without Glory*. Morel lives off his reputation for his one great achievement as a communist, a hunger strike which brought him to the edge of death and which forced the government to lift the ban on the party; and this, of course, is equivalent to Hardy's inability to exorcise the effects of his first novel.

The most recent attempt to carry through such an exorcism is *Who Shot George Kirkland?* in which Ross Franklyn—Hardy's pseudonym before the publication of *Power Without Glory,* and the counterpart of "Frank Hardy" in *The Hard Way*—debates the question of the factuality of the adultery scene in his novel *Power Corrupts*.[51] This story was given to him by an informant, Alan Hall, who was probably an undercover agent and perhaps an agent provocateur; Franklyn decides that the reliability of the adultery story is linked to the question of the reliability of another story told by Hall about his shooting of a gangster called George Kirkland.

The novel is divided into two parts, "Ross Franklyn recalls" and "Ross Franklyn recalled," the second of which concerns the recovery of the manuscript of Part 1 after Franklyn's death, and the extension of the quest by his biographer. Three modes of time are juxtaposed: the two times of writing, the time of memory, and fictional time.

Chapter headings date the use of each mode according only to its content, so that no narrative markers distinguish the status of any narrative segment. This means that, for example, an utterance attributed to Hall, standing independently and dated 1923, is entirely ambivalent. It is either an authorial reconstruction of an actual or possible event, or Hall's actual or reconstructed account of the event. And the only information the reader can use to try to fix the source and status of the utterance is negative: the fact that it is cross-textually undermined by evidence that Hall is a compulsive liar and internally undermined by the excessively positive and "literary" version it gives of Hall.

The interplay of discourses is reinforced by a complex structure of intertextual reference. The title of the novel is verbally the same as that of the manuscript of Part 1; chapter epigraphs in both parts are drawn from the text of Part 1; one of the preliminary epigraphs is taken "from a manuscript found in the National Library amongst the papers of Ross Franklyn, the author, who died in 1978"; another is ascribed to "Poisson," who turns up later as a character in the novel; and the protagonist of Part 2 quotes from his honors dissertation on Ross Franklyn, which apparently corresponds to "a thesis written by R. H. Cavenagh, *The Fiction of Frank Hardy*," to which "the author" gives acknowledgment on one of the unpaginated title pages. On a broader level the novel repeats other Hardy texts. Passages from *The Hard Way* are transcribed or closely summarized, but with the alteration of slight details: the story of the gambling win that allowed *Power Without Glory* to be typeset is reproduced almost verbatim, but in the later text the odds are given as fifty to one rather than thirty-three to one, and the win as £500 rather than £200 (*Who Shot George Kirkland?*, 40; cf. *The Hard Way*, 128). (In a 1976 article in *The Age*, Hardy is quoted as giving the odds as sixty-six to one and the win as $1,300;[52] this story should be compared with that of Wren's win on Carbine, obviously the product of the same imagination.) Hall is referred to as "something of a Peter Pan," which picks up and transforms a statement in the earlier text that "I haven't missed a Cup since Peter Pan's second win" (*Who Shot George Kirkland?*, 59; cf. *The Hard Way*, 154). In this process of rewriting, *The Hard Way* is in fact deleted: Franklyn writes as though that book had never existed, that act of exorcism never been performed. There is a similar form of rewriting of *Power Without Glory*: a long extract from that novel, dealing with Mrs. West's adultery with a construction worker, Bill Evans, is reproduced as a chapter of *Who Shot George Kirkland?* dated 1917, and with the single change that "Bill Evans" is now called "Bill Egan." There is an imitation of *But the Dead Are Many* in the reference to *"The Living Are Few,* my failed novel about the Communist who committed suicide because he had cast himself in a role he was incapable of playing" (84) and in the way Franklyn's suicide closely follows that of Morel. And in both parts of the novel the parodic voice of *The Outcasts of Foolgarah* is played off against other stylistic formations.

A major aspect of the rewriting-with-difference of earlier texts is the play of repression and revelation of proper names. Alan Hall's name was suppressed in *The Hard Way,* as was that of Evans/Egan's wife, a figure whose mysterious appearance in court was never explained. Evans's name was repressed during the trial by one of Wren's associates (a lapse which the defense eagerly seized on); the second-degree fictionalization of his name in *Who Shot George Kirkland?* re-produces a name that was always problematic as the signifier of an absent signified. Conversely, the name of the trade unionist George Seelaf figures prominently in *The Hard Way* but is here deliberately and mysteriously suppressed.

The major thematization of the status of the proper name concerns, of course, George Kirkland. The narrator of Part 2 finds evidence that Alan Hall, who claimed to have shot Kirkland, had indeed shot someone, but his victim's name was "Thomas Hamill." It seems possible, then, that "Kirkland" could be the fictitious name of a real person—that is, that it occupies the same ambivalent realm as the central proper names in *Power Without Glory.* After further research, the narrator uncovers the newspaper report of this shooting, which is quite different from the more dramatic and self-serving story told by Hall. He then manages to uncover a trace of the existence of George Kirkland; but, as in Hardy's fourth category of signification, this real proper name is inserted in an entirely different story. When he finally discovers the story of the shooting of George Kirkland, the multiplication of resemblances, differences, and obscurities makes it clear that the relation between name and story will never be adequately reconstructed. The story of this quest acts as a fable which is overtly thematized throughout the novel. Ross Franklyn discovers retrospectively that "the fictional world of the novel had become more real to me than the factual material I had gathered" (*Who Shot George Kirkland?,* 38). In later life "increasingly the real and the unreal merged in my human relationships: the events in my actual life blended with my obsessions and dreams to become recreated in my writing" (38). And he concludes that there is an "irreconcilable feud between literature and reality" (1) and that "truth does not live in verified facts, nor is it the opposite of falsehood; that fiction is not the opposite of truth, nor is it the equivalent of lies" (178).

A final thematic strand concerns a personal level of guilt, and this can be extended to cover the structure of repetition that is operative in all the novels. Ross Franklyn has stayed "relatively sane . . . only because I blotted the story out of my mind for nearly thirty years in a classically Freudian way" (75). What he had repressed was the act of aggression directed against Ellen Wren/Nellie West and against the father figure Wren/West. The narrator of Part 2 quotes a rumor, dating from 1950, that Franklyn was in fact Xavier, the supposedly dead son of Mrs. Wren/West and either Wren/West or "Bill Evans" (120); that he was, in other words, a character in his own novel, and one whose name, as Brennan points out, is both unusual and identical in the text of the novel and the text of the real.[53] Franklyn's crime was to have challenged the "menacing forces" (177) of West—a challenge repeated by his biographer, who masquerades as his son and becomes his "ghost" (142). There is a further twist to this, however. On the assumption that the adultery story, despite its having been written as fiction, was in fact true, it is conceivable that West/Wren might have used the trial as a way of publicly punishing his wife—in which case Ross Franklyn/Frank Hardy would have been acting as his unwitting accomplice (176). Franklyn therefore has no alternative but to deny the truth of the story, but thereby becomes guilty of having libeled an innocent woman. This double bind repeats the dilemma of the trial, in which the prosecution and the defense were compelled both to affirm and to deny the same proposition.

From *The Hard Way* to *Who Shot George Kirkland?* Hardy's texts can be read as compulsive repetitions of two aspects of *Power Without Glory:* the heroic myth of repression and victimization (repeated by Hardy *in propria persona* some years ago in a self-pitying interview with Bruce Molloy),[54] and the unresolved question of the ambivalence of fictional signification. *Power Without Glory* is in itself a radically incomplete text which has been continuously rewritten and transformed in the later books. Its problematic status as a text is confirmed by the scandal of its academic reception. It has been virtually absent from the orthodox literary histories, and when it is mentioned it is to be relegated to the status of a document—that is, to precisely that referential function that the later texts contest or problematize. Academic critics have imposed a normative closure on the text, and in the same methodological movement have reduced Hardy to the status of "author" of *Power Without Glory.* They have failed to analyze the extended process of constitution of the text in its reception and its rewriting: above all, its constitution as a political text in the *cause célèbre* of the trial and in the effect of the Australian television series.

In order to write the social history of this political text, it would be necessary to take into account not only Hardy's own rewritings but the politically conflicting readings and rewritings through which it is constructed as a heterogeneous text. Here I can give only a sketchy indication of the main ideological positions which contribute to this process. Schematically, I would isolate four groupings. The first is that of New Critical liberal humanism, which, in addition to the literary historians I have quoted earlier, would have to include critics like Clement Semmler and Cecil Hadgraft and cultural policemen like Max Harris. The second grouping, centered on *Quadrant,* is the Catholic right, together with lapsed communists like Fred Weller and Rupert Lockwood. From this perspective *Power Without Glory* is read as a political tract directed specifically against the Movement (the right-wing National Civic Council and its trade union and Labor Party cadres), and it is measured against a criterion of fidelity to the historical record (as though that record were not itself tendentiously constructed). Hardy is "placed" as a Stalinist hardliner, the author of only one other significant text, the notorious *Journey Into the Future*.[55] This group has the virtue of a declared interest in the political effects of texts. Its interventions have consequently occurred in two major waves: one in the early 1950s, when *Power Without Glory* was an issue in the literary politics of the Cold War and the Labor Party split (and when, as Brennan observes, "Wren's Catholic anti-Communist mates did more than anything else to ensure the continued sales and success of *Power Without Glory*" because "Hardy the Communist was a more dangerous figure in their eyes than Hardy the crashing bore who had laboriously turned out a vast and tedious work of questionable fiction");[56] and a second wave in 1976 as a reaction to the serialization of the novel for television, which was correctly perceived as marking the demise of *Quadrant*'s version of the historical record.

The third main grouping is that of the right and left wings of the Communist Party (and later the pro-Moscow Socialist Party of Australia). Here the fate of Hardy's texts coincides initially with the heroic myth of struggle against the suppression of democratic rights. Hardy himself gives the strongest version of this insertion of the literary into the general political struggle in *The Hard Way*. The later fate of his texts is inseparable from the faction fighting between the two wings of the party, peaking in 1957 and 1968.[57] The publication in 1969 of Hardy's "Stalin's Heirs" articles committed him to the left, "revisionist" wing of the party; but his increasing alienation from party politics means that his later work has had little political resonance (Eric Aarons's review of *But the Dead Are Many* is mainly anecdotal and avoids the theoretical problems the text poses).[58] The brunt of comment comes from the right. Jack Beasley's *Red Letter Days,* for example, is a savage personal attack, accusing Hardy of opportunism, class treachery, and plagiarism. It is noteworthy that Beasley's distinction between the "publicistic message" of *Power Without Glory* and its status as "literature," as well as that between its "public image" and its "real quality,"[59] reflects an insecurity about the political status and function of texts—an insecurity repeated in Jack Lindsay's question (mirroring that of the liberal-humanist literary historians): "Is it merely a document of great importance for the inner history of Australian politics and sports, or is it also a work of art in its own way?"[60]

The responsibility for shifting the kinds of questions asked of Hardy's texts would seem to lie most strongly with the fourth ideological grouping (in which my own work is situated), the New Left. Here, however, interest in Hardy has been belated and mostly unsatisfactory. John Docker's "study in context" of *But the Dead Are Many* is an excellent account of the stylistic and ideological weaknesses of the novel, but fails to move beyond seeing it as "a propaganda tract written on behalf of a victorious inner Party faction," and therefore as "analysis untransmuted into art."[61] Tim Rowse's review of *Red Letter Days* indicates the instability of political criteria in Beasley's reading of Hardy, and refers to the need for "a critique of language and narrative that may make us query the necessity of realism."[62] This project has only recently begun with Peter Williams's attempt to replace immanent and genetic readings of Hardy with a concern for the labor of intertextual production performed by the texts and for their political and institutional appropriation.[63]

Williams's argument for the pertinence of work "on the production of texts and the production of readings of them, which together constitute the structuration of textual 'meaning' through the reiteration of cultural codes"[64] is close to my argument that the significance of the text is inseparable from its historicity. *Power Without Glory* is constructed as a text in a contradictory network of private and public readings; in the trial and the attendant publicity; in its serialization for television; and in Hardy's own rewritings. There is no single, finite text external to our relation to it. Nor is there a closed corpus unproblematically defined by the trademark of its "author." If Hardy has devoted so much care to the "dismantling and splitting"[65] of the author function, it is surely presumptuous of critics simply to insist on the straightforward unity of this function.

The boundary of the text and its mode of signification are socially imposed; and on this basis the text is constituted heterogeneously within the process of Australian textual politics. It is made up of different modes and levels of intertextuality, each with a specific degree of cognitive privilege which is also socially ascribed. To say this is not to discard the concepts of text and of a specifically literary mode of discourse, nor does it involve a rejection of operations of evaluation. Rather, it means taking the structured field of evaluations and the critical concepts used to produce them as objects of analysis, and thereby integrating them into the textual process. Such a deconstruction of "the text" should lead us to focus on the interplay between text and system and on the social determinants of this process. Hardy's work has a particular value as a case study in that, standing as it does outside the orthodox canon, it challenges the ideological premises on which that canon is constructed, and indeed received conceptions of literary history itself.

8

Limits: The Politics of Reading

IN THIS LAST CHAPTER I work toward a sort of conclusion by writing about the politics of reading and of theorizing about literary texts. This involves, in particular, considering the concept of the situation(s) from which readings are undertaken and theories generated. How, for example, can a redefinition of the concepts of text, history, and system change the relations and the political dimensions within which these concepts are usually thought? How can an interested politics of reading relativize itself to an account of a limited, historically specific regime of reading? How can a theory of the literary system be thought as a *component* of the literary system?

In order to structure these questions, I begin by looking at an exchange which took place some years ago, between Derrida and Foucault.[1] This exchange combines an unusually intensive piece of textual analysis with a sharp distinction between two different ways of dealing with texts. I am not so much concerned with adjudicating between these positions (which in any case involve an element of caricature) as with exploring a small number of the methodological issues raised.

At the center of this confrontation is a passage from Descartes's *Méditations* which Derrida and Foucault unpack in different ways. Let me quote it in full in order to demonstrate the particular form of ellipsis which makes this possible:

> But [*sed forte*], although the senses sometimes deceive us, concerning things which are barely perceptible or at a great distance, there are perhaps many other things about which one cannot reasonably doubt, although we know them through the medium of the senses, for example, that I am here, sitting by the fire, wearing a dressing-gown, with this paper in my hands, and other things of this

nature. And how could I deny that these hands and this body belong to me, unless perhaps I were to assimilate myself to those insane persons whose minds are so troubled and clouded by the black vapours of the bile that they constantly assert that they are kings, when they are very poor; that they are wearing gold and purple, when they are quite naked; or who imagine that they are pitchers or that they have a body of glass. But these are madmen [*sed amentes sunt isti*], and I would not be less extravagant [*demens*] if I were to follow their example.

However [*praeclare sane*], I must here consider that I am a man, and consequently that I am in the habit of sleeping and of representing to myself in my dreams those same things, or sometimes even less likely things, which insane people do when they are awake.[2]

What is at issue here, in particular, is (1) the force of the relation between the example of madness and the example of dreaming; (2) the enunciative status of the *sed forte;* and (3) the discursive status and functions of the different terms designating madness. For Foucault the force of this sequence is to constitute a qualitative difference between the status of dreams and the status of madness; the former can represent "an instrument or stage of doubt" (9), but madness cannot. Insofar as madness undermines the rational Cogito itself, it becomes the Other of reason and must be excluded from the process of doubt. This exclusion of madness, this definition of the Cogito through the exclusion of madness, is what for Foucault constitutes a new historical economy of reason, an epistemological break which founds the status of madness in the modern (post-Cartesian) world. For Derrida the sequence reads differently. Rather than being the radically unthinkable Other of reason, madness is one case of sensory error; indeed, in this context, it is a less serious case than that of dreams. Foucault's attempt to write the history of the splitting—the "dissension" or division—of the logos into reason (the Cogito) and madness "runs the risk of construing the division as an event or a structure subsequent to the unity of an original presence, thereby confirming metaphysics in its fundamental operation" (40): whereas reason has always been constituted in relation to its Other. Either we recognize that the historicity of madness is always and repeatedly (re)constructed in this determinate relation, or we hypostatize madness as an indeterminate conceptual absolute, something like negativity, and so make impossible, precisely, a history of madness.

This is, very briefly, the larger argument. But what interests me here is the way two different readings of the passage from Descartes are built, and in particular the question of how the modality of the passage is constructed. Let me quote the passage of Derrida's text which Foucault quotes (in part) as the central moment of Derrida's critique:

> Now, the entire paragraph which follows [the *sed forte*] does not express Descartes's final, definitive conclusions, but rather the astonishment and objections of the nonphilosopher, of the novice in philosophy who is frightened by this doubt and protests, saying: I am willing to let you doubt certain sensory perceptions concerning "things which are hardly perceptible, or very far away," but the others! that you are in this place, sitting by the fire, speaking thus, this paper in your hands and other seeming certainties! Descartes then assumes the astonishment of this reader or naive interlocutor, pretends to take him into account when he writes: "And how could I deny that these hands and this body are mine, were it not perhaps that I compare myself to certain persons, devoid of sense, whose . . . and I should not be any the less insane were I to follow examples so extravagant."
>
> The pedagogical and rhetorical sense of the *sed forte* which governs this paragraph is clear. It is the "but perhaps" of the feigned objection. Descartes has just said that all knowledge of sensory origin could deceive him. He pretends to put to himself the astonished objection of an imaginary nonphilosopher who is frightened by such audacity and says: no, not all sensory knowledge, for then you would be mad and it would be unreasonable to follow the example of madmen, to put forth the ideas of madmen. Descartes *echoes* this objection: since I am here, writing, and you understand me, I am not mad, nor are you, and we are all sane. The example of madness is therefore not indicative of the fragility of the sensory idea. So be it. Descartes acquiesces to this natural point of view, or rather he feigns to rest in this natural comfort in order better, more radically and more definitively, to unsettle himself from it and to discomfort his interlocutor. So be it, he says, you think that I would be mad to doubt that I am sitting near the fire, etc., that I would be insane to follow the example of madmen. I will therefore propose a hypothesis which will seem much more natural to you, will not disorient you, because it concerns a more common, and more universal experience than that of madness: the experience of sleep and dreams. Descartes then elaborates the hypothesis that will ruin *all* the *sensory* foundations of knowledge and will lay bare only the *intellectual* foundations of certainty. This hypothesis above all will not run from the possibility of an insanity—an epistemological one—much more serious than madness.
>
> The reference to dreams is therefore not put off to one side—

quite the contrary—in relation to a madness potentially respected or even excluded by Descartes. It constitutes, in the methodical order which here is ours, the hyperbolical exasperation of the hypothesis of madness.   (50)

Derrida's strategy is to construct a play of voices in the text of Descartes—that is, a stratification of levels which breaks an expository monologue into a dialogue between the voice of the philosopher and the voice of a projected interlocutor. Bakhtin would say that such dialogism is constitutive of any argumentative discourse which anticipates possible objections and so builds possible counterpositions into its own progress. Effectively what we have is a passage of free indirect discourse, in which "Descartes" remains the only speaker but the position of utterance varies. Descartes *cites* an objecting voice and then *echoes* it, agreeing with it about madness the better then to unsettle it with the example of dreams. But since irony and free indirect discourse are not necessarily marked linguistically, the possibility of such a reading must depend on our judgment about the strategic force of a syllogism and on our knowledge of the rhetorical (generic) conventions governing the organization of such a discourse—conventions, that is, that would incorporate dialogism as a structural principle.

But it is precisely the question of generic conventions that Foucault seizes upon in his response. What Derrida has neglected is above all a "set of differences" which "controls all the others," and which "refers less to the signifying organization of the text than to the series of events (acts, effects, qualifications) which the discursive practice of meditation carries with it: it is a question of the modifications of the subject by the very exercise of discourse. And," he says, "I have a feeling that if a reader as remarkably assiduous as Derrida has missed so many literary, thematic or textual differences, then this is through having misunderstood those differences which are the principle of these others; namely, the 'discursive differences' " (18–19).

Let me quote at length from what follows, in order to foreground what I think is the decisive point at issue—the question of the mode of implication of subjects in discourse:

> We must keep in mind the very title of "meditations." Any discourse, whatever it be, is constituted by a set of utterances which are produced each in its place and time, as so many discursive events. If it is a question of a pure demonstration, these utterances can be read

as a series of events linked one to another according to a certain number of formal rules; as for the subject of the discourse, he is not implicated in the demonstration: he remains, in relation to it, fixed, invariable and as if neutralized. On the other hand, a "meditation" produces, as so many discursive events, new utterances which carry with them a series of modifications of the enunciating subject: through what is said in meditation, the subject passes from darkness to light, from impurity to purity, from the constraint of passions to detachment, from uncertainty and disordered movements to the serenity of wisdom, and so on. In meditation, the subject is ceaselessly altered by his own movement; his discourse provokes effects within which he is caught; it exposes him to risks, makes him pass through trials or temptations, produces states in him, and confers on him a status or qualification which he did not hold at the initial moment. In short, meditation implies a mobile subject modifiable through the effect of the discursive events which take place. From this, one can see what a demonstrative meditation would be: a set of discursive events which constitute at once groups of utterances linked one to another by formal rules of deduction, and a series of modifications of the enunciating subject which follow continuously one from another. More precisely, in a demonstrative meditation the utterances, which are formally linked, modify the subject as they develop, liberating him from his convictions or on the contrary inducing [*qui induisent*] systematic doubts, provoking illuminations or resolutions, freeing him from his attachments or immediate certainties, including new states: but inversely the decisions, fluctuations, displacements, primary or acquired qualifications of the subject make sets of new utterances possible, which are in their turn deduced regularly one from another.

The *Méditations* require this double reading: a set of propositions forming a *system,* which each reader must follow through if he wishes to feel their truth, and a set of modifications forming an *exercise,* which each reader must effect, by which each reader must be affected, if in turn he wants to be the subject enunciating this truth on his own behalf. And if there are indeed certain passages of the *Méditations* which can be deciphered exhaustively as a systematic stringing together of propositions—moments of pure deduction—there exist on the other hand sorts of "chiasma," where the two forms of discourse intersect, and where the exercise modifying the subject orders the succession of propositions, or controls the junction of distinct demonstrative groups. It seems that the passage on madness and dreaming is indeed of this order.   (19)

How many voices or "subjects" are there then in the text of Descartes—two or one? Or, more precisely, is there a single, constantly modified subject of the text, or are there a number of linked subject positions? This second formulation gets closer to the real difficulty, which has to do with what constitutes the forms of enunciative unity of a text. Whereas Derrida posits an interchange between two voices (but two voices both of which could be situated as moments of the discourse of the "philosopher"), Foucault speaks of "a series of modifications of the enunciating subject," a subject who is "ceaselessly altered by his own movement": a principle of diversity within unity, then, a mobility which is contained by the singleness of the enunciation. On this basis Foucault proceeds to denounce Derrida for his *invention* of "an alternation of voices which would displace, reject and drive out of the text itself the difficult exclamation: 'but just a moment—these are madmen' " (23). (And yet who speaks this "just a moment"? Is it not an *interruption*?) The failures of Derrida's reading (this judgment is the result of a much more extended critique than I have reproduced here) are "the omission of a certain number of *literary* elements . . . ; the elision of *textual* differences . . . ; finally and above all the erasure of the essential *discursive* determination (the double web of exercise and demonstration)"; and all of these failures stem from the initial fault of Derrida's having imagined "that other naive objecting voice behind Descartes' writing" (24).

And yet Foucault's reading, and above all his location of a " 'chiasma,' where the two forms of discourse intersect" (19), should surely support Derrida's analysis: there *is* a play of "voices" here—dialogism if not a dialogue. And it is precisely the "meditation" genre, which involves a *splitting* of the enunciating subject (the soul talking to itself, a sort of floating of discourse rather than the direct derivation of a discourse from an axiomatic), which provides the formal basis for this play. Foucault avoids the conclusions of his own account of the "discursive differences" by tying the movement of the discourse to its subject; this subject of the text is then opposed to Derrida's "invention of voices behind texts," which allows Derrida "to avoid having to analyse the mode of implication of the subject in discourses" (27).

But who is this "subject"? If it is "implicated" in discourses, must it not be an extradiscursive subject (either the author, Descartes, or the reader) articulated, bound into, constituted as a subject in language? But this surely cannot be the case, in the first instance, because this "enunciating subject" is opposed to "voices" posited as being *behind* the text, external to the text: so the subject of enunciation is not the substantial origin of discourse but a discursive effect, a positionality, a function. And this is borne out, secondly, by the fact that the reader can become "the subject enunciating this truth on his own behalf" only by following the "set of modifications forming an exercise" (19) which is the meditation. The reader inscribes himself within a set of subject positions in order to be constituted as subject of the enunciation; this latter *is* the effect of the occupation of these positions. But what guarantees the unity of these positions? Not the preconstituted subjectivity of the author and the reader; and not an effect of unity given by the text, because we are dealing precisely with "a mobile subject modifiable through the effect of the discursive events which take place" (19). Nothing, it seems to me, justifies Foucault, under these particular generic conditions, in assigning the "ownership" of a plurality of discursive positions to a single, unified subject of enunciation—nothing apart from a willful confusion of the discursive subject with "real," empirical speaking subjects. The point, of course—and Foucault tacitly acknowledges this by his use of the word *chiasma*—is that the genre of the meditation, with its controlled "floating" of arguments, tends to give rise to utterances whose assignment is ambivalent. Foucault is perfectly correct to focus his analysis on the generic conditions of utterance in this text; but he draws the wrong conclusions from this analysis.

The second aspect of Foucault's description of discursive determinations concerns the way the text plays off against each other terms designating madness which are drawn from quite different discursive domains. The word *insanus* belongs to medical terminology, whereas *demens* and *amens* are "terms that are in the first place juridical before being medical, and which designate a whole category of people incapable of certain religious, civil, and judicial acts; the *dementes* do not have total possession of their rights when it comes to speaking, promising, pledging, signing, starting a legal action, etc. *Insanus* is a characterizing term; *amens* and *demens* are disqualifying ones" (16). Derrida is therefore "wrong to say hastily that the question of right posed here concerns 'the truth of ideas'; when in fact as is clearly stated, it concerns the qualification of the subject" (17). Let me stress that what is in question here is not the opposition between an immanent textual analysis and a historical analysis; the difference is rather that between a simple textuality and the more complex textuality established by a play of intertextual relations. Derrida does make the mistake here, I think, of believing that his own practice of reading is somehow more "immanent" than Foucault's. In opposition to Foucault's analysis of

"an historical ensemble—notions, institutions, juridical and police meas-
ures, scientific concepts," Derrida himself proposes that the starting point
of any analysis must be "the internal and autonomous analysis of the
philosophical content of philosophical discourse," and that "only when
the totality of this content will have become manifest in its meaning for
me (but this is impossible) will I rigorously be able to situate it in its total
historical form" (44). By locating the effectivity of Descartes's text purely
within the system of Western philosophy, Derrida lays himself wide open
to Said's objection that he fails to analyze the constitution of this system,
remaining "within" it to the extent that he offers readings of a set of texts
taken as given and thereby neglecting "the implemented, effective power
of textual statement."[3] Derrida himself sets up this opposition between
discursive institutions and textuality which then allows Foucault to attack
him for a reduction of the former to the latter, for failing to "replac[e]
discursive practices in the field of transformations where they are carried
out," and thus for working within "a historically well-determined little
pedagogy . . . which teaches the pupil that there is nothing outside the
text, but that in it, in its gaps, its blanks and its silences, there reigns the
reserve of the origin; that it is therefore unnecessary to search elsewhere,
but that here, not in the words, certainly, but in the words under erasure,
in their *grid,* the 'sense of being' is said. A pedagogy which gives conversely
to the master's voice the limitless sovereignty which allows it to restate
the text indefinitely" (27).

It is important to be clear about what Foucault is attacking here: that
is, the practice of reading that he calls interpretation. He has written
elsewhere concerning the valorization of writing (and he is clearly referring
to Derrida) that it reintroduces "the religious principle of hidden meanings
(which require interpretation) and the critical assumption of implicit significations, silent purposes, and obscure contents (which give rise to commentary)."[4] To interpret is to accept at face value the givenness and the
rarity of statements, to fail to analyze what it is that makes interpretation
itself possible; it is naively to repeat a lack, or to try to fill it, rather than
enquiring into its conditions of existence.[5] And it is to restrict analysis to
the "meaning" of statements, the mode of validity they assign (or fail to
assign) to themselves without taking into account the fact that statements
"are invested in techniques that put them into operation, in practices that
derive from them, in the social relations that they form, or, through those
relations, modify."[6] To analyze a discursive formation is to take as object
the conditions of existence of discourse and the conditions of its effectivity.

But this does not mean "complementing" or "supplementing" textual analysis with an analysis of "context," as Michael Sprinker suggests at the end of his reading of this exchange ("Careful, rigorous, analytic study of texts must be complemented by historical investigations of the conditions of textual production and the place of texts in the cultural, economic, and political spheres that surround them").[7] Both Derrida and Foucault would agree in rejecting the relation of exteriority/interiority, or of supplementarity, proposed here: Foucault because he thinks of the institutional conditions of a discursive formation as a component of the formation,[8] Derrida because the question of the "edge" of discourse, and hence of the mediations between an "inside" and an "outside" of discourse, is fraught with difficulty. (I shall return to this question shortly.) Foucault's reading of the text of Descartes analyzes its generic conditions of possibility, and the discursive transformations it operates (the elaboration of medical and juridical discourses by the discourse of the meditation). It does not seek to derive these textual conditions from the administrative apparatus governing the segregation of madness, or vice versa (although it is true that in Foucault's earlier work the totalizing concept of the episteme is a problem in this respect). But at the same time it does not seek to defer an analysis of the "historical form" of the text until the impossible achievement of a total understanding of the text's philosophical content.

Foucault's practice of reading is here more efficient than Derrida's to the extent that it is able to thematize more fully the conditions of textual enunciation (even if it draws the wrong conclusions from this). But the larger question Derrida poses is whether Foucault can come to terms with the enunciative status of this thematization itself: whether it can pose the question of its own questions. What Foucault attempts to do in *Histoire de la folie* is "to write a history of madness *itself*" (33): that is, a history in which madness would speak for itself "on the basis of its own experience and under its own authority, and not a history of madness described from within the language of reason . . . that is to say, madness made into an object and exiled as the other of a language and a historical meaning which have been confused with logos itself" (34). The trap that Foucault has to avoid is that of "writing a history of untamed madness, of madness as it carries itself and breathes before being caught and paralysed in the nets of classical reason, from within the very language of classical reason itself" (34). Foucault avoids this in part by rejecting the language of reason (order) and seeking to evoke the *silence* of madness. But this is problematical: "First of all, is there a history of silence? Further, is not an archaeology, even of silence, a logic, that is, an organized language, a project, an order, a sentence, a syntax, a work? Would not the archaeology of silence be the most efficacious and subtle restoration, the *repetition,* in the most irreducibly ambiguous meaning of the word, of the act perpetrated against madness—and be so at the very moment when this act is denounced?" (35). This is to say that the crucial question is that of "the source and status of the language of this archaeology, of this language which is to be understood by a reason that is not classical reason" (35). In either the good or the bad sense of the word (and the issue should not be judged too quickly), Foucault's task is a paradox.

The form that Foucault's attempt to avoid the trap of reason takes is that of the deployment of a "relativity without recourse": that is, a language, at once necessary and impossible, which declines "to articulate itself along the lines of the syntax of reason" (37), which *gestures* to the silence of madness without giving it voice. But again the question this poses is that of the historical conditions of possibility of this language: "What, in the last resort, supports this language without recourse or support: who enunciates the possibility of nonrecourse? Who wrote and who is to understand, in what language and from what historical situation of logos, who wrote and who is to understand this history of madness?" (38). The rhetorical repetition of the question of the situation of utterance, bracketing as it does the linked questions of language and of the "historical situation of logos," refers us at once to the impossibility of such a history and to the conditions of its possibility and impossibility. But if Derrida is able to pose the question of these conditions in a way that outflanks Foucault and reveals something of the positivism of his enterprise (and perhaps of any construction of history which claims to be descriptive of its object), he is—at least at this stage—no more capable than Foucault of answering the question of these conditions. The gesture toward the "historical situation of logos" indicates the most banal, the most *philosophical* equation of the state of the real with the developed state of reason; and it robs Derrida's question of all its potentially *political* force.

LET US LEAVE this exchange, such as it is, having mapped out the problematic that I take to be of interest in it—that of the conditions of analysis of discourse, of the framework of analysis—and turn to another text by Derrida which addresses itself directly to the question of the frame and of the constitution of "internal" aesthetic spaces. At the very beginning of the essay "Le Parergon," there is a discussion of the institutional forms (curricula, examinations, staging, rhetorics) in which the teaching of philosophy, and specifically the systematic philosophical construction of the concept of art, are conducted in France. From this discussion Derrida deduces "the necessity for a deconstruction" of this institution, and goes on to describe what this would entail:

> The consequence of its logic would be to attack not just the internal structure [*édification*], both semantic and formal, of the philosophemes, but also what would wrongly be described as its external casing, the extrinsic conditions of its functioning: the historical forms of its pedagogy, the social, economic, or political structures of this pedagogic institution. It is because it affects solid structures, "material" institutions, and not only discourses or signifying representations, that deconstruction is always to be distinguished from an analysis or a "critique." And in order to be pertinent it works, as strictly as possible, in that place where the so-called internal arrangement of the philosophical is articulated in a necessary fashion (internal *and* external) with the institutional conditions and forms of teaching. To the point where the concept of institution itself would be submitted to the same deconstructive treatment.[9]

Commenting on this passage Samuel Weber points out that orthodox deconstruction has in practice failed to realize this critique (and certainly any dismantling) of its own conditions of existence; and he suggests that this is because, in "elaborating the aporetic, non-dialectical identity of the conditions of possibility and impossibility of systematic thought, such deconstruction has tended to ignore the forces and factors that always operate to institute and maintain certain sets of paradigms, notwithstanding (or even because of) their intrinsically aporetic structure."[10] "Or even because of": although it is surely just this cunning of power that a deconstructive theory should be able to notice, focusing as it does on the conditions of textuality. But my interest is again, at least initially, narrower: it is directed to the question of analytic interest; and to how the categorical opposition of the internal to the external (with the concomitant demands either for an immanent textual analysis or for a movement from the interior of the text to its external conditions of existence) is institutionally constructed and historically constitutive of the concept of art itself.

In discussing the nature of an intrinsic and disinterested aesthetic judgment Kant gives the example of a palace, and defines an appropriate aesthetic response by disqualifying a range of inappropriate responses, evaluations of the palace "as a function of *extrinsic* motifs, in terms of empirical psychology, economic relations of production, political structures, technical causality, etc." ("Le Parergon," 53). The aesthetic, the intrinsic, is what is left over after these responses have been disqualified; and Derrida suggests that "this permanent demand—to distinguish between the internal or proper meaning and the accidental circumstances of the object in question—organizes every philosophical discourse on art, the meaning of art, and meaning itself, from Plato to Hegel, Husserl, and Heidegger. It presupposes a discourse on the limit between the inside and the outside of the aesthetic object, in this case a *discourse on the frame*" (53).

Now, this discourse is lacking in *The Critique of Judgement;* or rather it is to be found only, displaced and decentered, in the obscure example of the ornament. Kant writes:

> Even what is called *ornamentation* [*Zierathen*] (*parerga*), i.e. what is only an adjunct, and not an intrinsic constituent in the complete representation of the object, in augmenting the delight of taste does so only by means of its form. Thus it is with the frames [*Einfassungen*] of pictures or the drapery on statues, or the colonnades of palaces. But if the ornamentation does not itself enter into the composition of the beautiful form—if it is introduced [*angebracht*] like a gold frame [*goldene Rahmen*] merely to win approval for the picture by means of its charm—it is then called *finery* [*Schmuck*] and takes away from the genuine beauty.[11]

The *parergon* is a supplement, an accessory, *hors d'oeuvre,* additional and external to the *ergon,* the work. But not entirely external: it "comes against, beside, and beyond the *ergon,* the work done, the fact of the work but it doesn't fall to one side; it touches and cooperates, from a certain outside, within the operation. It is neither simply within nor simply without" ("Le Parergon," 63). Because of its ambivalent status the examples Kant gives are difficult and inconclusive: where precisely does "drapery" *(Gewänder)* on a statue begin and end? What are we to make of a colonnade that is both structural and decorative? And what is the difference between a *parergon* and a background? For not every context (field, ground), however contiguous it may be, constitutes a *parergon:* thus "the natural site chosen for the erection of a temple is obviously not a *parergon,* nor is an artificial space: the square, the church, the museum" (69). It would seem, then, that drapery and colonnades are chosen not because of their separateness but because it is so hard to detach them from the work, and "without them, without their quasi-detachment, the lack within the work would appear" (69) (or—the same thing—would fail to). This is to say that "what constitutes them as *parerga* is not simply their exteriority but the internal structural link that binds them to the lack within the *ergon*. And this lack is constitutive of the very unity of the *ergon*. Without this lack the *ergon* would have no need of the *parergon*"—which nevertheless remains external to it (69).

The decisive example is that of the frame, for it is here that the paradoxical status, the doubleness of the *parergon* becomes fully apparent. The frame works not only against the "inside" of the work but simultaneously against the "outside":

> What is incomprehensible about the border, at the border, appears not only at the inner limit, which passes between the frame and the painting, the drapery and the body, the colonnade and the building, but also at the outer limit. *Parerga* have a thickness and a surface which separate them not only, as Kant would have it, from the integrity of the inside, the body of the *ergon* itself, but also from the outside, from the wall on which the painting is hung, from the space in which the statue or the colonnade is erected, and then gradually from the whole historical, economic, and political field of inscription in which the drive of the signature arises . . . No "theory," no "practice," no "theoretical practice" can intervene effectively in this field if it does not stress the frame, the invisible limit of (between) the interiority of meaning (protected by the whole hermeneutic, semiotic, phenomenological, and formalist tradition) *and* (of) all the empiricisms of the extrinsic which, not knowing how to see or how to read, miss the point of the question.   (71)

But this "thickness" and this work performed by the frame—this work which constitutes "the work"—is constitutively difficult to see; it gets lost in that double movement by which "in relation to the work which may function as its ground it disappears into the wall and then, little by little, into the general text. In relation to the ground established by the general text it disappears into the work which is set off against the general ground. Always a figure on a ground, the *parergon* is a figure which has traditionally been determined not by detaching itself but by disappearing, sinking in, effacing itself, dissolving at the moment when it is expending its greatest energy" (72–73). But at the same time the frame is potentially what disrupts the "interiority" of the work, betraying the *interest* by which it is delimited and the operation of valuation by which it is rarefied. Working inward and outward, on both "edges" at the same time, limiting and limited but also an energy, it cracks and dislocates itself even as it defines the space of the work (87). What it structures is neither an energy which would precede this structuration nor a determinate lack, but a play of differences it can never arrest. "There is no natural frame. There *is* framing, but the frame *has no existence*" (93).

Let me take the concept of frame as a metaphor for the frame structures of genre and literary system. This is at once a way of considering in "material" terms a set of abstract determinants and a way of formulating the paradox of systemic determination and of the textual modification of a system (so that the text is never the simple effect of its determinants, the inside of an outside). In these terms one can say that the ordered systems of signification governing the particular instance of a text establish for it a specific mode of aesthetic closure. This closure is marked by the particular distribution of the "real" and the "symbolic" within which the text operates at any one time, and it defines its appropriate degrees of fictionality and figurality and the kinds of use to which it can be put. I use the term *frame* to designate this limit, at once material and immaterial, literal and figurative, between adjacent and dissimilar ontological realms. The frame can be anything that acts as a sign of a qualitative difference, a sign of the boundary between a marked and an unmarked space. If this definition seems tautological it is because since Mauss, and in a different way since Duchamp, we know that the aesthetic space is not an anthropological constant but is constituted by a cultural recognition: the toilet seat hung in a museum is an aesthetic object because the museum sanctions its situation as aesthetic.

Any aesthetic object or process will tend to be defined by a particular configuration of framings. The frame of a painting may be reinforced by the broader frame of the museum; we could think of the "edge" of the work as a series of concentric waves in which the aesthetic space is enclosed. Theatrical space is defined by the borders of the stage, by the relation between the auditorium and the stage, and by the convention that the space of the stage is a privileged space of illusion.[12] Cinematic space is marked by the screen, by the darkness that surrounds the screen, by the projection apparatus and the theater situation, and by advertisements and billings (the visible frame of the industry). There is also an internal frame, the title sequence, which supplements and narrows down the predefinition of the kind of aesthetic space being outlined.

For a literary text the frame is particularly complex: it is made up, first of all, of the covers of a book, or the lines enclosing a poem in a journal (or by a recitation or reading situation); of the title pages, specifying genre and the expectations created by the date, by the signature, by dedicatory material, by the title, perhaps by the publishing house. Texts which have a special legitimacy often display special framing effects: that of a collected or standard edition, editorial exegesis (which may frame individual pages), an introduction stressing the canonic status of the text, expensive binding (corresponding to "the salient and richly ornamented enclosures that once . . . conveyed the idea of the preciousness of the work through its gilded mount"[13]—this is Kant's *goldene Rahmen*), and so on. A poem is usually framed, at a more intensive level, by the white margin that marks off line lengths (and this margin can be stressed in particular ways, as in the calligrams of Herbert or Apollinaire, or the attentive dispersal of the lines over the page of *Un Coup de dés*). For a narrative, the most intensive frame is that constituted by the beginning and, especially, the end of the narration. Jurij Lotman has constructed a typology of narrative modes on the basis of a distinction between those texts (for example myths or medieval chronicles) which emphasize origins and those which, like the novel, emphasize ends. The beginning of a text is governed by the modeling of causality, whereas the end stresses goals,[14] and this usefully links plot structure to the "edge" of the text, the point at which the text passes into, and is closed off from, nonaesthetic space, the "general text." The beginning of a text, finally, is the point at which the establishment of a particular distance between author and narrator usually occurs. The fourfold frame in which Scott encloses *The Heart of Midlothian,* for example, sets up a succession of redundant narrators in a strangely hesitant development of the narration which expresses something of the ambiguity of the novelistic speech situation. This distancing, like that effected by a prologue and epilogue, both reinforces the difference between the realm of narration and the realm of the narrated and eases the reader into the fictive world, sparing her the abruptness of a sudden passage.

The authority of the frame corresponds to that of the generic conventions it establishes. It works as a metacommunication specifying how to use the text, what one can expect to happen at different stages, and what to do if these expectations are not confirmed (for example, how to switch frame).[15] The "internal" structure of the text may either confirm this authority or react against it, or at the extreme it may break it. It is crucial that the text never completely *fills* the frame. But in all of these cases structure is made possible only by the presence of the frame, as norm or restriction and as the conventional sign of a closure which separates the limitedness of the text from the unlimitedness of the general text.[16] As a limit its importance lies precisely in this ambiguity of its threshold situation. Meyer Schapiro and Boris Uspensky both assign the frame of a painting to the space of the observer rather than to the illusory three-dimensional space of representation, although Schapiro does concede that the frame may also function as a compositional device.[17] Erving Goffman, by contrast, is fully aware of the ambivalence of its function. He distinguishes two levels of the frame: "One is the innermost layering, wherein dramatic activity can be at play to engross the participant. The other is the outermost lamination, the *rim* of the frame, as it were, which tells us just what sort of status in the real world the activity has, whatever the complexity of the inner laminations."[18] The frame of course is unitary, neither inside nor outside, and this distinction of levels is a fiction to express the "thickness" of the frame, its duality as a component of structure and a component of situation. For a literary text it works both as an enclosure of the internal fictional space and as an exclusion of the space of reality against which the text is set; but this operation of exclusion is also an inclusion of the text in this alien space. The text is closed and suspended, but as a constructional element the frame is internal to this closure and through it the text signifies difference, signifies what it excludes. Within the field of vision are included both the aesthetic space and the edge of aesthetic space. The extra-aesthetic is manifested negatively at this moment of passage, where the text reaches the limit and starts to become nontext. The energy of the frame thus radiates in two directions simultaneously: on the one hand, it conducts the trace of the excluded nonaesthetic area inward, so that the delimited space of the text is structured by its limit and becomes significant because of the restrictions operated by the frame. Thus the compositional structure of a painting—its perspective, the play of vectors, the foregrounding and backgrounding of motifs—is defined by the relation to the vertical and horizontal lines of the "edge"; and these are not simply the farthest point to which the painting reaches but are rather the dynamic moments which constitute the system and the semantic richness of the painting.

Similarly the margin around a poem is not an empty support of the printed text but actively breaks the poem off from its continuity with everyday life, suspending the line in arbitrary rhythmic or typographic lengths and isolating the poetic flower as *l'absente de tous bouquets*. And the end of a narrative shapes the plot, not as a static sequence of events but as a teleologically structured movement which characterizes the time of the text as a significant time in relation to the nonsignificant time against which it is set and from which it differentiates itself.[19] Yet the frame also situates the text within nonaesthetic space and thus transforms it into a function. The text is "quoted" by and within its context—the context of a particular kind of speech situation. This situation is variable: a text may be situated in the "normal" space of an aesthetic situation indicated by its frame (a play may be staged as an aesthetic object), or the frame may be ignored and the text "quoted" to nonaesthetic ends (the text of the play may serve as a moral or sociological example, or the play may be staged as a historical curiosity, so that it becomes a citation in a larger written or unwritten text). The frame signifies only the norm (the text as an aesthetic object, and the normative regime governing the reception of this object); as a sign of a conventionally guaranteed use of the text, it cannot account for deviant functions, including those which may bring about a reframing.

But the mere fact of the convergence of the internal structure and the contextual function of the text at the "edge" of the text indicates that the frame does not simply separate an outside from an inside but unsettles the distinction between the two. Changes in the literary system alter the valency of the frame and are thus translated into structural shifts in the text; and conversely, structural changes (new readings or uses of a text) become institutionalized as changes in the norm signified by the frame and so gradually alter the relevant "context." In this process the frame, as the conventionally regulated index of a demarcation, internalizes the "external" function of the text. The theater, where the frame is manifested largely as a visible architectural border and where genre structures can be closely correlated with this border (at least in the long term), provides a clear example of this. The change from the projecting Elizabethan stage to the pictorial space of the proscenium arch both corresponds to and reinforces a radically different kind of speech situation in which the whole status of the scenic illusion is modified. The alteration of the frame, in direct relation to modifications in the literary system (to the distance and the closed rigidity of frame characteristic of a neoclassical system) alters the nature of dramatic reality (the nature of the fictional space), and this is illustrated in exemplary fashion by modifications in the aesthetic object itself: modifications in interpretation of existing plays, for example of Shakespeare through new canons of performance (Tate's *Lear*) or through editorial restructuration of the texts; and in the production of new texts, for example the change between *Antony and Cleopatra* and *All for Love*.

As the index of a set of rules of usage, the frame thus corresponds roughly to what George Kubler calls the "self-signal" of a text,[20] its signification of itself as a function with a differential relation to reality. But the difficulty of coping with the concept of frame is the near invisibility of the frame. We have been taught to naturalize the space of the aesthetic object, to lose ourselves in an inside which is as unlimited as the world,[21] and this means that our "natural" inclination is to see the work in the same way we see the world, without awareness of the edge of our eyes' scan. The white margin around a poem, the beginning and end of reading, the darkness around the stage disappear as we focus on the presence of the text; they become an unapprehended negativity. And the frame is rightly an absence insofar as it is a purely relational moment, the point of crystallization of metadiscursive instructions. Like the meridian line dividing night from morning, it exists only as a sign of difference, and without a forcing of attention it is blotted out by the quasisubstantiality of its content. A *forcing* of attention: Derrida writes that the logic of the *parergon* is a "reflective operation" which affects the philosophy of art (and the empiricisms which are complicit with it) *necessarily,* and which is (or can "allow itself to be") "inscribed on the frame." It is the logic of "a certain repeated dislocation, an irrepressible regular deterioration which cracks the frame in general, embeds it in the corners of its angles and articulations, turns its inner limit into an outer limit, takes account of its thickness, lets us see the painting from the side of the canvas or the wood, etc." (85–86). The frame deconstructs itself; a work of deconstruction is always already written into the concept. Here and later Derrida appeals to the work of the frame, the work done by the frame. But a political analysis appeals instead (in Lesley Stern's words) to the work done *on* the text and on the frame, to the possibilities of laying bare the formal and institutional conditions of reading.[22]

WE HAVE MOVED from the frame of analysis to the framing of texts. I now want to retrace my steps in order to pose again the question of the conditions of theoretical enunciation, and in particular of the connection between the constitution of a distinctively or specifically aesthetic space and the historicity of the language which makes this possible. I want to approach this question initially from a very different direction—that of Gadamerian hermeneutics—because of the force with which it situates the reader/receiver of a text within the continuing process of constitution of the text ("All encounter with the language of art is an encounter with a still unfinished process and is itself part of this process"),[23] and because of its ability to skew the question of historical thinking back upon the question of its own historicality.

At the center of Gadamer"s attempt to redefine the validity of non-scientific knowledge is his opposition to the self-obliteration of the knowing subject in nineteenth-century *Historismus*. The bases for a reconstruction of a theory and practice of historical mediation are Hegel's conception of historical understanding as a self-recognition of the Spirit (100), and Heidegger's displacement of this unity of subject and object from an ontological to a historical realm. As Gadamer phrases it: "The coordination of all knowing activity with what is known is not based on the fact that they are essentially the same but draws its significance from the particular nature of the mode of being that is common to both of them. It consists in the fact the neither the knower nor the known are present-at-hand in an 'ontic' way but in a historical one, i.e., they are of the mode of being of historicalness" (232). The mediation of historical subjectivity occurs through language, which constitutes the guarantee and the limit of our understanding of otherness (xxii); but if language unites us with the past (and this possibility of "recognition" is partial and often indirect), history anchors us in a separateness and a particularity which is the unconscious precondition of our being:

> In fact history does not belong to us, but we belong to it. Long before we understand ourselves through the process of self-exami-nation, we understand ourselves in a self-evident way in the family, society and state in which we live. The focus of subjectivity is a distorting mirror. The self-awareness of the individual is only a flick-ering in the closed circuit of historical life. That is why the prejudices of the individual, far more than his judgments, constitute the his-torical reality of his being.   (245)

This self-evidentiality and unconsciousness of institutionally regulated meanings corresponds closely to what I mean by ideology, and Gadamer relates it causally to the concept of Authority. But this Authority seems to have no relation to social structure. Its dimensions are restricted to the personal and charismatic. By setting the discussion of prejudice in the con-text of the Enlightenment's mechanistic opposition of Authority to the autonomy of Reason (247), Gadamer argues that insofar as prejudice sets a limit to the absoluteness of reason, we must recognize the relative validity of prejudice, and this means recognizing that Authority is the source of both prejudice and truth (or of truth in the form of prejudice, 247). This in turn leads Gadamer to a legitimation of Authority: of "real" Authority, that is, which is rooted in the individual—"the teacher, the superior, the expert" (249)—outside of any social context, and which is based not on subjection (*Unterwerfung*) but on recognition (*Anerkennung*) (248). This recognition is part of the larger consensus which guarantees social order and which (as in the case of the psychoanalyst, who must engage in his hermeneutic activity only in his professional capacity),[24] sets the limits to critical reflection: "Hermeneutic reflection teaches us that social community, despite all its tensions and divisions, always goes back to a social consensus through which it exists,"[25] and this "genuine" order is opposed to "the disorder of naked violence."[26]

But it is precisely ideology which—on the basis of "consensus"—transforms naked force into "order." As Habermas writes, "violence becomes permanent anyway only through the objective appearance of the non-violence of a pseudo-communicative consensus"; and Gadamer's argument presupposes "that the legitimating recognition and the consensus which is constitutive of Authority work without violence."[27] Because of his exclusion of this dimension of power (of the asymmetry of nearly all communication), Gadamer characterizes the hermeneutic situation as a "conversation" between two autonomous "Thou's" (321, 330)—a conversation between fully present, fully constituted subjects on a basis of equality. If a relation to Authority is involved—for example to the authority of "tradition" (249) or of the "classic" (258)—this is nevertheless an innocent relation because there is no necessary connection between systems of meaning and systems of power. And language works in this conversation as a transparent or potentially transparent window, not as a productive practice.[28]

What is problematic in Gadamer's argument is his failure to situate tradition in the social function to which it has been assimilated:

> The Enlightenment knew something that Gadamer forgets: that the "conversation" that Gadamer says we "are" is also a power relationship, and to that extent is not a conversation . . . The universal claims of the hermeneutic approach can be maintained only if we proceed from an understanding that the network of tradition [*der Überlieferungszusammenhang*], as the locus of possible truth and factual agreement, is simultaneously the locus of factual untruth and of persistent violence.[29]

Thinking through within a Marxist practice of reading the idea that our own historical situation is an essential factor of historical understanding would entail both a challenge to the postulation of historical continuity (a questioning of the very possibility of historical understanding) and a greater concession to the foreignness and distance of the transmitted text. In Gadamer's writings this distance is masked by the legitimation of authority and of the normativeness of the "classic." Prejudice comes to be seen not as a limitation to understanding which must itself be exposed to hermeneutic reflection, but as a justification of the limits of reflection, just as Gadamer's recognition of the omnipresence of tradition turns into a "recognition" of its authority. The inability to see the symbolic order as being riven by relations of power means that Gadamer fails to understand what makes all understanding doubtful, the historically determined ideological function of language and tradition, which situates us in a symbolic power relation at the same time as it appears to purify this situation of any political dimension.

The knowledges produced by texts are always relative to a definite social regulation of the uses and boundaries of interpretation. The historical problem of assessing the ideological intensity of a text, the degree of its break with ideological norms and the level at which this occurs is finally the problem of the historicity of reading: what we notice in a text is guided and limited by our situation within a field of ideological struggle. A concern with the lines of power which structure this situation precludes the relegation of the text to the apparently closed context of its initial writing. It can be situated neither in an unmediated pastness nor in an unmediated presence. This is all the more a methodological necessity because of the way in which capitalism constructs the past, in a massive totalization of human history over and above the global extension of the capitalist mode of production, as a moment of the present. Through industrialized tourism, through films and television documentaries, through academic and popular historiography, through a constant productive flow of discourses and images, the past is not just recovered, displayed, interpreted but is written within and by the present as a sign of difference from the present. But in recognizing this we must also be wary of assuming the homogeneous temporality of the present and the uninterrupted totality of the capitalist mode of production. Part of what is involved in integrating our own history as a component of the textual process is an awareness that the "present" is not a homogeneous conjunctural presence but is crossed by polychronic lines of force; that, in Frank Lentricchia's words, "it is in the sign conceived as trace that the present as an in-itself is broken up and reconstituted as a synthesis of retentions and protentions, a relation to both as a past and a future."[30] Thus a "classic" text (the Bible, the Homeric epics) has the complex presence of a Scripture (which blocks, reifies its iteration in and appropriation by other systems of writing) and at the same time of a repertory of disseminated forms and topoi whose status approximates that of the popular subgenres.

The situation of reception is thus a relation to a process which can be defined, in shorthand form, as a relation to the authority of the textual frame. Readers react to the authority of the transmitted text (where the text has been absorbed into the canon) either by reproducing (confirming) it or by contesting it; and in this respect their situation—like that of Menard, first inventing and then rejecting variants—is parallel to that of the producer of a new text. Reading is only immediately an act of simple consumption; it is, more important, an act of production (or of reproduction) on the basis of previous acts of readerly production and reproduction. We can carry the economic metaphor a little farther and say that the authority of the text is equivalent to its value: not an isolated use value but an exchange value, which is created by its integration into a market system, the system of valorization of cultural objects, where it becomes a cultural token, an automatized "official" value. The text which has acquired normative status represents a storing up of such value (through the prolonged injection of value in the course of its appropriations), and so a cultural capital which is denied to subordinate classes and which has the double function of exclusion, and of legitimation of the social order. It has a symbiotic relation to the dominant form of social capital, a relation of both disguise and representation.

The task of the reader who is trying to come to terms with this stored-up symbolic value and who is concerned with a reflexive integration of his or her own situation cannot be that of a "correct" interpretation of the text, nor can it simply be the practical one of transferring this value to those dispossessed of "legitimate" culture; these two choices entail only a reinvestment or a redistribution of cultural capital, and this leaves the text within the sphere of legitimacy, where it continues to be the property of the dominant class and its administrators. Rather than reproducing the text's official value, the reader must undertake a negative revalorization by "unframing" it, appropriating it in such a way as to make it subversive of its own legitimacy and so *useful* in the class struggle. The possibility of doing this is not inherent in the text, but it is possible to construct the moment of initial intertextual productivity as an image of such a possibility. To construct this moment (which has no given form and no fixed textual markers) is to break the commodity character of the text, to comprehend its immediacy as a historical result which is based on an earlier act of critical production. This is neither the restoration of an "original" text (and an "original" intertextuality) nor an absolute negativity (the break with dominant norms is only ever partial and its limits are historically conditioned) but rather the bringing together of two productive activities: that of the text in its initial relation (its reading constructed in our reading) to the literary system, and that of a reading which attempts to release the text from its accretion of normative values. The chance is that of converting the text's criticality into a use value and of using our appropriation of the text against the socially normative appropriation. For example, the slight ambivalence toward the theological order in Dante's *Commedia,* through both the hierarchical polyvalence of its symbols (with their materialist resonance at the lower end of the scale) and the overconstruction of the "system" (which becomes an intrusive frame, laying bare the paradox of an absolute order that claims to encompass human freedom), allows us, as *part* of a reading, to read the poem as a metaphor at various non- or antitheological levels (as a political poem, a poem about poetry, a poem about the contradiction between maternal presence and the Law of the Father, and so on).

The interpretive emphasis, then, is thrown onto the use that we can make of the text, rather than concentrating on a self-contained recollection or revelation of meaning. The productive role of the reader, fusing with the image of textual productivity, represents a break with a dominant regime of reading and with the institutional context of reading which directly or indirectly sustains this regime. It thus sets up a connection (however tenuous it may be in itself) to other political practices. To "politicize" the situation of reception therefore means no more than to make evident a political dimension it already contains; but an enormous effort is necessary to bring to evidence that which is invisible as a condition of its effectiveness. In this, the interpretation (use) of literary texts is a part of the larger problem of interpreting and actively transforming "past" history. If it is true that the capitalist present is constantly constructing the past as a massively derealized simulacrum, it is also true that this present is nothing more than the putting to work of a stored-up pastness (stored-up labor in capital, stored-up power-knowledge in technology, stored-up power-value in culture, stored-up violence in the law and the state). This repetitious weight of the past is an oppression from which we can rescue ourselves only by political choices. Marxism is not the predestined heir of history but the possibility of a radical break with its patterns—which are patterns of oppression and repression, of violence and suffering. But just as literary texts have a double form of existence, as normative models endowed with ideological authority, and as a stock of reusable material, so past history has a potential productivity in that it can be rescued from its "possession" by a dominant class. Benjamin has written extensively about this possibility: a genuinely creative understanding of history—as distinct from that monumental conception of history that Nietzsche condemned—can be achieved when we recognize that the past is only fleetingly graspable and when we confront it in "the critical constellation . . . in which precisely this fragment of the past encounters precisely this present."[31] This fragment of the past is experienced as unique and momentary;[32] it flashes up only when it is threatened by the danger of appropriation, of becoming a weapon in the hands of the ruling class, and disappears when its relevance is not lived.[33] This is to say that the past becomes available only as a function of repetition—that, in Deleuze's words, "repetition is the historical condition under which something new is effectively produced."[34] Rather than historical continuities, the ever-present availability of tradition, we have access only to a past which is radically discontinuous with the present; and this discontinuity is directly bound up with radical inequalities of power in the present. The possibility of redeeming the past depends entirely on the interests and energies, the play of forces mobilized by political struggle.

"The decree of the past is always an oracular decree; only as an architect of the future, with a true knowledge of the present, will you understand it."[35] Nietzsche's linking of historical understanding to political practice may serve to indicate again the inadequacy of a purely "aesthetic" interpretation of the "classic" texts: as Jauss has argued, the destruction of the aesthetic distance between these texts and the contemporary horizon of literary norms means the approximation of the classic to kitsch.[36] The social function of the classical text is in the first place to *be* a classical text, to signify its own value as cultural capital. It is entirely a self-signal, a solid and empty frame, and it is therefore withdrawn from the realm of heterosignification. This can be restored only if we contest the function itself and displace the text from its ideal nontime, restoring a historical distance and strangeness to it. To put this differently, the text has not only an intertextual relationship to previous texts (in the case of the classics this is usually effaced) but also an intertextual relationship to itself as canonized text. The responsibility is ours for making this relation one of difference from itself, of self-estrangement, rather than of conformity with itself. In this respect Logue's "translation" of Homer is exemplary. Its fragmentation of epic unity, its refusal of antiquarian reconstruction, its disrespect for the authoritative and authoritarian textuality which is its object constitute a fully productive misreading, one which, in abolishing historical difference, converting the *Iliad* into a modernist text, at the same time restores (produces) the contradictions of the multiple historicities and the multiple textualities of its text.

TO DESCRIBE, from within a literary system, the interpretive limits set by the system is at once to describe a set of constraints and to interrupt the limits, the enclosing frame, by framing them within a larger closure. This process is neither revolutionary nor endless. The possibility of unsettling limits is always both given and limited by an actual condition of power. There is no outside of power. But to write, within discursive limits, with a recognition of what these limits are and of the forms of discursive objects and relations delimited by a discursive formation is to push at these limits, to lay them open to the inspection of a counterpower whose force is not completely contained or foreseen. Without this possibility no system could ever change, it could only collapse from its own inertia.[37]

This problematic of limits is characteristically that of Derridean deconstruction: Derrida's writings focus relentlessly on the concepts of limit, border, genre, closure, context, margin, frame. One way of unifying this thematic repetition would be to say that it concerns the status of a theoretical metadiscourse, and so the possibility of closure (or grounding) of discourse. The activity of deconstruction is one of constantly undermining any such possibility by indicating that this act of closure can itself be subsumed within a further series at a higher logical level; whatever marks the edge of a set, "the closing that excludes itself from what it includes,"[38] can itself be folded into another set.[39] But such a demonstration, such a reframing, would itself be no more than a further exercise of the authority of closure. Rather than repeating this demarcation between an inside and an outside, a center and a periphery, and without claiming to transcend the problematic of systemic closure, deconstruction seeks to problematize the problematic, to make it irresolvable; and it does this by stressing either the potential infinity of metacommunicative closures or the internal ambiguity, the paradoxicality, the marginality of any centralizing or totalizing act of closure. But this deferral of judgment and authority, this refusal to occupy the place of law, has ambivalent political consequences.

Here are two descriptions of how deconstruction constructs beginnings and endings. In the first, Sprinker writes that each time Derrida addresses the quesion of who or what produces a critical reading, he begs the question by "producing yet another reading which does not establish the grounds of its own possibility but rather shows how the attempt to reach such a stable beginning point or ground is always already differentiated into oppositions that undermine the project of such a pure beginning."[40] In the second, Jonathan Culler writes that "since deconstruction treats any position, theme, origin, or end as a construction and analyses the discursive forces that produce it, deconstructive writings will try to put in question anything that might seem a positive conclusion and will try to make their own stopping points distinctly divided, paradoxical, arbitrary, or indeterminate."[41] The two descriptions are almost identical, but the first is a condemnation and the second is, presumably, written in approval. The question of the politics of deconstruction has been exhaustively discussed,[42] and I do not want to pursue it at any length here. It is in part the wrong question to ask, insofar as it relies upon a unification of deconstruction as a movement or a more or less systematic critical strategy, and consequently upon the question of the relation between Derrida's writings and institutionalized American deconstruction (a question which depends upon a problematic of fidelity or infidelity to an origin, a problematic of responsibility). But there can certainly be little doubt about the political implications of mainstream "American" deconstruction. As Christopher Fynsk argues, it relies upon a self-serving critique of the political which problematizes the category of decision by demonstrating that any stance is an instance in a play of difference and deferral, that any act or performance is a representation, and vice versa; but the criticism stops there, and so "remains critical in a traditional sense—it is not itself carried into the movement of its own deconstructive process."[43] But this is equally true of the literary politics of academic deconstruction. Its critical practice and its pedagogy entirely reproduce the traditional literary canon and traditional exegetical procedures based on the supposition of intrinsic textual properties (the self-deconstructing activity of literary texts); and it has never disturbed disciplinary boundaries.

The object of the practice of deconstruction is closed formal systems. But any formal system is a component of a system of institutionalized practices. In the case of the former it makes sense to stress the impossibility of closure and limitation; in the case of the latter it usually makes sense to stress, in the first instance, the real limitations imposed by such systems and the strategic difficulty of breaking these limitations (since the breaking of the closure of systems of practice does not depend upon an act of will or demonstration). This division is of course itself open to question, but I think it is an important distinction to make if it is done in the way that any political positioning should be undertaken: provisionally, and in accordance with necessities which are conjunctural. Such a positioning is in principle quite alien to that constitutive positioning by which, say, the metadiscourse of aesthetics establishes (or screens the establishment of) the concept of art, and it has a quite opposite attitude toward the question of aesthetic interest. Remember the responses to the question of the beauty of the palace that Kant disqualifies in his attempt to clarify an intrinsically aesthetic response:

> I may, perhaps, reply that I do not care for things of that sort that are merely made to be gaped at. Or I may reply in the same strain as that Iroquois *sachem* who said that nothing in Paris pleased him better than the eating-houses. I may even go a step further and inveigh with the vigour of a *Rousseau* against the vanity of the great who spend the sweat of the people on such superfluous things. Or, in fine, I may quite easily persuade myself that if I found myself on an uninhabited island, without hope of ever again coming among men, and could conjure such a palace into existence by a mere wish, I should still not trouble to do so, so long as I had a hut there that was comfortable enough for me.[44]

All of these judgments might be interesting, but none of them would constitute an intrinsically aesthetic judgment. But suppose that there is no interest, no "disinterested interest," apart from this heterogeneous array of possible interests. To suggest this is not to open the way to a pluralist eclecticism; I have made it clear throughout that I think interpretive interest should be focused on the overdetermination of discourse by power. But it does mean that there should be no normative regulation of an aesthetically (or politically or morally) "correct" mode of reading and theorizing. The "point" of literary study is various and open.

But these interests, these ends of reading, are nevertheless susceptible of systematic description in terms of the interpretive regimes which govern them, and which make them something other than individual responses. To describe can easily become a positivism which, giving itself no other justification than that of producing an exact knowledge of textual for-

234 Marxism and Literary History

mations, can link up only with academic practices of knowing, with practices of closure. The alternative to this must be a practice which can continually, and effectively, pose to itself the question of its own use and usefulness, the question of the extent to which it reproduces or transforms institutional structures of knowing, the question of its ability to generate a textual politics (a political positioning of texts). These questions do not allow of simple answers in the case of literary study, precisely because of the highly mediated relations between social class, power, and literary discourse. Certainly I do not believe that, within current institutional structures, literary study can relate directly to the political needs of the working class or that it can contribute directly to the formation of organic working-class intellectuals[45] (and I think that self-deception about this can be politically dangerous). But it may well be the case that literary study has an exemplary value in relation to other discursively based disciplines. Leo Bersani argues that "literature may not *have* much power, but it should certainly be read as a display of power; and it is a peculiarly instructive model of that play of complicity and resistance which characterizes the innumerable local confrontations of power in human life."[46] It would perhaps be more accurate to say that this "instructiveness" is a function not so much of literary discourse as of the focus, or the possible focus, of literary analysis. The whole weight of recent literary theory has been on the *constitutive* status of language, on the impossibility of linguistic transparency, on the agonistic rhetorical strategies of discourse, and on the shaping of language by the forces of power and desire. The effect of this emphasis should be in the first place to redefine the traditional objects of literary knowledge, and in particular the forms of valorization of writing which have prevailed in most forms of literary study. But beyond this it should have the effect of calling into question the boundaries established between "high" and "popular" literary discourse, and between "literary" and "nonliterary" discourse. The necessary consequence of such a questioning would be the disruption of that disciplinary organization which excludes from literary study such genres and media as jokes, "natural" narratives, biography and autobiography, pornography and popular romances, journalism, and the genres of film and television.[47] This disruption would then involve the construction of a general poetics. But the most radical and yet most logical effect of the shifts in emphasis which have taken place in literary theory would be an extension of the strategies and interests of literary analysis to nonaesthetic discursive domains: to legal discourse, scientific discourse, historiography, philosophy; to moral and religious discourses; and to everyday language. It is no accident that two of the most thorough (but also in many ways very conservative) exercises in poetics in recent times, those of Frye and of Todorov, have concluded with a call for the self-abolition of poetics and its transformation into a general rhetoric.[48] This call has frequently been repeated, and with greater degrees of political awareness, since then.[49] The construction of a general poetics would be a necessary moment of its own self-abolition. This movement, with its progressive extension and radicalization of the question of discursive power, is one that at once completes and exceeds the argument of this book.

Notes

Index

Notes

1. Introduction

1. Edward Said, *Beginnings: Intention and Method*, 2nd ed. (1975; reprint, Baltimore: Johns Hopkins University Press, 1978), p. xiii.
2. Norman O. Brown, *Hermes the Thief: The Evolution of a Myth*, 2nd ed. (1947; reprint, New York: Vintage, 1969), p. 45.
3. Said, *Beginnings*, p. 6.
4. John Brenkman, "Theses on Cultural Marxism," *Social Text*, 7 (1983), 19.
5. Stanley Fish, "Profession Despise Thyself: Fear and Self-Loathing in Literary Studies," *Critical Inquiry*, 10, no. 2 (1983), 349–364.
6. Samuel Weber, "The Limits of Professionalism," *Oxford Literary Review*, 5, nos. 1 and 2 (1982), 68–69.
7. Ibid., p. 71.
8. Edward Said, "Opponents, Audiences, Constituencies, and Community," *Critical Inquiry*, 9, no. 1 (1982), 16. The editor's introduction to the collection in which this essay appears mentions that "these essays were first presented as lectures at *Critical Inquiry*'s symposium on 'The Politics of Interpretation,'" and that "special thanks are due to the Rockefeller Foundation, the Exxon Education Foundation, and the National Endowment for the Humanities for their generous support of this project" (vii–viii).
9. Ibid., p. 17.
10. Edward Said, *The World, the Text, and the Critic* (Cambridge, Mass.: Harvard University Press, 1983), p. 174.
11. Eduard Parow, *Die Dialektik des symbolischen Austauschs* (Frankfurt am Main: Europäische Verlagsanstalt, 1973), pp. 16–18.
12. Bernard Sharratt, *Reading Relations: Structures of Literary Production: A Dialectical Text/Book* (Brighton: Harvester, 1982), p. 14.
13. Cf. in particular Herbert Marcuse, *Soviet Marxism*, 2nd ed. (1958; reprint, Harmondsworth: Penguin, 1971); Oskar Negt, "Marxismus als Legitima-

tionswissenschaft: Zur Genese der stalinistischen Philosophie," introduction to Nicolai Bukharin and Abram Deborin, *Kontroversen über dialektischen und mechanistischen Materialismus* (Frankfurt am Main: Suhrkamp, 1974); Rossana Rossanda, *Über die Dialektik von Kontinuität und Bruch,* trans. B. Kroeber (Frankfurt am Main: Suhrkamp, 1975); and the first two volumes of Charles Bettelheim, *Les Luttes de classe en URSS* (Paris: Maspéro/Seuil, 1974, 1977).

14. Henri Arvon, *Marxist Aesthetics,* trans. H. Lane (Ithaca: Cornell University Press, 1973), p. 41.

15. Karel Kosík, *Dialectics of the Concrete,* trans. K. Kovanda and J. Schmidt, Boston Studies in the Philosophy of Science, vol. 52 (Boston: Reidel, 1976), p. 78.

16. V. F. Pereveržev, "Voraussetzungen der marxistischen Literaturwissenschaft," in *Marxistische Literaturkritik,* ed. V. Žmegač (Bad Homburg: Athenäum, 1970), p. 20.

17. Quoted in Francisco Posada, *Lukács, Brecht y la situación actual del realismo socialista* (Buenos Aires: Editorial Galerna, 1969), p. 176.

18. Cf. Ístvan Mészáros, *Lukács' Concept of Dialectic* (London: Merlin Press, 1972), p. 61.

19. "In our time the most substantial corpus of Marxist literary analysis, that of Lukács, has been genre-oriented from beginning to end (seeming, indeed, to recapitulate some ideal trajectory from a Hegelian interrogation of genre, in *Sociology of Modern Drama* and *The Theory of the Novel,* to an Aristotelian emphasis in the late two-volume *Aesthetik*"; Fredric Jameson, "Magical Narratives: Romance as Genre," *New Literary History,* 7, no. 1 (1975), 160.

20. Paul Hernardi, *Beyond Genre* (Ithaca: Cornell University Press, 1972), p. 115.

21. Georg Lukács, *The Theory of the Novel,* trans. A. Bostock (Cambridge, Mass.: MIT Press, 1971), p. 93.

22. Georg Lukács, "Hegels Ästhetik," in *Probleme der Ästhetik, Werke,* vol. 10 (Neuwied: Luchterhand, 1969), p. 118.

23. Lothar Baier, "Streit um den schwarzen Kasten," in *Lehrstück Lukács,* ed. Jutta Matzner (Frankfurt am Main: Suhrkamp, 1974), p. 250.

24. Helga Gallas, *Marxistische Literaturtheorie: Kontroversen im Bund proletarisch-revolutionärer Schriftsteller* (Neuwied: Luchterhand, 1971), p. 154.

25. Lukács, *Theory of the Novel,* p. 46.

26. Ibid., p. 37.

27. Ibid., p. 72.

28. Georg Lukács, *Writer and Critic,* trans. A. D. Kahn (New York: Grosset and Dunlap, 1971), p. 126.

29. Ibid., p. 127.

30. Ibid.

31. Alberto Asor Rosa, "Der junge Lukács—Theoretiker der bürgerlichen Kunst," in Matzner, *Lehrstück Lukács,* p. 101.

32. Cf. Paul de Man, "Georg Lukács' Theory of the Novel," in *Blindness and Insight* (New York: Oxford University Press, 1971), pp. 58–59.
33. Gerhard Fehn, "Georg Lukács: Erkenntnistheorie und Kunst," in Matzner, *Lehrstück Lukács,* p. 235.
34. Lukács, "Art and Objective Truth," in *Writer and Critic,* p. 31.
35. Ibid., pp. 31–32.
36. Lukács, "Über die Besonderheit als Kategorie der Ästhetik," in *Probleme der Ästhetik,* p. 670.
37. Lukács, "Art and Objective Truth," p. 34.
38. Lukács, "Über die Besonderheit," p. 757.
39. Ibid., p. 755.
40. Cf. ibid., p. 683: "The independent form of the work is therefore a reflection of essential connections and forms of appearance of reality itself."
41. Horst Althaus, *Georg Lukács, oder Bürgerlichkeit als Vorschule einer marxistischen Ästhetik* (Bern: Francke Verlag, 1962), p. 48.
42. Georg Lukács, "Tendenz oder Parteilichkeit," in *Essays über Realismus: Probleme des Realismus I, Werke,* vol. 4 (Neuwied: Luchterhand, 1971), p. 32.
43. Gallas, *Marxistische Literaturtheorie,* pp. 150–151.
44. "In the beginning he mumbles a couple of times 'period of bourgeois decadence,' and then after that just 'period of decadence'—it's the whole lot that's decaying, not the bourgeoisie"; Bertolt Brecht, *Arbeitsjournal I* (Frankfurt am Main: Suhrkamp, 1973), p. 13.
45. Hans Robert Jauss, "Literary History as a Challenge to Literary Theory," in *Toward an Aesthetic of Reception,* trans. Timothy Bahti, Theory and History of Literature, vol. 2 (Minneapolis: University of Minnesota Press, 1982), p. 194, n. 38.
46. Georg Lukács, *Essays on Thomas Mann,* trans. Stanley Mitchell (New York: Grosset and Dunlap, 1965), p. 16.
47. Ibid., p. 100.
48. Lukács, "Art and Objective Truth," p. 38.
49. Posada, *Lukács, Brecht,* p. 303.
50. Georg Lukács, *The Historical Novel,* trans. H. and S. Mitchell (Harmondsworth: Penguin, 1969), p. 290.
51. Gallas, *Marxistische Literaturtheorie,* p. 164.
52. Lukács, "Art and Objective Truth," p. 52.
53. Gallas, *Marxistische Literaturtheorie,* p. 51.
54. Bertolt Brecht, *Schriften zur Literatur und Kunst II, Gesammelte Werke,* vol. 19 (Frankfurt am Main: Suhrkamp, 1967), p. 317.
55. Ibid., p. 291.
56. Lukács, quoted in Posada, *Lukács, Brecht,* p. 30.
57. Cf. especially "The Intellectual Physiognomy in Characterization," in Lukács, *Writer and Critic,* pp. 149ff.

58. Georg Lukács, "Aus der Not eine Tugend," in *Essays über Realismus,* pp. 55ff.
59. Posada, *Lukács, Brecht,* p. 30.
60. Klaus Völker, "Brecht und Lukács: Analyse einer Meinungsverschiedenheit," *Kursbuch,* 7 (1966); Gallas, *Marxistische Literaturtheorie.*
61. For example, Cesare Cases, "Introduction," in Matzner, *Lehrstück Lukács.*
62. Werner Mittenzwei, "Die Brecht-Lukács Debatte," *Sinn und Form,* 19, no. 1 (1967), 244.
63. Brecht, *Arbeitsjournal I,* p. 25.
64. Brüggemann speaks in this respect of the merely formal mediating role between class consciousness and totality assigned in *History and Class Consciousness* to the party: it functions as a transcendental guarantee of knowledge of the social-historical totality. Heinz Brüggemann, *Literarische Technik und soziale Revolution: Versuche über das Verhältnis von Kunstproduktion, Marxismus und literarischer Tradition in den theoretischen Schriften Bertolt Brechts* (Reinbek bei Hamburg: Rowohlt, 1973), p. 91.
65. Mészáros, *Lukács' Concept of Dialectic,* pp. 80–81.
66. Ibid., p. 81.
67. Ibid.
68. Ibid., p. 82.
69. Rosa, "Der junge Lukács," p. 101.

2. Marxism and Structuralism

1. Pierre Macherey, *Pour une théorie de la production littéraire* (Paris: Maspéro, 1966); in English, *A Theory of Literary Production,* trans. Geoffrey Wall (London: Routledge and Kegan Paul, 1978); Terry Eagleton, *Criticism and Ideology* (London: New Left Books, 1976). References in the text to these and other works cited in the notes will give the page number and, where necessary, the title or the name of the author.
2. See Pierre Macherey and Etienne Balibar, "Literature as an Ideological Form: Some Marxist Propositions," trans. Ian McLeod et al., *Oxford Literary Review,* 3, no. 1 (1978), 4.
3. Francisco Posada, *Lukács, Brecht y la situación actual del realismo socialista* (Buenos Aires: Editorial Galerna, 1969), p. 217.
4. Macherey and Balibar, "Literature as an Ideological Form," p. 10.
5. Louis Althusser, "Contradiction and Overdetermination: Notes for an Investigation," in *For Marx,* trans. Ben Brewster (New York: Vintage Books, 1970), p. 101.
6. Ibid., p. 113.
7. Louis Althusser, "On the Materialist Dialectic: On the Unevenness of Origins," in *For Marx,* p. 213.

8. Louis Althusser and Etienne Balibar, *Reading Capital,* trans. Ben Brewster (London: New Left Books, 1970), p. 94; hereafter cited in the text.

9. Louis Althusser, "A Letter on Art in Reply to André Daspré," in *Lenin and Philosophy and Other Essays,* trans. Ben Brewster (New York: Monthly Review Press, 1971), p. 222.

10. Macherey and Balibar, "Literature as an Ideological Form," p. 12.

11. Catherine Gallagher, "The New Materialism in Marxist Aesthetics," *Theory and Society,* 9 (July 1980), 637, 639.

12. Terry Eagleton, "Aesthetics and Politics," *New Left Review,* 107 (February 1978), 22.

13. Tony Bennett, *Formalism and Marxism* (London: Methuen, 1979), p. 12.

14. Bennett, *Formalism and Marxism,* p. 112.

15. Philip Lewis, "The Post-Structuralist Condition," *Diacritics,* 12, no. 1 (Spring 1982), 12.

16. Ibid.

17. Ibid., p. 18.

18. Vincent Descombes, *Modern French Philosophy,* trans. L. Scott-Fox and J. M. Harding (Cambridge: Cambridge University Press, 1980), pp. 13, 75.

19. Fredric Jameson, *The Political Unconscious: Narrative as a Socially Symbolic Act* (London: Methuen, 1981), p. 9; hereafter cited in the text.

20. Fredric Jameson, *Marxism and Form* (Princeton, N.J.: Princeton University Press, 1971), p. 9, n. 2.

21. Fredric Jameson, *The Prison-House of Language* (Princeton, N.J.: Princeton University Press, 1972), p. 109.

22. Terry Eagleton, "Fredric Jameson: The Politics of Style," *Diacritics,* 12, no. 3 (Fall 1982), 19.

23. Cf. his comments, "Interview with Fredric Jameson," *Diacritics,* 12, no. 3 (Fall 1982), esp. 85–86.

24. Jameson, *Marxism and Form,* p. 74.

25. Terry Eagleton, *Walter Benjamin, or, Towards a Revolutionary Criticism* (London: Verso, 1981), p. 76; hereafter cited in the text.

26. V. I. Lenin, *Materialism and Empirio-Criticism: Critical Comments on a Reactionary Philosophy* (New York: International Publishers, 1927), pp. 38, 120–121.

27. Terry Eagleton, *The Rape of Clarissa: Writing, Sexuality and Class Struggle in Samuel Richardson* (Oxford: Blackwell, 1982), pp. 66–67.

3. *Discourse and Power*

1. Friedrich Engels, *The Condition of the Working Class in England,* in Marx/ Engels, *Collected Works,* vol. 4 (London: Lawrence and Wishart, 1975), pp. 347–348; hereafter cited in the text. I have interpolated occasional words or

phrases from the German edition, Karl Marx and Friedrich Engels, *Werke,* vol. 3 (Berlin: Dietz Verlag, 1969).

2. Stephen Marcus, *Engels, Manchester and the Working Class* (New York: Random House, 1975), p. 170.

3. One could perhaps define a further position—that of the petty bourgeois, the very ambivalence of whose class position would play a major role in the production of ideological effects. Engels's text is interesting in terms of the buffer role of this class, but there is no suggestion that it has an autonomous ideological position. The model I am using is not that of a direct correspondence between class position and ideological position; it is that of a contradictory coding, within which the noncategorical classes fit themselves.

4. Marcus, *Engels,* p. 172.

5. Paul Hirst, *On Law and Ideology* (London: Macmillan, 1979), p. 41.

6. Maurice Godelier, "Système, structure et contradiction dans 'le Capital,' " *Les Temps modernes* (November 1966), 832.

7. Barry Hindess and Paul Hirst, *Pre-Capitalist Modes of Production* (London: Routledge and Kegan Paul, 1975), p. 318.

8. Barry Hindess and Paul Hirst, *Mode of Production and Social Formation* (London: Macmillan, 1977), p. 20.

9. Ibid., pp. 11–17.

10. Ibid., p. 8.

11. Hirst, *On Law and Ideology,* p. 63.

12. Ibid., p. 19, n. 2.

13. Perry Anderson, *In the Tracks of Historical Materialism* (London: Verso, 1983), pp. 45–47; hereafter cited in the text.

14. Terry Lovell, *Pictures of Reality: Aesthetics, Politics and Pleasure* (London: BFI, 1980), p. 16.

15. Ibid., p. 17.

16. Cf. Anthony Wilden, *System and Structure* (London: Tavistock, 1972), p. 204.

17. Ferruccio Rossi-Landi, *Linguistics and Economics,* Janua Linguarum, Series Maior 81 (The Hague: Mouton, 1975), p. 16. The ultimate material irreducibility of the body is the basis of the social and of power, the limit to meaning, the final source and measure of value. But the body then in turn *becomes* meaning in the social order; it is the canvas for elaborate semiotic differentiations, in particular for the construction of gender, and it is the measure of other signifying systems: it feels pain and joy, but it also talks.

18. Michel Foucault, *Power/Knowledge,* ed. and trans. Colin Gordon (New York: Pantheon, 1980), p. 118.

19. Anthony Giddens argues that the concept of ideology "is *empty of content* because what makes belief systems ideological is their incorporation within systems of domination," and that "to understand this incorporation we must analyze the mode in which patterns of signification are incorporated within

the medium of *day-to-day practices*"; "Four Theses on Ideology," *Canadian Journal of Political and Social Theory,* 7, nos. 1 and 2 (1983), 18.

20. Nicos Poulantzas, *Political Power and Social Classes,* trans. Timothy O'Hagan (London: New Left Books and Sheed and Ward, 1973), p. 203.

21. Antonio Gramsci, *Selections from the Prison Notebooks,* ed. and trans. Quinton Hoare and Geoffrey Nowell Smith (New York: International Publishers, 1971), p. 55.

22. Nicholas Abercrombie, Stephen Hill, and Bryan S. Turner, *The Dominant Ideology Thesis,* 2nd ed. (1980; reprint, London: George Allen and Unwin, 1984), p. 185.

23. Cf. Georg Lukács, *History and Class Consciousness,* trans. Rodney Livingstone (Cambridge, Mass.: MIT Press, 1971), p. 86.

24. Mikhail Bakhtin/V. N. Vološinov, *Marxism and the Philosophy of Language,* trans. L. Matejka and I. R. Titunik (New York: Seminar Press, 1973), p. 10.

25. Ibid., p. 9.

26. Rossi-Landi, *Linguistics and Economics,* p. 139.

27. Cf. Charles K. Ogden and Ivor A. Richards, *The Meaning of Meaning,* 8th ed. (1923; reprint, New York: Harcourt, Brace, 1956), p. 11.

28. Ferdinand de Saussure, *Course in General Linguistics,* trans. Wade Baskin (New York: McGraw-Hill, 1966), p. 112.

29. Ibid., p. 65.

30. Umberto Eco, *A Theory of Semiotics* (Bloomington: Indiana University Press, 1976), p. 61.

31. Jacques Derrida, *Of Grammatology,* trans. Gayatri Chakravorty Spivak (Baltimore: Johns Hopkins University Press, 1976), p. 49.

32. Eco, *Theory of Semiotics,* p. 68.

33. Michel Foucault, *The Archaeology of Knowledge,* trans. A. M. Sheridan Smith (London: Tavistock, 1972), pp. 87–88, 99; hereafter cited in the text. On Bakhtin's parallel distinction between sentence and utterance in his *Estetika* (1979) ("A sentence . . . lacks the capability of determining a response; it acquires this capability . . . only in the entirety comprised by an utterance"), cf. Michael Holquist, "Answering as Authoring: Mikhail Bakhtin's Trans-Linguistics," *Critical Inquiry,* 10, no. 2 (1983), 313.

34. Holquist, "Answering as Authoring," p. 311.

35. For the second position, cf. Teun van Dijk, *Text and Context: Explorations in the Semantics and Pragmatics of Discourse* (London: Longman, 1977), p. 91.

36. Hermann Parret, *Language and Discourse,* Janua Linguarum, Series Minor 119 (The Hague: Mouton, 1971), pp. 275–276.

37. Bakhtin/Vološinov, *Marxism and the Philosophy of Language,* p. 20.

38. Ibid., p. 21; cf. Bakhtin, *Estetika,* p. 258 (translated in Holquist, "Answering as Authoring," p. 314): "To learn to speak means to learn to construct utterances . . . We learn to cast our speech in generic forms and, when we hear

others' speech, we deduce its genre from the first words; we anticipate in advance a certain volume (that is, the approximate length of the speech whole) as well as a certain compositional structure. We foresee the end; that is, from the very beginning we have a sense of the speech whole."

39. M. A. K. Halliday, *Language as Social Semiotic* (London: Edward Arnold, 1978), p. 111; hereafter cited in the text.

40. Tzvetan Todorov, *Les Genres du discours,* Collection Poétique (Paris: Seuil, 1978), p. 23.

41. Michel Pêcheux, *Les Vérités de la Palice,* Collection Théorie (Paris: Maspéro, 1975), p. 81.

42. But cf. Paul Hirst and Penny Woolley's caution that "prayer . . . does not have one universal form, nor are the attributes of the subjects who support forms of prayer universal. The mechanical repetition of the *Ave Maria* and the earnest dialogue with God imply and produce very different subjects"; Hirst and Woolley, *Social Relations and Human Attributes* (London: Tavistock, 1982), p. 120.

43. Cf. Bernard Edelman, *Ownership of the Image: Elements for a Marxist Theory of Law,* trans. Elizabeth Kingdom (London: Routledge and Kegan Paul, 1979), p. 29.

44. David Crystal and Derek Davy, *Investigating English Style* (London: Longman, 1969), p. 213.

45. Cf. Bakhtin's argument that "one of the main subjects of human speech is discourse itself," that metadiscursivity is a generalized usage of language. M. M. Bakhtin, *The Dialogic Imagination,* trans. Caryl Emerson and Michael Holquist (Austin: University of Texas Press, 1981), p. 355.

46. Crystal and Davy insist that "linguistic features do not usually correlate in any neat one-for-one way with the situational variables in an extra-linguistic context," and that linguists should therefore be concerned rather with "*ranges* of appropriateness and acceptability of various uses of language to given situations" (*Investigating English Style,* p. 62). While it is important to register the point that language cannot be read off from context, and vice versa, it should be noted that M. A. K. Halliday's "situation of context" is not a particular empirical context but (1) a *semiotic* environment and (2) a *type*.

47. Jacques Derrida, "The Law of Genre," trans. Avital Ronell, *Glyph,* 7 (1980), 203.

48. Ibid., p. 206.

49. David Silverman and Brian Torode, *The Material Word* (London: Routledge and Kegan Paul, 1980), p. 337.

50. Derrida, "The Law of Genre," p. 212.

51. Ibid., p. 206.

52. Jonathan Culler has argued that "meaning is context-bound, but context is boundless," in the first place because discourse is always open to further de-

scription or new framings, and second because "any attempt to codify context can always be grafted onto the context it sought to describe, yielding a new context which escapes the previous formulation"; *On Deconstruction* (London: Routledge and Kegan Paul, 1983), p. 123. It is true that discourse *may* not be limited; but the occurrence of discourse is always particular, and it always yields particular effects of knowledge and power.

53. Pêcheux, *Les Vérités de la Palice*, p. 144.

54. Cf. Robert Hodge and Gunther Kress, *Language as Ideology* (London: Routledge and Kegan Paul, 1979), p. 9.

55. Paul Henry, "On the Processing of Message Referents in Contexts," in *Social Contexts of Messages*, ed. E. Carswell and R. Rommetveit (London: Academic Press, 1971), p. 79.

56. Bakhtin's concept of "carnivalesque" discourse covers the same phenomenon. Mikhail Bakhtin, *Rabelais and His World*, trans. Hélène Iswolsky (Cambridge, Mass.: MIT Press, 1968).

57. Basil Bernstein, *Class, Codes and Control*, vol. I, 2nd ed. (1971; reprint, St. Alban's: Paladin, 1973).

58. Pierre Bourdieu and Jean-Claude Passeron, *Les Héritiers: les étudiants et la culture* (Paris: Minuit, 1964); Pierre Bourdieu, *Reproduction in Education, Society and Culture*, trans. Richard Nice (London: Sage Publications, 1977).

59. Mary Douglas, *Implicit Meanings* (London: Routledge and Kegan Paul, 1975), p. 177.

60. Michael Gregory and Susan Carroll, *Language and Situation: Language Varieties and Their Social Context* (London: Routledge and Kegan Paul, 1978), p. 80.

61. Bernstein, *Class, Codes and Control*, p. 197.

62. Ibid., p. 199.

63. Ibid., p. 200.

64. Hirst and Woolley, *Social Relations and Human Attributes*, p. 136.

65. Louis Althusser, "Ideology and Ideological State Apparatuses," in *Lenin and Philosophy*, trans. Ben Brewster (New York: Monthly Review Press, 1971), p. 161.

66. Colin MacCabe, "On Discourse," *Economy and Society*, 8, no. 4 (1979), 302.

67. Althusser, "Ideology and Ideological State Apparatuses," p. 171.

68. Stephen Heath, "Notes on Suture," *Screen*, 18, no. 4 (1977–1978), 73.

69. Emile Benveniste, *Problèmes de linguistique générale*, vol. 1 (Paris: Gallimard, 1966), p. 259.

70. Ibid., p. 130.

71. V. N. Vološinov, *Freudianism: A Marxist Critique*, trans. I. R. Titunik (New York: Academic Press, 1976), p. 101.

72. Henry, "On the Processing of Message Referents," p. 88.

73. A. J. Greimas, *Sémiotique et sciences sociales* (Paris: Seuil, 1976), p. 21.

74. Paul Henry, *Le mauvais outil: langue, sujet et discours* (Paris: Klincksieck, 1977), pp. 58–59.
75. M. A. K. Halliday and Ruqaiya Hasan, "Text and Context: Aspects of Language in a Social-Semiotic Perspective," *Sophia Linguistica,* 6 (1980), 76.
76. Donald Barry, "Knowledge Without Epistemology? A Study of Three Possibilities" (honors diss., Griffith University, Brisbane, Australia, 1982), p. 38.
77. Michel Foucault, *The History of Sexuality,* vol. I, trans. Robert Hurley (Harmondsworth: Penguin, 1981), p. 96.
78. Dana B. Polan, "Fables of Transgression: The Reading of Politics and the Politics of Reading in Foucauldian Discourse," *Boundary 2,* 10, no. 3 (1982), 366.
79. Jacques Donzelot, *The Policing of Families,* quoted in Polan, "Fables of Transgression," p. 372.
80. Silverman and Torode, *The Material Word,* p. 185.

4. Russian Formalism and the Concept of Literary System

1. See especially Hans Günther, ed., *Marxismus und Formalismus* (Munich: Hanser, 1973); Leon Trotsky, *Literature and Revolution* (Ann Arbor: University of Michigan Press, 1960); Galvano Della Volpe, "Settling Accounts with the Russian Formalists," *New Left Review,* nos. 113–114 (1979), 133–145; Christopher Pike, ed., *The Futurists, the Formalists and the Marxist Critique* (London: Pluto, 1980).
2. Fredric Jameson, *The Prison-House of Language* (Princeton, N.J.: Princeton University Press, 1972), pp. 92–93.
3. Jurij Tynjanov and Roman Jakobson, "Problems in the Study of Literature and Language," in *Readings in Russian Poetics,* ed. and trans. Ladislav Matejka and Krystyna Pomorska (Cambridge, Mass.: MIT Press, 1971), p. 79.
4. Jurij Striedter, "Zur formalistischen Theorie der Prosa und der literarischen Evolution," in *Russischer Formalismus,* ed. Jurij Striedter, 2nd ed. (1969; reprint, Munich: Fink, 1971), p. lxxi.
5. Jurij Tynjanov, "Das literarische Faktum," in Striedter, *Russischer Formalismus,* p. 401.
6. Jurij Tynjanov, quoted in Boris M. Ejxenbaum, "The Theory of the Formal Method," in Matejka and Pomorska, *Readings in Russian Poetics,* p. 31.
7. René Wellek, "The Concept of Evolution in Literary History," in *Concepts of Criticism* (New Haven: Yale University Press, 1963), p. 40.
8. Viktor Šklovskij, "Art as Technique," in *Russian Formalist Criticism: Four Essays,* ed. L. Lemon and M. Reis (Lincoln: University of Nebraska Press, 1965), p. 11.
9. Jameson, *The Prison-House of Language,* p. 75.

10. Šklovskij, "Art as Technique," p. 12.
11. Striedter, "Zur formalistischen Theorie," p. xxiii.
12. Quoted in Exjenbaum, "Theory of the Formal Method," p. 12.
13. Viktor Šklovskij, "Sterne's *Tristram Shandy*," in Lemon and Reis, *Russian Formalist Criticism*, pp. 30–31.
14. Cf. Boris I. Arvatov, "Poetische und praktische Sprache (Zur Methodologie der Kunstwissenschaft)," in Günther, *Marxismus und Formalismus*, p. 225: "Šklovskij has forgotten that form lives not only in art but in every cell of life, and in this respect he has fallen to the same level as his opponents: neither they nor Šklovskij was able to recognize the social nature of form."
15. Cf. Ingrid Strohschneider-Kohrs, *Literarische Struktur und geschichtlicher Wandel* (Munich: Fink, 1971), p. 13.
16. Viktor Šklovskij, "The Connection between Devices of *Syuzhet* Construction and General Stylistic Devices," in *Russian Formalism*, ed. S. Bann and J. Bowlt, Twentieth Century Studies (New York: Barnes and Noble, 1973), p. 53.
17. Tynjanov, "Das literarische Faktum," p. 413.
18. Pavel N. Medvedev/Mikhail M. Bakhtin, *The Formal Method in Literary Scholarship: A Critical Introduction to Sociological Poetics,* trans. Albert J. Wehrle (Baltimore: Johns Hopkins University Press, 1978; reprint, Cambridge, Mass.: Harvard University Press, 1985), p. 145.
19. Ibid., p. 149.
20. Quoted in Viktor Ehrlich, *Russian Formalism,* 3rd ed. (1955; reprint, The Hague: Mouton, 1969), p. 109.
21. Striedter, "Zur formalistischen Theorie," p. xxx.
22. Peter Steiner, "Three Metaphors of Russian Formalism," *Poetics Today,* 2, no. 1b (1980–1981), 67.
23. Graham Pechey, "Bakhtin, Marxism, and Post-Structuralism," in *The Politics of Theory,* ed. Francis Barker et al. (Colchester: University of Essex, 1983), p. 236.
24. Steiner, "Three Metaphors," p. 79.
25. Ibid., p. 89.
26. Ibid., p. 95.
27. Pechey, "Bakhtin, Marxism, and Post-Structuralism," p. 238.
28. Roman Jakobson, "The Dominant," in Matejka and Pomorska, *Readings in Russian Poetics,* p. 85.
29. Jurij Tynjanov, "On Literary Evolution," in Matejka and Pomorska, *Readings in Russian Poetics,* p. 68.
30. Striedter, "Zur formalistischen Theorie," p. lxii.
31. Tynjanov, "On Literary Evolution," p. 69.
32. Ibid., p. 72.
33. Tynjanov and Jakobson, "Problems in the Study of Literature and Language," p. 79.

34. Tynjanov, quoted in Ejxenbaum, "The Theory of the Formal Method," p. 28.
35. Tynjanov, "On Literary Evolution," p. 77.
36. Ibid.
37. Ibid., p. 73.
38. Ibid., p. 74.
39. Ibid., pp. 73–74.
40. Ehrlich, *Russian Formalism,* p. 135.
41. Jakobson, "The Dominant," p. 84.
42. Roman Jakobson, "Fragments de 'La Nouvelle Poésie Russe,' " in *Questions de Poétique* (Paris: Seuil, 1973), p. 15.
43. Jakobson, "The Dominant," p. 84.
44. Roman Jakobson, "What Is Poetry?" in *Selected Writings,* vol. 3 (The Hague: Mouton, 1981), p. 750.
45. Ibid.
46. Ibid., pp. 749–750.
47. Jan Mukařovský, *Aesthetic Function, Norm and Value as Social Facts,* trans. M. Suino, Michigan Slavic Contributions, no. 3 (Ann Arbor: University of Michigan, 1970), p. 3.
48. Jan Mukařovský, "Zur tschechischen Übersetzung von Šklovskij's *Theorie der Prosa,*" *Alternative,* 80 (October 1971), 166.
49. Mukařovský, *Aesthetic Function,* p. 9.
50. Ibid., p. 3.
51. Hans Günther, *Struktur als Prozess* (Munich: Fink, 1973), p. 20.
52. Jan Mukařovský, "Der Standard der ästhetischen Funktion unter den übrigen Funktionen," in *Kapitel aus der Ästhetik* (Frankfurt am Main: Suhrkamp, 1970), p. 113.
53. Mukařovský, "Zur tschechischen Übersetzung von Šklovskij's *Theorie der Prosa,*" p. 170; for a critical analysis of the theoretical consequences of this cf. Kurt Konrad, "Der Streit um Inhalt und Form," *Alternative,* 80 (October 1971).
54. Mukařovský, *Aesthetic Function,* p. 67.
55. Ibid., p. 88.
56. Mukařovský, "Der Standard der ästhetischen Funktion," pp. 126, 134.
57. Strohschneider-Kohrs, *Literarische Struktur und geschichtlicher Wandel,* p. 24.
58. Kvetoslav Chvatik, *Strukturalismus und Avantgarde: Aufsätze zur Kunst und Literatur,* trans. H. Gaertner (Munich: Hanser, 1970), p. 88.
59. For example, Tony Bennett, *Formalism and Marxism* (London: Methuen, 1979); Pechey, "Bakhtin, Marxism, and Post-Structuralism."
60. Gary Morson, "The Heresiarch of *Meta,*" *PTL,* 3, no. 3 (1978), 408.
61. Medvedev/Bakhtin, *The Formal Method,* pp. 75–76; hereafter cited in the text.
62. M. M. Bakhtin, *The Dialogic Imagination,* trans. Caryl Emerson and Michael Holquist (Austin: University of Texas Press, 1981), p. 328; cf. Paul de Man, "Dialogue and Dialogism," *Poetics Today,* 4, no. 1 (1983), 104.

63. For example, V. N. Vološinov/M. M. Bakhtin, *Marxism and the Philosophy of Language,* trans. Ladislav Matejka and I. R. Titunik (New York: Seminar Press, 1973), p. 77; Bakhtin, *The Dialogic Imagination,* p. 281.

64. For example, Bakhtin, *The Dialogic Imagination,* p. 292.

65. Francisco Posada, *Lukács, Brecht y la situación actual del realismo socialista* (Buenos Aires: Editorial Galerna, 1969), p. 267.

66. Michel Foucault, *The Discourse on Language,* in *The Archaeology of Knowledge* (New York: Pantheon, 1972), p. 216.

67. Gilles Deleuze, *Différence et répétition* (Paris: Presses Universitaires Françaises, 1968), pp. 12, 97.

68. Pierre Bourdieu, *Outline of a Theory of Practice,* trans. Richard Nice (London: Cambridge University Press, 1977), pp. 78–87.

69. Cf. Viktor Šklovskij, "The Resurrection of the Word," in *Russian Formalism,* ed. Bann and Bowlt, p. 44; automatized texts "cease to be seen and begin to be recognized"; they "have become covered with the glassy armour of familiarity."

70. Heinz Brüggemann, *Literarische Technik und soziale Revolution—Versuche über das Verhältnis von Kunstproduktion, Marxismus und literarischer Tradition in den theoretischen Schriften Bertolt Brechts* (Reinbek bei Hamburg: Rowohlt, 1973), p. 176.

71. Ferrucio Rossi-Landi, *Semiotik, Ästhetik und Ideologie,* trans. Burkhart Kroeber (Munich: Hanser, 1976), pp. 100–102; hereafter cited in the text.

72. Bennett, *Formalism and Marxism,* p. 136.

5. For a Literary History

1. But it should not be confused with the Althusserian *coupure épistémologique* because I use it without the teleological sense of a transition from one order of knowledge to another (from "ideology" to "science," or from "illusion" to "fiction," for example).

2. Jan Mukařovský, *Aesthetic Function, Norm and Value as Social Facts,* trans. M. Suino, Michigan Slavic Contributions, no. 3 (Ann Arbor: University of Michigan, 1970), p. 33.

3. Michel Foucault, *The Archaeology of Knowledge,* trans. A. M. Sheridan Smith (London: Tavistock, 1972), pp. 21–22. Let me note in passing Foucault's rejection of a bipolar model of antagonistic succession through the opposition of the norm and new production; his argument is that the "new" is already inscribed in the general conditions of discourse, and that an archaeology of knowledge must be concerned not with the alternation of regularity and irregularity but with the systematic regularity of discursive practice (pp. 144–145). It seems to me that it is precisely here that a very traditional notion of epochal unity creeps back into Foucault's thought. Obviously the new literary

product is never *radically* new, but it is *other* than what was; it encroaches, however slightly, upon the excluded space of the inconceivable.

4. V. N. Vološinov/M. Bakhtin, *Marxism and the Philosophy of Language,* trans. L. Matejka and I. R. Titunik (New York: Seminar Press, 1973), pp. 55, 77.

5. H. R. Jauss, "Literary History as a Challenge to Literary Theory," in *Toward an Aesthetic of Reception,* trans. Timothy Bahti, Theory and History of Literature, vol. 2 (Minneapolis: University of Minnesota Press, 1982), p. 25.

6. Ian Gough, "Marx's Theory of Productive and Unproductive Labour," *New Left Review,* 76 (November–December 1972), 50.

7. Jean Baudrillard, *L'Echange symbolique et la mort* (Paris: Gallimard, 1976), p. 77.

8. Jacques Attali, *Bruits: essai sur l'économie politique de la musique* (Paris: Presses Universitaires Françaises, 1977); cf. Wlad Godzich, "The Semiotics of Semiotics," *Australian Journal of Cultural Studies,* 2, no. 2 (1984).

9. Bertolt Brecht, "Der Dreigroschenprozess," in *Schriften zur Literatur und Kunst I, Gesammelte Werke,* vol. 18 (Frankfurt am Main: Suhrkamp, 1967), pp. 156, 158; cf. John Frow, "Film, Commodity Production and the Law: Brecht's 'Sociological Experiment,'" *Australian Journal of Cultural Studies,* 2, no. 1 (1984), 4–5.

10. Francisco Posada, *Lukács, Brecht y la situación actual del realismo socialista* (Buenos Aires: Editorial Galerna, 1969), p. 153.

11. Bertolt Brecht, "Fünf Schwierigkeiten beim Schreiben der Wahrheit," in *Schriften zur Literatur und Kunst I, Gesammelte Werke,* vol. 18, p. 230.

12. Brecht, "Der Dreigroschenprozess," p. 159.

13. Ibid., pp. 156–158.

14. This hierarchy is based on a scale of legitimacy which constantly loses its upper register as newly legitimate genres—the novel in the nineteenth century, the *conte* in the late Middle Ages—force their way in from below. Pierre Bourdieu gives a detailed table of relations of legitimacy at the present time in *Un Art moyen* (Paris: Ed. de Minuit, 1965), p. 136. It should be noted, however, that with the rise of a mass audience for the arts, there now exists in fact a double standard of legitimacy, one canonical and one noncanonical—what Gans calls the upper- and lower-middle "taste-cultures"; Herbert J. Gans, "The Politics of Culture in America: A Sociological Analysis," in *Sociology of Mass Communications,* ed. D. McQuail (Harmondsworth: Penguin, 1972), pp. 375, 378.

15. Claudio Guillén, *Literature as System* (Princeton, N.J.: Princeton University Press, 1971), p. 384.

16. Jean Baudrillard, "The Precession of Simulacra," in *Simulations,* trans. Paul Foss, Paul Patton, and Philip Bleitchman, Foreign Agents Series (New York: Semiotext(e), 1983), pp. 2ff. This should be contrasted with Gilles Deleuze's account of the simulacrum in *Différence et répétition* (Paris: Presses Universitaires Françaises, 1968). Deleuze describes a similar world of simulacra in

which all identities are simulated in the play of difference and repetition (pp. 1, 355); but, in a tone that lacks all of Baudrillard's melancholy, Deleuze uses the concept to overthrow a residual Platonism which insists on "the primacy of an original over the copy, of a model over the image" (p. 92). The concept of simulacrum can thus be understood not as "a simple imitation but rather as the act by which the very idea of a model or of a privileged position is challenged" (p. 95).

17. In *The Mirror of Production,* trans. Mark Poster (St. Louis: Telos Press, 1975), Jean Baudrillard writes that in the system of monopoly capitalism, "the signified and the referent are now abolished to the sole profit of the play of signifiers, of a generalized formalization in which the code no longer refers back to any subjective or objective 'reality,' but to its own logic. The signifier becomes its own referent and the use value of the sign disappears to the benefit of its commutation and exchange value alone. The sign no longer designates anything at all. It approaches its true structural limit which is to refer back only to other signs" (pp. 127–128). A few pages later he adds: "Against the spoken word, political economy supports *discourse* in which everything that is exchanged is put under the instance of the code. At the side of all the discriminations, the markings and demarkings of which we have spoken, the system produced a fundamental separation of the signifier from signified. Through it and the whole logic of communications that it institutes, the system has succeeded, slowly but inexorably, in neutralizing the symbolic power of the spoken word" (p. 137).

18. Walter Benjamin, "The Work of Art in the Age of Mechanical Reproduction," in *Illuminations,* trans. Harry Zohn (New York: Schocken, 1969), pp. 218ff.

19. Ibid., pp. 249–250, n. 17.

20. Walter Benjamin, "Zentralpark," in *Illuminationen,* 2nd ed. (1955; reprint, Frankfurt am Main: Suhrkamp, 1966), pp. 255–259.

21. George Kubler, *The Shape of Time* (New Haven: Yale University Press, 1962), pp. 39, 72.

22. Karl Marx, *The German Ideology,* in *Marx-Engels Collected Works,* vol. 5 (London: Lawrence and Wishart, 1976), p. 37.

23. Friedrich Engels, "Ludwig Feuerbach und der Ausgang der klassischen deutschen Philosophie," in *Marx-Engels Werke,* vol. 21 (Berlin: Dietz Verlag, 1973), p. 303.

24. Jane Harrison, "From Ritual to Art," in *Sociology of Literature and Drama,* ed. Tom and Elizabeth Burns (Harmondsworth: Penguin, 1973), p. 327.

25. H. R. Jauss, "Theory of Genres and Mediaeval Literature," in *Toward an Aesthetic of Reception,* trans. Timothy Bahti, Theory and History of Literature, vol. 2 (Minneapolis: University of Minnesota Press, 1982), p. 94.

26. The analogy between artistic and social work must not be taken too literally, because of the relative stability of the mode of aesthetic production, and

because of the special problems associated with "unproductive" labor. But cf. Marx's passage on Raphael in *The German Ideology,* pp. 393–394.

27. Aristotle, *Poetics* 4.1449a15.

28. Kubler, *The Shape of Time,* pp. 35, 53.

29. Ibid., p. 85.

30. Ibid., p. 64.

31. Ibid., p. vii.

32. Quoted in Viktor Ehrlich, *Russian Formalism,* 3rd ed. (1955; reprint, The Hague: Mouton, 1969), pp. 255–256.

33. René Wellek, "The Theory of Literary History," *Travaux du Cercle Linguistique de Prague,* 6 (1936), 190–191; cf. also "The Concept of Evolution in Literary History," in *Concepts of Criticism* (New Haven: Yale University Press, 1963), p. 49.

34. I am assuming that Wellek means by this "the history which we write," because otherwise he is begging the question of the objectivity of "tendencies" and values in history.

35. Jurij Tynjanov and Roman Jakobson, "Problems in the Study of Literature and Language," in *Readings in Russian Poetics,* ed. Ladislav Matejka and Krystyna Pomorska (Cambridge, Mass.: MIT Press, 1971), p. 80.

36. Kubler, *The Shape of Time,* p. 13.

37. Julia Kristeva, *Desire in Language,* ed. Leon S. Roudiez, trans. Thomas Gora, Alice Jardine, and Leon S. Roudiez (Oxford: Blackwell, 1980), p. 69.

38. Umberto Eco, *Einführung in die Semiotik,* trans. J. Trabant (Munich: Fink, 1972), pp. 145, 151.

39. Jochen Schulte-Sasse, "Theory of Modernism versus Theory of the Avant-Garde," foreword to Peter Bürger, *Theory of the Avant-Garde,* trans. Michael Shaw, Theory and History of Literature, vol. 4 (Minneapolis: University of Minnesota Press, 1984), p. viii.

40. Bürger, *Theory of the Avant-Garde,* p. 87.

41. Fredric Jameson, "The Ideology of the Text," *Salmagundi,* nos. 31–32 (1975–1976), p. 242.

42. Ibid., p. 243.

43. Didier Coste, "Rehearsal: An Alternative to Production/Reproduction in French Feminist Discourse," in *Innovation/Renovation: New Perspectives on the Humanities,* ed. I. and J. Hassan (Madison: University of Wisconsin Press, 1983), p. 250.

44. H. R. Jauss, "Racines und Goethes *Iphigenie,*" *Neue Hefte für Philosophie,* 4 (1973), 45.

45. Jurij Lotman, *The Structure of the Artistic Text,* trans. R. Vroon, Michigan Slavic Contributions, no. 7 (Ann Arbor: University of Michigan, 1977), pp. 289–291.

46. Bertolt Brecht, Notes to *Aufstieg und Fall der Stadt Mahagonny,* in *Schriften zum Theater III, Gesammelte Werke,* vol. 17, p. 1005.

47. Walter Benjamin, "The Author as Producer," in *Understanding Brecht,* trans. Anna Bostock (1973; reprint, London: Verso, 1983), pp. 93–94.

48. Karl Marx, Postface to the 2nd ed., *Capital,* vol. 1, trans. Ben Fowkes (Harmondsworth: Penguin, 1976), p. 101. The words are quoted approvingly by Marx from a reviewer's summary of the method of *Capital.*

49. Barbara Herrnstein Smith, "Contingencies of Value," *Critical Inquiry,* 10, no. 1 (1983), 23. Cf. Richard Ohmann, "The Shaping of a Canon: U.S. Fiction, 1960–1975," ibid., pp. 199–223; and Frank Kermode, "Institutional Control of Interpretation," *Essays on Fiction, 1971–82* (London: Routledge and Kegan Paul, 1983), pp. 168–184.

50. But for a more differentiated account cf. Tony Bennett, "Marxism and Popular Fiction," *Literature and History,* 7 (1981), 138–165; "Marxist Cultural Politics: In Search of 'The Popular,'" *Australian Journal of Cultural Studies,* 1, no. 2 (1983), 2–28.

51. Terry Lovell, *Pictures of Reality: Aesthetics, Politics and Pleasure* (London: BFI, 1980), p. 91.

6. *Intertextuality*

1. Michael Riffaterre, "Syllepsis," *Critical Inquiry,* 6 (1980), 625.

2. Hans Robert Jauss, "Literary History as a Challenge to Literary Theory," in *Toward an Aesthetic of Reception,* trans. Timothy Bahti, Theory and History of Literature, vol. 2 (Minneapolis: University of Minnesota Press, 1982), p. 22; hereafter cited in the text.

3. Julia Kristeva, *Desire in Language,* ed. Leon S. Roudiez, trans. Thomas Gora, Alice Jardine, and Leon S. Roudiez (Oxford: Blackwell, 1980), p. 66.

4. Julia Kristeva, *Semeiotikè: Recherches pour une sémanalyse* (Paris: Seuil, 1969), p. 255.

5. Kristeva, *Desire in Language,* pp. 64–65.

6. Julia Kristeva, "Problèmes de la structuration du texte," in *Théorie d'ensemble* (Paris: Seuil, 1968), p. 311.

7. Theodor W. Adorno and Max Horkheimer, *Dialectic of Enlightenment,* trans. John Cumming (London: Allen Lane, 1973), pp. 130–131.

8. John Frow, "Mediation and Metaphor: Adorno and the Sociology of Art," *Clio,* 12, no. 1 (1982), 57–65.

9. Ross Chambers, *Story and Situation: Narrative Seduction and the Power of Fiction,* Theory and History of Literature, vol. 12 (Minneapolis: University of Minnesota Press, 1984), p. 34.

10. Ibid., pp. 25–26.

11. *The Satyricon of Petronius,* trans William Arrowsmith (Ann Arbor: University of Michigan Press, 1959), pp. 122–125. The Latin text, taken from *Petronii Saturae,* ed. F. Buecheler, 8th ed. (1862; reprint, Berlin: Weidmannsche Verlagsbuchhandlung, 1963), pp. 136–142, is as follows: "Matrona quaedam

Ephesi tam notae erat pudicitiae, ut vicinarum quoque gentium feminas ad spectaculum sui evocaret. haec ergo cum virum extulisset, non contenta vulgari more funus passis prosequi crinibus aut nudatum pectus in conspectu frequentiae plangere, in conditorium etiam prosecuta est defunctum, positumque in hypogaeo Graeco more corpus custodire ac flere totis noctibus diebusque coepit. sic adflictantem se ac mortem inedia persequentem non parentes potuerunt abducere, non propinqui; magistratus ultimo repulsi abierunt, comploratoque singularis exempli femina ab omnibus quintum iam diem sine alimento trahebat. adsidebat aegrae fidissima ancilla, simulque et lacrimas commodabat lugenti et quotienscunque defecerat positum in monumento lumen renovabat. una igitur in tota civitate fabula erat: solum videlicet illud adfulsisse verum pudicitiae amorisque exemplum omnis ordinis homines confitebantur, cum interim imperator provinciae latrones iussit crucibus adfigi secundum illam eandem casulam, in qua recens cadaver matrona deflebat. proxima ergo nocte, cum miles, qui cruces asservabat, ne quis ad sepulturam corpus detraheret, notasset sibi et lumen inter monimenta clarius fulgens et gemitum lugentis audisset, vitio gentis humanae concupiit scire, quis aut quid faceret. descendit igitur in conditorium, visaque pulcherrima muliere primo quasi quodam monstro infernisque imaginibus turbatus substitit. deinde ut et corpus iacentis conspexit et lacrimas consideravit faciemque unguibus sectam, ratus scilicet id quod erat, desiderium extincti non posse feminam pati, adtulit in monumentum cenulam suam coepitque hortari lugentem, ne perseveraret in dolore supervacuo ac nihil profuturo gemitu pectus diduceret: omnium eundem esse exitum [sed] et idem domicilium, et cetera quibus exulceratae mentes ad sanitatem revocantur. at illa ignota consolatione percussa laceravit vehementius pectus ruptosque crines super pectus iacentis imposuit. non recessit tamen miles, sed eadem exhortatione temptavit dare mulierculae cibum, donec ancilla vini certe ab eo odore corrupta primum ipsa porrexit ad humanitatem invitantis victam manum, deinde refecta potione et cibo expugnare dominae pertinaciam coepit et 'quid proderit' inquit 'hoc tibi, si soluta inedia fueris, si te vivam sepelieris, si ante quam fata poscant, indemnatum spiritum effuderis?

    id cinerem aut manes credis curare sepultos?

vis tu revivescere? vis [tu] discusso muliebri errore, quam diu licuerit, lucis commodis frui? ipsum te iacentis corpus ammonere debet, ut vivas.' nemo invitus audit, cum cogitur aut cibum sumere aut vivere. itaque mulier aliquot dierum abstinentia sicca passa est frangi pertinaciam suam, nec minus avide replevit se cibo quam ancilla, quae prior victa est. ceterum scitis, quid plerumque soleat temptare humanam satietatem. quibus blanditiis impetraverat miles, ut matrona vellet vivere, isdem etiam pudicitiam eius adgressus est. nec deformis aut infacundus iuvenis castae videbatur, conciliante gratiam ancilla ac subinde dicente:

'placitone etiam pugnabis amori?'
[nec venit in mentem, quorum consederis arvis?]

quid diutius moror? ne hanc quidem partem corporis mulier abstinuit, vic-
torque miles utrumque persuasit. iacuerunt ergo una non tantum illa nocte,
qua nuptias fecerunt, sed postero etiam ac tertio die, praeclusis videlicet con-
ditorii foribus, ut quisquis ex notis ignotisque ad monimentum venisset, pu-
taret expirasse super corpus viri pudicissimam uxorem. ceterum delectatus
miles et forma mulieris et secreto, quicquid boni per facultates poterat, coe-
mebat et prima statim nocte in monumentum ferebat. itaque unius cruciarii
parentes ut viderunt laxatam custodiam, detraxere nocte pendentem supre-
moque mandaverunt officio. at miles circumscriptus dum desidet, ut postero
die vidit unam sine cadavere crucem, veritus supplicium mulieri, quid acci-
disset, exponit: nec se expectaturum iudicis sententiam, sed gladio ius dic-
turum ignaviae suae. commodaret ergo illa perituro locum et fatale
conditorium . . . familiari ac viro faceret. mulier non minus misericors quam
pudica 'ne istud' inquit 'dei sinant, ut eodem tempore duorum mihi carissi-
morum hominum duo funera spectem. malo mortuum impendere quam vivum
occidere.' secundum hanc orationem iubet ex arca corpus mariti sui tolli atque
illi, quae vacabat, cruci adfigi. usus est miles ingenio prudentissimae feminae,
posteroque die populus miratus est, qua ratione mortuus isset in crucem."

12. Yuri K. Scheglov, "Matrona iz Efesa," in *Sign-Language-Culture,* ed. A. J.
Greimas (The Hague: Mouton, 1970), pp. 591–600; cited in L. M. O'Toole,
"Analytic and Synthetic Approaches to Narrative Structure," in *Style and Struc-
ture in Literature,* ed. R. Fowler (Oxford: Blackwell, 1975), p. 148; cf. also
Yuri K. Scheglov and A. Zholkovsky, "Towards a 'Theme—(Expression De-
vices)—Text' Model of Literary Structure," trans. L. M. O'Toole, *Russian
Poetics in Translation,* 1 (1975), 6–50.

13. Mikhail Bakhtin, *The Dialogic Imagination,* trans. C. Emerson and M. Holquist
(Austin: University of Texas Press, 1981), p. 222; hereafter cited in the text.

14. Jurij Lotman, *The Structure of the Artistic Text,* trans. Ronald Vroon, Michigan
Slavic Contributions, no. 7 (Ann Arbor: University of Michigan, 1977), pp.
236–238.

15. Sigmund Freud, *Jokes and Their Relation to the Unconscious,* trans. J. Strachey
(London: Routledge and Kegan Paul, 1966), p. 100.

16. Don DeLillo, *Running Dog* (New York: Vintage, 1978), p. 49; hereafter cited
in the text.

17. Robert Ludlum, *The Gemini Contenders* (London: Granada, 1977), pp. 135,
141.

18. The text used is that in *Hölderlin: Sämtliche Werke,* Kleine Stuttgarter Ausgabe,
ed. Friedrich Beissner, vol. 2 (Stuttgart: Kohlhammer, 1965), pp. 58–59.

19. Cf. Theodor W. Adorno, "Parataxis," in *Noten zur Literatur III* (Frankfurt
am Main: Suhrkamp, 1965), p. 198.

20. Peter Szondi, following W. Binder, denies that Hölderlin equates Kronos and Chronos; Szondi, *Einführung in die literarische Hermeneutik* (Frankfurt am Main: Suhrkamp, 1978), pp. 247–248. Although the equation does seem to be supported by the appellations of *Kronion* and *Sohn der Zeit* given to Jupiter, either reading gives, eventually, the same sense.

21. Lotman, *Structure of the Artistic Text,* p. 95.

22. Riffaterre does at times seem to define the *mimesis* in a traditionally positivist way: representation, he claims, "is founded upon the referentiality of language, that is, upon a direct relationship of words to things"; *Semiotics of Poetry,* 2nd ed. (1978; reprint, London: Methuen, 1980), p. 2; hereafter cited in the text. A note on p. 168 does, however, suggest a more tenable version of the concept: "Whether the reader believes the mimesis is grounded in a genuine reference of words to things, or realizes the mimesis is illusory and is in truth built upon an entirely verbal, self-sufficient system, the impact of the representation of reality upon his imagination is the same. It has to be a norm before the well-formedness of any of its components can appear questionable."

23. Anne Freadman, *"Riffaterra Cognita:* A Late Contribution to the Formalism Debate," *SubStance,* 42 (1983), 35.

24. Riffaterre, "Syllepsis," p. 627.

25. Ibid., p. 626.

26. Riffaterre, "Hermeneutic Models," *Poetics Today,* 4, no. 1 (1983), 7.

27. Jonathan Culler, *The Pursuit of Signs: Semiotics, Literature, Deconstruction* (London: Routledge and Kegan Paul, 1981), p. 117; hereafter cited in the text.

28. Laurent Jenny, "The Strategy of Form," in *French Literary Theory Today,* ed. T. Todorov, trans. R. Carter (Cambridge: Cambridge University Press, 1982), pp. 40–41; hereafter cited in the text.

29. Riffaterre, "Syllepsis," p. 627.

30. Gustave Flaubert, *Madame Bovary,* ed. E. Maynial (Paris: Garnier, 1961), p. 35: "Emma se graissa donc les mains à cette poussière des vieux cabinets de lecture."

31. Paul de Man, *Allegories of Reading* (New Haven: Yale University Press, 1979), p. 17.

32. Barbara Herrnstein Smith, *On the Margins of Discourse* (Chicago: Chicago University Press, 1978), p. 25.

33. David Silverman and Brian Torode, *The Material Word* (London: Routledge and Kegan Paul, 1980), p. 8.

34. Bakhtin, *The Dialogic Imagination,* p. 264.

35. Cf. Janusz Slawinsky, *Literatur als System und Prozess,* trans. Rolf Fieguth (Munich: Nymphenburger, 1975), p. 93.

36. Cf. Roy Pascal, *The Dual Voice* (Manchester: Manchester University Press, 1977); Ann Bainfield, "Narrative Style and the Grammar of Direct and Indirect Speech," *Foundations of Language,* 10 (1973), 1–29; Brian McHale, "Free Indirect Discourse: A Survey of Recent Accounts," *PTL,* 3, no. 2 (1978);

and, on the function of "hybrid constructions" in *Little Dorrit*, cf. Bakhtin, *The Dialogic Imagination*, p. 304. For my use of the concept of modality, cf. R. Hodge and G. Kress, *Language as Ideology* (London: Routledge and Kegan Paul, 1979), pp. 85 and 91.

37. Roland Barthes, *S/Z: An Essay*, trans. Richard Miller (New York: Hill and Wang, 1974), pp. 41–42.
38. Charles Dickens, *Little Dorrit* (1857; reprint, Harmondsworth: Penguin, 1967), pp. 181–182; hereafter cited in the text.
39. Cf. Pascal, *The Dual Voice*, p. 10.
40. Mikhail Bakhtin, *Problems of Dostoevsky's Poetics*, trans. R. W. Rotsel (Ann Arbor: Ardis, 1973), pp. 153ff; Bakhtin, *The Dialogic Imagination*, p. 276.
41. Cf. Dianne Sadoff, "Storytelling and the Figure of the Father in *Little Dorrit*," *PMLA*, 95 (1980), 240: "*Little Dorrit*'s version of incest represents this double bond of incest—familial desire and the temporal collapse of generation. The narrative collapses the family onto two figures: the daughter whom the father seduces becomes the mother who nurtures him, while the fatherly figure of the law becomes, through regression, the son. This dyad combines all the roles possible in an incest matrix."
42. Henry James, *Selected Literary Criticism*, ed. Morris Shapira, 2nd ed. (1963; reprint, Harmondsworth: Penguin, 1968), pp. 32–33.
43. In *Fantasy: The Literature of Subversion* (London: Methuen, 1981), p. 132, Rosemary Jackson discusses Dickens's use of the grotesque, and in particular that inversion by which material objects are animated at the same time as "character" is constructed synecdochically through the fragmentation of bodies.

7. Text and System

1. Jorge Luis Borges, "Pierre Menard, Author of Don Quixote," in *Fictions*, ed. Anthony Kerrigan (London: John Calder, 1965); hereafter cited in the text.
2. Mike Gane, "Borges/Menard/Spinoza," *Economy and Society*, 9, no. 4 (November 1980), 411; cf. Pierre Macherey, *A Theory of Literary Production*, trans. Geoffrey Wall (London: Routledge and Kegan Paul, 1978), p. 250.
3. Alicia Borinsky, "Repetition, Museums, Libraries: Jorge Luis Borges," *Glyph*, 2 (1977), 92, 97.
4. Gane, "Borges/Menard/Spinoza," p. 416.
5. Tony Bennett, *Formalism and Marxism* (London: Methuen, 1979), p. 59.
6. George Chapman, *Homer's Iliad* (London: George Routledge and Sons, 1903), p. 218; Alexander Pope, *The Iliad of Homer*, ed. Maynard Mack, Twickenham Edition of the Poems of Alexander Pope, vol. 8 (London and New Haven: Methuen and Yale University Press, 1967), pp. 273–274; Andrew Lang, Walter Leaf, and Ernest Myers, *The Iliad of Homer* (London: Macmillan, 1883), p. 334; *The Iliad of Homer*, trans. Richmond Lattimore (Chicago: University

of Chicago Press, 1951), pp. 347–348; Christopher Logue, *Patrocleia of Homer* (Ann Arbor: University of Michigan Press, 1963), pp. 41–42—a slightly different version is published in Logue's *War Music* (1981; reprint, Harmondsworth: Penguin, 1984), pp. 32–33.

7. The concept of keying is taken from Erving Goffman, *Frame Analysis: An Essay on the Organization of Experience* (New York: Harper and Row, 1974), p. 44, where it is defined as a modulation to a secondary ontological framework.

8. Peter Bürger, *Theory of the Avant-Garde,* trans. Michael Shaw, Theory and History of Literature, vol. 4 (Minneapolis: University of Minnesota Press, 1984), p. 12.

9. Marthe Robert, *The Old and the New,* trans. Carol Cosman (Berkeley: University of California Press, 1977), p. 75; hereafter cited in the text.

10. Matthew Arnold, "On Translating Homer," lectures 1–3 (1861–1862), and Francis W. Newman, "Homeric Translation in Theory and Practice" (1861), in *Essays by Matthew Arnold* (London: Oxford University Press, 1914).

11. Karl Marx, "Introduction," *Grundrisse: Foundations of the Critique of Political Economy,* trans. Martin Nicolaus (Harmondsworth: Penguin, 1973), p. 111. On this passage cf. particularly O. K. Werckmeister, "Marx on Literature and Art," *New Literary History,* 4, no. 3 (Spring 1973), 518.

12. Milman Parry, *The Making of Homeric Verse: The Collected Papers of Milman Parry,* ed. Adam Parry (Oxford: Oxford University Press, 1971); Albert Lord, *The Singer of Tales* (Cambridge, Mass.: Harvard University Press, 1960); Walter J. Ong, *Orality and Literacy: The Technologizing of the Word* (London: Methuen, 1982), pp. 17–30.

13. E. C. Mack, *Public Schools and British Opinion Since 1860,* cited in Jacqueline Rose, *The Case of Peter Pan, or The Impossibility of Children's Fiction* (London: Macmillan, 1984), p. 152.

14. Cf. Renée Balibar et al., *Les Français fictifs* (Paris: Hachette, 1974).

15. Pierre Macherey, "Problems of Reflection," trans. John Coombes, *Literature, Society and the Sociology of Literature: Proceedings of the Conference Held at the University of Essex, July 1976* (Colchester: University of Essex, 1977), p. 45.

16. David Morley, *The "Nationwide" Audience: Structure and Decoding,* BFI Television Monograph 11 (London: BFI, 1980), p. 31.

17. Paul Willemen, "Notes on Subjectivity," *Screen,* 19, no. 1 (Spring 1978).

18. Morley, *The "Nationwide" Audience,* p. 158.

19. Ibid., p. 161.

20. Claire Johnston, "The Subject of Feminist Film Theory/Practice," *Screen,* 21, no. 2 (Summer 1980), 30.

21. Morley, *The "Nationwide" Audience,* p. 162. The other major theoretical problems with Morley's analysis are the assumption that the reconstructed readings are the transparent representation of an experience rather than the conventional discursive construction of an interview answer; the fact that as a result of the distinction between an "ideological problematic" and an enunciative "mode

of address" (p. 139) the latter is implicitly excluded from the former and so marginalized; and that this marginalization is then used to render less problematical the "oppositional" stance of some socially conservative groups.

22. Stanley Fish, *Is There a Text in This Class?: The Authority of Interpretive Communities* (Cambridge, Mass.: Harvard University Press, 1980), pp. 153–154; hereafter cited in the text.

23. Mircea Marghescou, *Le Concept de littérarité* (The Hague: Mouton, 1974), p. 47.

24. Didier Coste, "Trois conceptions du lecteur et leur contribution à une théorie du texte littéraire," *Poétique,* 43 (1980), 357.

25. Wolfgang Iser, *The Implied Reader* (Baltimore: Johns Hopkins University Press, 1974); *The Act of Reading: A Theory of Aesthetic Response* (Baltimore: Johns Hopkins University Press, 1978), esp. pp. 34–35 and 167.

26. Marx describes the categories of bourgeois economics as being "forms of thought which are socially valid (*gültig*), and therefore objective, for the relations of production belonging to this historically determinate mode of social production." Karl Marx, *Capital: A Critique of Political Economy, I,* trans. Ben Fowkes (Harmondsworth: Penguin, 1976), p. 169.

27. Cf. Keith Tribe, "Literary Methodology," *Economy and Society,* 9, no. 2 (May 1980), 248.

28. Tony Bennett, "Text, Readers, Reading Formations," *Literature and History,* 9, no. 2 (Autumn 1983), 218.

29. *The Oxford History of Australian Literature,* ed. Leonie Kramer (Melbourne: Oxford University Press, 1981), pp. 130–131.

30. H. M. Green, *A History of Australian Literature* (Sydney: Angus and Robertson, 1961), II, 1130–1131.

31. *The Literature of Australia,* ed. Geoffrey Dutton (Harmondsworth: Penguin, 1964), p. 217.

32. Walter Benjamin, "Eduard Fuchs: Collector and Historian," in *The Essential Frankfurt School Reader,* ed. Andrew Arato and Eike Gebhardt (New York: Urizen Books, 1978), p. 226.

33. Frank Hardy, *The Hard Way: The Story Behind "Power Without Glory"* (London: T. Werner Laurie, 1961), pp. 214–215; hereafter cited in the text.

34. On the concept of repetition see Gilles Deleuze, *Différence et répétition* (Paris: Presses Universitaires Françaises, 1968), and Jeffrey Mehlman, *Revolution and Repetition: Marx/Hugo/Balzac* (Berkeley: University of California Press, 1977).

35. Frank Hardy, *Power Without Glory* (1950; reprint, London: Panther, 1975), p. 32.

36. Niall Brennan, *John Wren, Gambler: His Life and Times* (Melbourne: Hill of Content, 1971), pp. 211–212.

37. John Searle, *Speech Acts: An Essay in the Philosophy of Language* (Cambridge: Cambridge University Press, 1969), pp. 171–172.

38. Brennan, *John Wren,* p. 206.

39. "Basking in Reflective Glory," *The Age,* 8 June 1976, p. 2.
40. Hugh Buggy, *The Real John Wren* (Melbourne: Widescope, 1977); hereafter cited in the text.
41. Brennan, *John Wren,* p. vii.
42. Frank Hardy, review of Brennan, *The Review,* 20–26 November 1971, p. 186.
43. Frank Hardy, *The Four-Legged Lottery* (London: T. Werner Laurie, 1958), p. 90; hereafter cited in the text.
44. Frank Hardy, author's note, *The Outcasts of Foolgarah* (Melbourne: Allara Publishing, 1971), pp. 232–245.
45. Jack Beasley, *Red Letter Days: Notes from Inside an Era* (Sydney: Australasian Book Society, 1979), pp. 80–81, 90.
46. Mikhail Bakhtin, *Rabelais and His World,* trans. Hélène Iswolsky (Cambridge, Mass.: MIT Press, 1968).
47. Mikhail Bakhtin, *Problems of Dostoevsky's Poetics,* trans. R. W. Rotsel (Ann Arbor: Ardis, 1973).
48. Frank Hardy, *But the Dead Are Many: A Novel in Fugue Form* (Sydney: Bodley Head, 1975), p. 29.
49. John Docker, "A Study in Context: And the Dead Are Many," *Arena,* 41 (1976), 50.
50. Cecil Hadgraft, "Indulgence," in *Studies in the Recent Australian Novel,* ed. K. G. Hamilton (St. Lucia: University of Queensland Press, 1978), p. 223.
51. Frank Hardy, *Who Shot George Kirkland? A Novel about the Nature of Truth* (Melbourne: Edward Arnold, 1981); hereafter cited in the text.
52. "Basking in Reflective Glory," p. 2.
53. Brennan, *John Wren,* p. 206.
54. Bruce Molloy, "An Interview with Frank Hardy (1973)," *Australian Literary Studies,* 7 (1976), 356–374.
55. See Patrick Morgan, "The Hard Way and the Soft Way," *Quadrant,* 20, no. 12 (1976), 25–30; Gerard Henderson, "Would You Believe?" *Quadrant,* 20, no. 12 (1976), 31–33; Rupert Lockwood, "One Night in the Life of Frank Hardy," *Nation Review,* 17–23 October 1975, p. 24.
56. Brennan, *John Wren,* p. 208.
57. For material on the Communist Party split, see W. Higgins, "Reconstructing Australian Communism," in *The Socialist Register 1974,* ed. Ralph Miliband and John Saville (London: Merlin Press, 1974), pp. 151–188, and issues 18–22 of *Arena.*
58. Eric Aarons, "Hardy Novel Bares Dilemmas of Our Times," *Tribune,* 1 October 1975, p. 7.
59. Beasley, *Red Letter Days,* pp. 60, 62.
60. Jack Lindsay, introduction, in Hardy, *Power Without Glory,* p. 18.
61. Docker, "A Study in Context," pp. 61, 55.
62. Tim Rowse, "Jack Beasley's *Red Letter Days,*" *New Literature Review,* 6 (1979), 44.

63. Peter Williams, "Interventions and Obsessions: The Work of Frank Hardy," *Southern Review,* 14 (1981), 168–191, and "Plagiarism and Rewriting: The Case of Frank Hardy," *New Literature Review,* 10 (1982), 45–53.
64. Williams, "Interventions and Obsessions," p. 172.
65. Ibid.

8. Limits: The Politics of Reading

1. Jacques Derrida, "Cogito and the History of Madness," in *Writing and Difference,* trans. Alan Bass (London: Routledge and Kegan Paul, 1978), pp. 31–63; Michel Foucault, "My Body, This Paper, This Fire," trans. Geoff Bennington, *Oxford Literary Review,* 4, no. 1 (1979), 9–28, first published as an appendix to the second (1972) edition of *Histoire de la folie;* hereafter both essays will be cited in the text. In addition to the essays by Said and Sprinker cited in notes 3 and 7, there are useful readings of the exchange by Shoshana Felman, "Madness and Philosophy, *or* Literature's Reason," *Yale French Studies,* 52 (1975), 206–228, and Robert D'Amico, "Text and Context: Derrida and Foucault on Descartes," in *The Structural Allegory: Reconstructive Encounters with the New French Thought,* ed. John Fekete, Theory and History of Literature, vol. 11 (Minneapolis: University of Minnesota Press, 1984), pp. 164–182.
2. René Descartes, *Discourse on Method and the Meditations,* trans. F. E. Sutcliffe (Harmondsworth: Penguin, 1968), p. 96. Since questions of textual detail are crucial in this debate, I reproduce below the Latin and French texts of this passage, taken from Descartes, *Oeuvres philosophiques,* vol. 2 (1638–1642), ed. Ferdinand Alquié (Paris: Garnier, 1967), p. 178 (Latin) and pp. 405–406 (French):

"Sed forte, quamvis interdum sensus circa minuta quaedam & remotiora nos fallant, pleraque tamen alia sunt de quibus dubitari plane non potest, quamvis ab iisdem hauriantur: ut jam me hic esse, foco assidere, hyemali toga esse indutum, chartam istam manibus contrectare, & similia. Manus vero has ipsas, totumque hoc corpus meum esse, qua ratione posset negari? nisi me forte comparem nescio quibus insanis, quorum cerebella tam contumax vapor ex atra bile labefactat, ut constanter asseverent vel se esse reges, cum sunt pauperrimi, vel purpura indutos, cum sunt nudi, vel caput habere fictile, vel se totos esse cucurbitas, vel ex vitro conflatos; sed amentes sunt isti, nec minus ipse demens viderer, si quod ab iis exemplum ad me transferrem.

"Praeclare sane, tanquam non sim homo qui soleam noctu dormire, & eadem omnia in somnis pati, vel etiam interdum minus verisimilia, quam quae isti vigilantes."

"Mais, encore que les sens nous trompent quelquefois, touchant les choses peu sensibles et fort éloignées, il s'en rencontre peut-être beaucoup d'autres,

desquelles on ne peut pas raisonnablement douter, quoique nous les connais-
sions par leur moyen: par exemple, que je sois ici, assis auprès du feu, vêtu
d'une robe de chambre, ayant ce papier entre les mains, et autres choses de
cette nature. Et comment est-ce que je pourrais nier que ces mains et ce corps-
ci soient à moi? si ce n'est peut-être que je me compare à ces insensés, de qui
le cerveau est tellement troublé et offusqué par les noires vapeurs de la bile,
qu'ils assument constamment qu'ils sont des rois, lorsqu'ils sont très pauvres;
qu'ils sont vêtus d'or et de pourpre, lorsqu'ils sont tout nus; ou s'imaginent
être des cruches, ou avoir un corps de verre. Mais quoi? ce sont des fous, et
je ne serais pas moins extravagant, si je me réglais sur leurs exemples.

"Toutefois j'ai ici à considérer que je suis homme, et par conséquent que
j'ai coutume de dormir et de me représenter en mes songes les mêmes choses,
ou quelquefois de moins vraisemblables, que ces insensés, lorsqu'ils veillent."

3. Edward Said, *The World, the Text, and the Critic* (Cambridge, Mass.: Harvard
University Press, 1983), p. 214.

4. Michel Foucault, "What Is an Author?" in *Language, Counter-Memory, Practice,*
trans. Donald Bouchard (Ithaca, N.Y.: Cornell University Press, 1977), p.
120.

5. Michel Foucault, *The Archaeology of Knowledge,* trans. A. M. Sheridan-Smith
(London: Tavistock, 1972), p. 120.

6. Ibid., p. 123.

7. Michael Sprinker, "Textual Politics: Foucault and Derrida," *Boundary 2,* 8
(1980), 92.

8. Foucault, *Archaeology of Knowledge,* p. 163.

9. Jacques Derrida, "Le Parergon," in *La Vérité en peinture* (Paris: Flammarion,
1978), p. 23; hereafter cited in the text.

10. Samuel Weber, "The Limits of Professionalism," *Oxford Literary Review,* 5,
nos. 1 and 2 (1982), 60.

11. Immanuel Kant, *The Critique of Judgement,* trans. James Creed Meredith (Oxford: Oxford University Press, 1952), p. 68.

12. Erving Goffman, *Frame Analysis: An Essay on the Organization of Experience*
(New York: Harper and Row, 1974), pp. 124–125.

13. Meyer Schapiro, "On Some Problems in the Semiotics of Visual Art: Field
and Vehicle in Image-Signs," *Semiotica,* 1, no. 3 (1969), 227–228.

14. Jurij Lotman, *The Structure of the Artistic Text,* trans. R. Vroon, Michigan
Slavic Contributions, no. 7 (Ann Arbor: University of Michigan, 1977), pp.
212–213; cf. Barbara Herrnstein Smith, *Poetic Closure: A Study of How Poems
End* (Chicago: University of Chicago Press, 1968).

15. Cf. M. Minsky, "A Framework for Representing Knowledge," in Dieter Metz-
ing, ed., *Frame Conceptions and Text Understanding,* Research in Text Theory
Series, vol. 5 (Berlin: De Gruyter, 1980), p. 1.

16. Lotman, *Structure of the Artistic Text,* p. 210. Note, however, Goffman's cau-

tion (*Frame Analysis,* p. 46) that "keying," the modulation to a secondary framework, is a shift not from the unframed to the framed but from the imperceptible primary frame of everyday experience to a perceptible secondary frame.

17. Boris Uspensky, *A Poetics of Composition,* trans. V. Zavarin and S. Wittig (Berkeley: University of California Press, 1973), p. 143; Schapiro, "On Some Problems in the Semiotics of Visual Art," p. 227.

18. Goffman, *Frame Analysis,* p. 82.

19. Frank Kermode, *The Sense of an Ending* (London: Oxford University Press, 1966), p. 46.

20. George Kubler, *The Shape of Time* (New Haven: Yale University Press, 1962), p. 24.

21. Although it is true that much of the defamiliarizing effort of modernist art has been directed to a foregrounding of the frame, to stressing the arbitrariness of the limit of the text; cf. Dégas's *Tête-à-tête dîner,* in which the frame cuts off half of the man's face, or Godard's technique of having his characters walk casually in and out of a "badly composed" frame.

22. Lesley Stern, "Fiction/Film/Femininity I," *Australian Journal of Screen Theory,* nos. 9–10 (1981), 39.

23. Hans Georg Gadamer, *Truth and Method,* trans. G. Barden and J. Cumming (New York: Seabury Press, 1975), p. 88; hereafter cited in the text.

24. Hans Georg Gadamer, "Rhetorik, Hermeneutik und Ideologiekritik," in *Hermeneutik und Ideologiekritik,* ed. Jürgen Habermas (Frankfurt am Main: Suhrkamp, 1971), p. 81.

25. Ibid., p. 82.

26. Ibid., p. 73.

27. Jürgen Habermas, "Der Universalitätsanspruch der Hermeneutik," in *Hermeneutik und Ideologiekritik,* pp. 156–157.

28. Gadamer, "Rhetorik, Hermeneutik und Ideologiekritik," p. 64.

29. A. Wellmer, *Kritische Gesellschaftstheorie und Positivismus,* quoted in Habermas, "Der Universalitätsanspruch der Hermeneutik," p. 153.

30. Frank Lentricchia, *After the New Criticism* (London: The Athlone Press, 1980), p. 175.

31. Walter Benjamin, "Eduard Fuchs: Collector and Historian," in *The Essential Frankfurt School Reader,* ed. Andrew Arato and Eike Gebhardt (New York: Urizen Books, 1978), p. 227.

32. Walter Benjamin, "Theses on the Philosophy of History," in *Illuminations,* trans. Harry Zohn (New York: Schocken, 1969), p. 225.

33. Ibid., and Benjamin, "Eduard Fuchs," p. 227.

34. Gilles Deleuze, *Différence et répétition* (Paris: Presses Universitaires Françaises, 1968), p. 121.

35. Friedrich Nietzsche, "Vom Nutzen und Nachteil der Historie für das Leben,"

Unzeitgemässe Betrachtungen, Zweites Stück, Werke, ed. Karl Schlechta, vol. 1, 6th ed. (Munich: Hanser, 1969), p. 251.

36. Hans Robert Jauss, "Literary History as a Challenge to Literary Theory," *Toward an Aesthetic of Reception,* trans. Timothy Bahti, Theory and History of Literature, vol. 2 (Minneapolis: University of Minnesota Press, 1982), pp. 25–26.

37. Cf. Jean-François Lyotard, *The Post-Modern Condition: A Report on Knowledge,* trans. Geoff Bennington and Bryan Massumi, Theory and History of Literature, vol. 10 (Minneapolis: University of Minnesota Press, 1984), p. 17: "The limits the institution imposes on potential language 'moves' are never established once and for all (even if they have been formally defined). Rather, the limits are themselves the stakes and provisional results of language strategies, within the institution and without"; and "reciprocally, it can be said that the boundaries only stabilize when they cease to be stakes in the game."

38. Jacques Derrida, "The Law of Genre," trans. Avital Ronell, *Glyph,* 7 (1980), 212.

39. Cf. Michael Ryan, *Marxism and Deconstruction: A Critical Articulation* (Baltimore: Johns Hopkins University Press, 1982), p. 16.

40. Sprinker, "Textual Politics," p. 79.

41. Jonathan Culler, *On Deconstruction* (London: Routledge and Kegan Paul, 1983), p. 259.

42. Cf. Ryan, *Marxism and Deconstruction;* Terry Eagleton, *Walter Benjamin, or, Towards a Revolutionary Criticism* (London: Verso, 1981); Jonathan Arac, Wlad Godzich, and Wallace Martin, eds., *The Yale Critics: Deconstruction in America,* Theory and History of Literature, vol. 6 (Minneapolis: University of Minnesota Press, 1983).

43. Christopher I. Fynsk, "A Deceleration of Philosophy," *Diacritics,* 8, no. 6 (1978), 87.

44. Kant, *Critique of Judgment,* p. 43.

45. But cf. Stuart Hall's argument in "Cultural Studies and the Centre: Some Problematics and Problems," in Stuart Hall et al., eds., *Culture, Media, Language* (London: Hutchinson, 1980), pp. 46–47.

46. Leo Bersani, "The Subject of Power," *Diacritics,* 7, no. 3 (1977), 6.

47. But of course an extension of the curriculum may not in itself change anything; cf. Noel King, "The Place of Film in an English Department," *Australian Journal of Cultural Studies,* 1, no. 1 (1982), 47.

48. Northrop Frye, *The Anatomy of Criticism* (New York: Antheneum, 1967), p. 350: "The argument of our last essay . . . led to the principle that all structures in words are partly rhetorical, and hence literary, and that the notion of a scientific or philosophical verbal structure free of rhetorical elements is an illusion. If so, then our literary universe has expanded into a verbal universe, and no aesthetic principle of self-containment will work." Tzvetan Todorov,

Introduction to Poetics, trans. Richard Howard, Theory and History of Literature, vol. 1 (Minneapolis: University of Minnesota Press, 1981), p. 72: "Poetics is . . . called upon to play an eminently *transitional* role, even a transitory one: it will have served as an 'indicator' of discourses, since the least transparent kinds of discourse are to be encountered in poetry; but this discovery having been made, the science of discourses having been instituted, its own role will be reduced to little enough: to the investigation of the reasons that caused us to consider certain texts, at certain periods, as 'literature.' No sooner born than poetics finds itself called upon, by the very power of its results, to sacrifice itself on the altar of general knowledge. And it is not certain that this fate must be regretted."

49. For example, David Silverman and Brian Torode, *The Material Word* (London: Routledge and Kegan Paul, 1980), p. 257; Terry Eagleton, *The Function of Criticism* (London: Verso, 1984), pp. 123–124; Colin MacCabe, "Towards a Modern Trivium—English Studies Today," *Critical Quarterly,* 26, nos. 1, 2 (1984), 79; Graham Pechey, "Bakhtin, Marxism, and Post-Structuralism," in *The Politics of Theory,* ed. Francis Barker et al. (Colchester: University of Essex, 1983), p. 245.

Index